ARCHITECTURE, LANDSCAPE, AND AMERICAN CULTURE SERIES
Katherine Solomonson and Abigail A. Van Slyck, Series Editors

Medicine by Design: The Architect and the Modern Hospital, 1893–1943
Annmarie Adams

Manhood Factories: YMCA Architecture and the Making of Modern Urban Culture
Paula Lupkin

194X: Architecture, Planning, and Consumer Culture on the American Home Front
Andrew M. Shanken

A Manufactured Wilderness: Summer Camps and the Shaping of American Youth, 1890–1960
Abigail A. Van Slyck

The Architecture of Madness: Insane Asylums in the United States
Carla Yanni

MANHOOD FACTORIES

MANHOOD FACTORIES

YMCA Architecture and the
Making of Modern Urban Culture

PAULA LUPKIN

ARCHITECTURE, LANDSCAPE,
AND AMERICAN CULTURE SERIES

University of Minnesota Press
Minneapolis • London

This book is supported by a grant from the Graham Foundation for Advanced Studies in the Fine Arts.

The University of Minnesota Press gratefully acknowledges the work of Edward Dimendberg, editorial consultant, on this project.

Contemporary drawing plans, maps, and illustrations were created by Marisa Miller and Paula Lupkin.

Portions of chapter 4 previously appeared as "A Temple of Practical Christianity: Chicago's YMCA Skyscraper," *Chicago History* 24 (Fall 1995): 22–41. Portions of chapter 5 previously appeared as "Manhood Factories: Architecture, Business, and the Evolving Role of the YMCA, 1869–1915" in *Men and Women Adrift: The YMCA and YWCA in the City, 1869–1960,* edited by Nina Mjagkij and Margaret Spratt (New York: New York University Press, 1997).

Copyright 2010 by Paula Lupkin

All rights reserved. No part of this publication may be reproduced, stored in a retrieval system, or transmitted, in any form or by any means, electronic, mechanical, photocopying, recording, or otherwise, without the prior written permission of the publisher.

Published by the University of Minnesota Press
111 Third Avenue South, Suite 290
Minneapolis, MN 55401-2520
http://www.upress.umn.edu

Library of Congress Cataloging-in-Publication Data

Lupkin, Paula.
  Manhood factories : YMCA architecture and the making of modern urban culture / Paula Lupkin.
       p. cm. — (Architecture, landscape, and American culture series)
    Includes bibliographical references and index.
    ISBN 978-0-8166-4834-4 (hc : alk. paper) — ISBN 978-0-8166-4835-1 (pb : alk. paper)
    1. YMCA—Buildings. 2. Architecture—Moral and ethical aspects—United States.
  3. Architecture and society—United States. 4. Space (Architecture)—United States. I. Title.
    BV1110.L87 2010
    726′.9—dc22   2009009243

Printed in the United States of America on acid-free paper

Designed by Yvonne Tsang and copyedited by Nancy Evans, both at Wilsted & Taylor Publishing Services

The University of Minnesota is an equal-opportunity educator and employer.

17 16 15 14 13 12 11 10   10 9 8 7 6 5 4 3 2 1

For my parents

CONTENTS

Acknowledgments xi

Introduction *The YMCA and the Cultural Landscape of Modernity* xv

1. **RECONCILING MORALITY AND MAMMON** 1
   A Christian Club for Clerks

2. **INVENTING THE YMCA BUILDING** 37

3. **ACCEPTING THE CALL TO BUILD** 73
   Architectural Evangelism on Main Street

4. **BEDROOMS, BILLIARDS, AND BASKETBALL** 111
   Retooling the YMCA

5. **FROM GREENSBORO TO CHINA** 137
   YMCA Architecture as International Business

Epilogue *Influences Radiate . . .* 181

Notes 199

Bibliography 221

Illustration Credits 241

Index 243

ACKNOWLEDGMENTS

So many people contributed to and supported this project, and I am delighted to acknowledge them. David Brownlee gave unstintingly of his time, his ideas, and his enthusiasm. His perceptive criticisms of my work and insight into the problems it addresses shaped my scholarship and served as a model of collegiality; my appreciation can never be adequately expressed. Thanks also to Elizabeth Johns, Robert Bruegmann, Kathleen James-Chakraborty, Jeffrey Cody, Julia Rosenbaum, Parker James, Angela Miller, Margaret Garb, Joseph Heathcott, Rebecca Ginsburg, Amy Weisser, Nina Mjagkij, Thomas Winter, Janis Zubalick, Inbal Ben-Asher Gitler, Catherine Bishir, Pieter Martin, and Edward Dimendberg, for their interest and help during the long gestation of this book. Kate Solomonson and Abigail Van Slyck's dedication to the project and editorial acumen have made the book better in every way.

I am grateful for the financial support I received while working on this project from the University of Pennsylvania in the form of a William Penn Fellowship and a School of Arts and Sciences Dissertation Fellowship. The funds provided by the Clarke Chambers Travel Fellowship, administered by the University of Minnesota, allowed me to pursue necessary research in the Kautz Family YMCA Archives. The Graham Foundation for Advanced Study in the Fine Arts provided a generous publication grant that made my fruitful collaboration with Marisa Miller in the digital production of maps and models possible. Christine Boyer's mapping of the geography of the Ladies' Mile was an essential foundation for the maps of New York, as was Tim Gilfoyle's work on New York's "Temples of Love."

A fellowship at the Charles Warren Center for Studies in American

History provided a wonderful opportunity to engage in new research and benefit from collaboration with my fellow-fellows Danny Abramson, Eric Avila, Alice Friedman, Paul Groth, Jane Kamensky, Martha McNamara, Ann Whitson Spirn, and Ellen Stroud. Kudos to Liz Cohen and Margaret Crawford for organizing and leading such a stimulating, enriching experience that significantly advanced the interdisciplinary study of the American built environment.

The assistance of various archival and library professionals was invaluable at every stage of the project. David Carmichael, Dagmar Getz, and Andrea Hinding at the Kautz Family YMCA Archives welcomed me warmly in the midst of a Minneapolis January and offered their knowledge of and enthusiasm for the rich materials under their supervision. They and the staff, including Ryan Bean, have been staunch supporters of this project at every step along the way. Geoffrey Palmer and Colin Lees generously shared their knowledge of the British YMCA with me. I would also like to thank Mary Woolever at the Burnham Library of Architecture; Tony Wrenn at the Archives of the American Institute of Architects; Eileen Carroll at the Building and Furnishings Service of the YMCA of the USA; Madeleine Ford and Sean Conolly at the YMCA of Greater New York; Daniel Lee of the YMCA of Metropolitan Chicago; Rosemary Adams, Lesley Martin, and Archie Motley at the Chicago Historical Society; Steve Siegel at the Ninety-second Street YMCA; Madeleine Duet of the YWCA of New York; and Paige Roberts and Jeffrey Monseau at Springfield College.

The staff at the University of Pennsylvania and the Washington University Libraries was creative, generous, and patient with my requests. Micheline Nilsen, Crystal Springer, Elizabeth Williams, Jane Darcovich, and especially Betha Whitlow provided help with visual materials with speed and goodwill. Without the administrative and research support and good humor of Sandy Brennan, Sandy Cooper, Jamie Giganti, Lori Turner, and most especially Lindsey Girard I would not have been able to complete this project. Laura Antonacos helped to reconstruct a long-demolished building from written descriptions; Ted LaBoube introduced me to Geographic Information Systems (GIS); and Eric Cesal provided critical support with illustrations at the eleventh hour. Nancy Evans most skillfully and patiently copyedited the manuscript. Jill Davis opened her home to a traveling scholar on more than one occasion. In addition to sharing his scholarly expertise, Joshua Lupkin offered emergency research assistance. My parents, Rona and Joseph Lupkin, gave their love and moral support. Thanks most of all to the people who kept things in perspective: Andrew, who was there from the beginning, and Jacob, whose knowledge of the YMCA is thus far limited to the lyrics of the Village People.

929 — Y. W. C. A. and Y. M. C. A. Buildings, Portland, Oregon

INTRODUCTION

*The YMCA and the
Cultural Landscape of Modernity*

Between the Civil War and World War I the Young Men's Christian Association was responsible for the construction of more than one thousand buildings on Main Streets across the United States. The typical Main Street YMCA building's form—brick, three or four stories tall, with some classicizing detail—is so standardized and well known that it is often taken for granted, a set piece in the American downtown. One model railroading supply company, Model Power, even manufactures an N-Scale YMCA building kit (Figure I.1), which it sells to

FIGURE I.1. Model Power N-Scale YMCA building model railroad kit, ca. 1999.

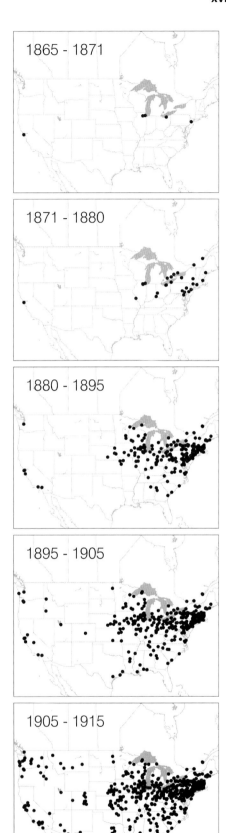

FIGURE I.2. YMCA building construction map, 1865–1915.

hobbyists constructing their ideal town layouts, along with its bank, library, town hall, railroad station, and drugstore. The YMCA, a typically typical building, has not attracted much attention from architectural historians.[1] Its conservative styling and understated formal qualities do not lend themselves to the aesthetic narrative of modern architecture in the United States. Nor has it been the subject of vernacular architecture studies.[2] Although it is part of the everyday landscape of American cities, it has pretensions (minimal though they may be in some cases) to the status of Architecture, including authorship by a professional designer. Betwixt and between high and low, YMCA buildings are common, yet in many senses extraordinary, features of the modern urban landscape.

YMCA buildings appeared in spurts on the national map, emerging in response to patterns of economic growth and depression (Figure I.2). The first three appeared in New York, Chicago, and San Francisco during the bonanza economy that followed the Civil War. The financial downturn of the 1870s meant that few communities could afford to construct their own YMCAs, but during the recovery of the 1880s hundreds appeared in cities across the East and Midwest. Just after the turn of the twentieth century the developing urban centers of the West acquired their own YMCA buildings. By the onset of the Great Depression most urban communities in the United States could boast of a "modern" YMCA building, as could cities abroad, especially in heavily industrializing nations like China. By the end of the 1920s, this Protestant evangelical organization was responsible for a network of what Theodore Roosevelt dubbed "manhood factories": buildings intended to mass-produce properly socialized, practically educated, and morally upright young men for the modern age.[3] Explicitly intended to cater to the needs of young men, this national network of buildings has a significance that extends beyond a strictly gendered interpretation.

Through its provision of these standardized buildings the Y helped to mediate the shift from an agrarian past to a corporate urban future, from the country's Puritan heritage to the rise of mass culture. The conception, design, construction, and reception of a YMCA building were important processes in the development of a new physical and social order for modernity. In the increasingly large, urbanized, and mobile society at the turn of the century, space was an important tool for constructing identity, negotiating change, and inscribing unified cultural values. The YMCA building, with its leisure spaces, dormitory rooms, and educational facilities, was a key element of a complex, spatially segmented system of class, race, ethnicity, age, *and* gender identity that helped define and maintain a culture of corporate capitalism.[4] Through the process of conceiving, siting, constructing, and programming these buildings, the YMCA took an active role as an impresario of a modern, yet moral public culture.

Interpreting the YMCA as a Male Space

Manhood Factories complicates the nineteenth-century middle-class moral geography of separate spheres as scholars currently understand it.[5] In the late nineteenth century, middle-class women were making their way into the public sphere and, as Abigail Van Slyck, Alison Isenberg, and Daphne Spain show in their work, were beginning to play central roles in shaping the welfare of the nation's urbanizing regions.[6] Recent scholarship has emphasized the porosity of normative gender boundaries by focusing on the extension of this female role in urban reform activities but does not address similar male gender-bending activities.

The "central" YMCA building on Main Street is a key entry point into a critical analysis of the national, white, Anglo-Saxon Protestant, commercial, and masculine urban downtown that many feminist studies of architecture and the built environment take for granted.[7] As a "Christian clubhouse," the YMCA was intended as a homosocial world in which an upright, principled masculinity would be cultivated through contact with other men, rather than women. With both parlors and gyms, it structured an alternative vision of manhood that navigated between the "sporting life" and evangelical culture.

In recent years scholars of social history have begun to interpret the YMCA as a site for the construction of identity based on class, race, and sexuality, as well as the lived experience of working-class men, African-American men, and gay men.[8] Although they do not explicitly analyze the built environment, these studies all acknowledge the importance of space to the organization. This is especially true of John Gustav-Wrathall's and George Chauncey's works on gay male culture in the YMCA, and Thomas Winter's book on YMCAs for working-class men at the turn of the twentieth century.[9] All of these authors focus upon the YMCA building space as a site of gender formation.[10]

This book builds upon the scholarship on space and identity, but places the building front and center as the subject of inquiry. Like William Moore's study of Masonic architecture, the present work demonstrates that the process of making and using buildings and urban spaces helped middle-class men restructure modern manhood.[11] YMCAs and fraternal buildings used space in complementary ways to redefine rapidly shifting male identity at the end of the nineteenth century.

Such shifts in gender identity are not uncommon precisely because gender is not a fixed category, but (in Gail Bederman's words) a dynamic "historical, ideological process."[12] Yet, in the aftermath of the Civil War, white middle-class men, especially native-born men, confronted shifts in their work life that challenged their power, autonomy, and mobility to an unprecedented degree. The decisive shift from a regional, rural, agrarian system to a national industrial economy linked by rails had a profound effect on the identity of middle-class men in the United States. Fewer men had the chance to ascend to a position of economic independence. Instead, they were positioned within an increasingly rigid structure governed by managerial authority: a structure they helped to shape, but could not escape.[13]

Responding to this change, the YMCA (and the business community that financed it) sought to bridge the traditional religious values of the agrarian past and the modern, corporate, capitalist future, maintaining the authority of the traditional evangelical values of manhood within a new national political and economic system. This transition was both masked and facilitated by a variety of fictive strategies. Horatio Alger stories, advice books, and the biographies of men like Andrew Carnegie and George Pullman mythologized and perpetuated the traditional antebellum American image of an autonomous, mobile, and democratic white manhood. These fantasies maintained the allure of useful Protestant virtues like delayed gratification and hard work in an age when men were being asked to take on new and contradictory roles as mid-level employees and consumers.

New leisure institutions housed in prominently designed and sited buildings, like the YMCA and Masonic Lodges, were an attempt to define men's lives and help them make sense of their place and their roles within this evolving system. Although they shared a common goal and a similar spatial strategy, the Y and the Masons used different means to achieve their ends. While the Masons enacted supposedly timeless rituals to shore up their vision of manhood, the YMCA's program, sponsored by employers, was very much anchored in a pragmatic, useful preparation for a productive and successful, if increasingly limited, work life. Both groups, however, employed a degree of fantasy in their model of manhood, emphasizing ascent and progress through a hierarchical structure that was not always present on the job. The Masons moved up through degrees of brotherhood, and, as a 1906 advertisement suggests, Y members could avoid the tough climb of the job ladder by taking the elevator from "a job" to life as a "captain of industry" (Figure I.3).

In both cases the buildings are essential frames for the pantomime of mobility. Masonic temples, as portrayed by Moore, are literal stage sets for dramatic ritual. Although the YMCA was certainly also a staged environment for masculine display, its gymnasium, classrooms, library, and later its pool and dormitories made it more overtly a leisure center for the managers and minions of the emerging corporate culture. Activi-

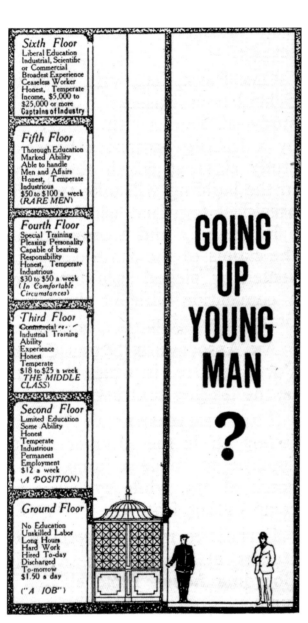

FIGURE I.3. "Going Up Young Man?" Advertisement in *Association Men*, ca. 1905.

ties at the Y were designed to meet the needs of both constituencies, offering individualism, mobility, and consumption in an age of system and conformity. Promoted and supported by leaders and pioneers in railroads, investment banking, insurance, manufacturing, and retailing, the YMCA building was an important attempt to mold modern white-collar manhood.

Yet the YMCA's model of manhood was itself dynamic and open to change. By the turn of the century the antebellum evangelical ideal of upright Christian manliness, invested with self-control, charity, and paternal responsibility, had given way to a more physical, bodily embodiment of masculinity. The YMCA strove to adapt and maintain its appeal to members, adhering to the tenets of muscular Christianity and promoting physical fitness within a frame of productivity. At the Brooklyn YMCA, for example, low- and mid-level white-collar employees could enjoy the social, athletic, and residential amenities of a club for a minimal price. Its new building, opening in 1913, offered members the opportunity to take a "hot cabinet bath" after a hard day at work to offset the pressures of fast-paced modern life (see Plate 8). This mechanical contraption was a descendant of the more sensual and decadent Turkish bath: a sweating experience intended to cleanse the skin and promote relaxation. Yet, unlike the recumbent and relaxed sweating enjoyed by members of elite clubs, these cubicles modestly enclosed a bather from the neck to the feet in an upright posture, efficiently heating the space around him. A period of sweating would be followed by a rough towel-down and possibly a massage. At the YMCA, leisure and relief from the work world were provided to the individual member, albeit within a carefully defined environment intended to manufacture strong bodies. The cabinet baths were representative of the YMCA's modern fusion of religion, sport, and masculinity, an ideal that was, through its buildings, accepted and integrated as a central element of the American urban landscape.

Gender, Segregation, and the Landscape of Capitalism

This book does more than address lacunae in the history of masculine space. The YMCA building was, from the beginning, undoubtedly a men's institution. The fundamental emphasis on the masculine, and the provision (by the wives and daughters of YMCA leaders) of a corresponding and subordinate feminine space in the YWCA, suggests this fundamental gender division (Figure I.4). Yet, as Bederman has observed, nineteenth-century Americans did not compartmentalize "gender" and "cultural" issues as today's historians sometimes do. Instead, these men "addressed their cultural crisis in gendered terms, and their masculinity crisis in cultural terms."[14] In the late nineteenth century Americans faced the crisis to national identity and individuality posed by incorporation. Beginning with the construction of a unified republic in the early nineteenth century, white manhood was a tool used to cultivate an identity that transcended the barriers of ethnic, religious, political, regional, and state differences. As Dana Nelson has suggested, an

FIGURE I.4. YWCA and YMCA buildings, Taylor Street, between Sixth and Seventh streets, Portland, Oregon, 1908. The two organizations purchased the land, raised money, and planned their buildings jointly. The relative size of the buildings reflected a proportional division of funds raised, with three-tenths going to the construction of the YWCA and seven-tenths to the YMCA.

ideological conception of national manhood existed from the beginnings of the United States, an imagined fraternity of white men whose alliance confirmed authority over women and others and papered over difference. This "national manhood" was revived in the wake of the Civil War, as part of the political project of Reconstruction and the economic project of incorporation. As Nelson argues, "Men whose interests had been temporarily unified in wartime were increasingly encountering their peers not as fellow citizens but as competitors in an unstable, rapidly changing postwar economy."[15] Gender was an abstract way to deal with individualistic competition and unite men in difference against the other.

The importance of the YMCA, then, goes beyond its role as a purveyor of gendered space precisely because it offers insights into the broader role that gender and other forms of identity played in the construction of the modern built environment. These male spaces were designed as part of a larger system of spatial segregation and classification embedded in the landscape of capitalism. This creation of new, gendered, leisure spaces was part of a larger reconception of the moral and spatial organization of urban society under corporate capitalism. As Alan Trachtenberg has shown, in the three decades following the Civil War—a period he calls the "age of incorporation"—Americans were deeply engaged in processes of cultural change, a "reorganization of perceptions . . . about the individual, the relation between public and private realms, and the character of the nation."[16] The shift in the scale and structure of American capitalism from its mercantile origins to the dominance of hierarchically organized and managed corporations meant changes in all aspects of life, especially economic, social, cultural, and spatial organization.

The age of incorporation was a pivot point in the spatial production of modernity in the United States. Newly national and even international forms of organization, communication, finance, and production dislodged established modes of thinking and doing and initiated the dynamic process of creative destruction that would bring about a "second nature," William Cronon's term for that seemingly natural, yet man-made ecology imposed atop existing geography. Linked by railroad lines and flows of capital, second nature connects city and country together in a coordinated system of raw materials, processing, manufacturing, and distributing.[17]

Alongside and intertwined with the systematic transformation of the economy came fundamental shifts in the built environment, producing a distinctive cultural landscape of modernity. This landscape is most obviously visible in the buildings constructed to serve industry and business: factories, worker housing, and office buildings. Yet the corporate reorganization of American culture affected the rest of the built environment as well, requiring reformulation of spatial ideas about gender and class.

From the scale of the nation, to the city, and down to the individual building and the human body, incorporation emphasized regimentation, planning, management, and separation; unity was achieved through subordination of the individual to the whole.[18] At the World's Fair and in the cities it influenced, all people and things were spatially categorized and carefully assigned a place within a singular controlling scheme.[19] Women, blacks, and ethnic "others" were incorporated along with native-born white men into a mosaic of distinct but interlocking spheres. The YMCA's buildings are an important part of this more complicated pattern.

From its beginnings the YMCA was invested in defining class, race, and ethnicity as well as gender through its buildings. The "central" YMCA, the subject of this book, was the flagship of the organization's building program, but only one aspect of its efforts to shape society through architecture. As early as the 1860s, when the New York YMCA planned its seminal Twenty-third Street building, the central YMCA building was understood as a white-collar clubhouse. At the same time that its young leaders planned lavish facilities for clerks, it also initiated plans to rent separate spaces in lower Manhattan, branch Ys that would cater to blue-collar workers, blacks, and German men. Indeed, the inclusion of stores on the ground level of the Twenty-third Street building was intended to finance these outreach programs.

When the Chicago YMCA celebrated its architectural achievements in 1923, the "city" of YMCA buildings it assembled into one image included not only the central YMCA skyscraper and hotel, but the neighborhood branch buildings, the Wabash YMCA for "colored" men, the Sears Roebuck Y for industrial workers, and the railroad Y buildings, financed by the Chicago,

FIGURE I.5. Composite picture of the department buildings of the Young Men's Christian Association of Chicago, 1923.

Burlington, and Northwestern as well as other lines for their employees (Figure I.5).[20] Never as well-funded as enterprises for urban white-collar workers, these suborganizations were often housed in rented quarters long after the city had a permanent, purpose-built central building.

I have chosen to focus on the construction of the central "main" buildings not only as a means of understanding the construction of modern white manhood, but also because these structures are emblematic of the complex role of gender in the modern cultural landscape. As an advertisement for the Pittsfield YMCA shows, the influence of the building "radiates all over town," permeating the distinct bubbles of home, school, store, office, business, church, mine, factory, smelter, and pleasure resort (Figure I.6).

The YMCA, Modern Architecture, and the Modern Urban Landscape

The late-nineteenth and early-twentieth-century building program of the YMCA, shaped so strongly by the economic forces of capitalism, offers an interesting perspective on the relationship between architecture and society in the modern period. On the surface its buildings appear conservative, and do not "look" modern in the way we have come to understand the term. But as the story of the YMCA suggests, the forces of modernity not only produced

FIGURE I.6. "The Center of Things": fundraising image for the Pittsfield, Massachusetts, YMCA, 1908.

individual monuments, but also shaped the entire landscape, as well as the processes of making and using buildings. When we map the contours of modern life, we must include the YMCA alongside the department store, the factory, the library, the skyscraper, the slum, and the suburbs. These buildings were not individual elements, but threads woven into the patterned fabric of the modern American city, fashioned on the loom of incorporation.

This book explores a wider conception of the modern in architecture, treating all the elements of the building process as functions of modernity: determining the functional program, raising the funds, choosing a site, selecting an architect, determining the exterior style, arranging the interior spaces, furnishing those interior spaces, using those spaces, and representing the buildings in a range of printed materials, newspaper articles, and postcards.[21] This emphasis on the *process* of making space and meaning, rather than the final *product*, reveals architecture's great social significance and can substantially enrich our understanding of the relationship between design and modern life.

I present the architectural biography of the American YMCA in five chapters and an epilogue, which move between social history, institutional policy, and architectural analysis to address the subject at different scales.

Chapter 1, "Reconciling Morality and Mammon: A Christian Club for Clerks," introduces the concept of the modern YMCA as an organization, its roots in evangelical culture, and its transformation into an architectural vehicle for the making of modern urban culture during the Civil War. Central to this development is the active engagement of a new group of leaders, elite young New Yorkers, including J. P. Morgan. With their Yankee upbringing, they were attracted to the YMCA's evangelical mission and focus on the needs of young white-collar men. The architectural vision of this group, the New York YMCA building of 1869, is the central focus of chapter 2, "Inventing the YMCA Building." A detailed analysis of its design presents the concept of the modern YMCA building. From this singular building the organization attempted to shape urban culture across the United States. Chapter 3, "Accepting the Call to Build: Architectural Evangelism on Main Street," traces the efforts of these New Yorkers to place a building on every American Main Street. In addition to documenting this effort to unify Americans in a modern but respectable middle-class culture, this chapter also tracks the response of local and regional communities to this call to build.

In chapter 4, "Bedrooms, Billiards, and Basketball: Retooling the YMCA," I return to an examination of the YMCA building's form, tracing changes in its functional program and design as it adapted to the introduction of a mass culture based on commercial leisure. Chapter 5, "From Greensboro to China: YMCA Architecture as International Business," is about the importance of the building process in the development of the modern YMCA building, and the challenges an international construction campaign offered the organization and its architects. The Epilogue concludes this study with a consideration of buildings influenced by the YMCA—Young Men's Hebrew Associations, schools, social centers, and community centers—and raises the question of resistance to the male, middle-class, Protestant basis of the organization by Progressive reformers on behalf of working-class and immigrant culture. However, the reliance of these groups on the YMCA as a conceptual and architectural model ultimately reflects on the impact of the YMCA's architectural activities on both the modern urban landscape and the American concept of leisure and manhood in the twentieth century.

I

RECONCILING MORALITY AND MAMMON

A Christian Club for Clerks

AT THE END OF THE CIVIL WAR, the New York Young Men's Christian Association was struggling: for money, for members, and for a clearly defined purpose. Once more than a thousand strong, this active brotherhood of clerks and clerics had dwindled to a few dozen members. Heated debate over the issue of slavery and then enlistment had slowly denuded it of its membership, and money available for the spiritual needs of young men was directed to soldiers in the field rather than clerks in the countinghouses. Nearly bankrupt, the Y was forced to move to cheap rented quarters in the Bible House on Astor Place. The small library and parlor, located down a dark hallway away from the street, did not draw new members. As one leader lamented, "We have found our present attractions repulsive, young men will not come or be induced to frequent our rooms." Instead, they flocked to the rowdy concert saloons and other commercial entertainments on the Bowery, only a few blocks away. The future of this innovative evangelical organization seemed bleak. According to one board member, in 1864 the organization was "theoretically and practically" dead. Borrowing Abraham Lincoln's architectural metaphor of the "house divided," he compared the current state of the YMCA to an edifice with decayed beams, crumbling foundations, and broken walls.[1]

Within five years the New York YMCA would be reborn, emerging from the ashes of war as a dynamic force in the cultural and economic reconstruction of the United States. Between 1864 and 1869 a handful of young New Yorkers, including the scions of the wealthy Dodge, Stokes, and Morgan families, re-visioned the antebellum YMCA, transformed its structure and methods, and moved from the Bible House to a grand new clubhouse they constructed for themselves in the fashionable entertainment district emerging around Madison Square. This transformation, both programmatic and architectural, made a new place for the organization in the cultural landscape of modernity, and positioned it as a site for the production of a national manhood for the industrial age.

The Civil War stands in the middle of this transformation, a catalytic event in the organization's history. *Any* organization devoted to the interests of young men would of course be transformed by the enlistment of its members. Many if not most Y members in the North and Midwest, too poor to buy their way out of service, joined the Union Army, leaving their local organizations bereft and often bankrupt. The few existing southern YMCAs, never as firmly rooted as their Yankee counterparts, disappeared entirely during the conflict and its aftermath. For the YMCA the importance of the war went well beyond a loss of members. The war transformed the organization's identity. The marshalling and deployment of men and materiel on a national scale catalyzed a rethinking of its very mission, methods, and purpose. During the conflict between the states the YMCA undertook widespread evangelical work among soldiers. In the process it metamorphosed from a voluntary evangelical association to a bureaucratically organized vehicle of organization and managerial control.

From its origins as a British evangelical voluntary association, the Young Men's Christian Association was transformed by a group of young but powerful New York businessmen into an innovative gendered organization during the Civil War. Their mission, embodied in the development of a Christian clubhouse for aspiring young men, spatially and conceptually restructured male identity, respectability, and leisure within the emerging culture of corporate capitalism.

Origins

Americans first became acquainted with the YMCA during the 1851 Great Exhibition in London. On display alongside the furniture and machinery inside the Crystal Palace was a small exhibit on a voluntary association for young men that had started in 1844. In that year a young London clerk named George Williams, with help from like-minded friends, founded a group called the Young Men's Christian Association. Its mission was "the improvement of the spiritual condition of young men engaged in the drapery and other trades." This was a very specific goal, focused upon the population of approximately 150,000 young men working in the City of London as clerks in banks, countinghouses, the offices of professional men, and in the various departments of wholesale and retail trade.

To Williams and his friends, active members of Dissenter churches, the social and spiritual problems of these young men were intertwined. If young men could be religiously converted, improvement in their behavior and morals would inevitably follow, and vice versa. Williams understood that in order to lead young men toward more Christian lives he had to meet their special needs for mutual support and spiritual improvement outside of the back rooms of the pub, where voluntary groups frequently rented space.[2] Gradually, with the encouragement and financial help of employers and other benefactors in the business community, the London YMCA came to see that well-furnished rooms could be used as a powerful evangelical tool to draw men away from the pub and prepare them to accept God.

It was to this clubhouse that visitors to the YMCA booth at the Great Exhibition were invited. At least one American, George H. Petrie, a young importer from New York, took up the invitation. So struck was he by the rooms that, upon his return, Petrie "was to describe them more vividly than the exhibits he had examined in the Crystal Palace." On the first floor he encountered a series of comfortably furnished reading rooms with local and international newspapers and periodicals. Upstairs was a library of seven thousand volumes, and the third floor housed several classrooms for the study of French, German, Latin, Greek, Hebrew, mathematics, history, and other subjects (Figure 1.1).[3]

In many ways the London YMCA "rooms," as they were called, resembled spaces that might have been familiar to many Americans. The amenities, earnest atmosphere, and genteel fellowship of clerks closely matched the character of mercantile libraries, rooms of debating societies, and other self-improvement groups that appeared in cities and towns throughout the United States in the 1830s and 1840s. There was, however, one distinct difference between the YMCA and these earlier organizations: religious purpose. Although mercantile libraries, with their mission of self-improvement, implicitly promoted the values of middle-class evangelical culture, their function (and that of other types of fraternal organizations, like the Masons and the Odd Fellows) was not spiritual. In contrast, the YMCA's mission focused primarily on the souls of young men, and its rooms and social activities were conceived as tools of moral suasion.

First organized in Boston in 1854, the American YMCA was a laymen's evangelical organization that restricted full membership to those who were active members of one of the mainstream Protestant evangelical denominations: Congregational, Baptist, Episcopal, Methodist, Presbyterian, Lutheran, and related sects. Ostensibly the American YMCA espoused a universal mission to all young men, including special efforts to organize meetings for "colored" and German immigrant young men. Nonetheless, the organization's main mission, its culture, and its architecture were shaped by and for middle-class, Anglo-Saxon, evangelical Protestants.[4]

The idea quickly spread to New York, Philadelphia, and most large cities. It was especially popular in smaller cities and towns of the "burned-over district" of western New York, and in northern and midwestern states that had experienced a period of religious fervor and evangelical revival in the 1820 and 1830s, during the Second Great Awakening. With its Yankee origins and urban focus the YMCA was less popular in the South, but

even there young men gathered together and organized local chapters. Each group raised funds to rent rooms and build libraries like those in London. Typically these spaces were located in the heart of the business district, near merchant houses and shops where young men worked.

By 1856 the YMCA was well established in North America. Young men, with the help of clergy and employers, had organized more than fifty-six associations from Toronto to Brooklyn, Dayton to Natchez, Houston to Peoria. Despite sectional tensions and arguments over states' rights during the period leading up to the Civil War, the cause of young men's souls united groups from North and South into a national organization, led by the "Central Committee," which met in convention several times to discuss and debate its mission, goals, and methods.

The widespread appeal and popularity of this British organization in the United States lay in a shared religious culture. With their common roots in Puritanism, American evangelicals had much in common with British Dissenters, including Williams, the Y's founder. For both evangelical groups conversion was an essential act, the sole meaning of existence. With no birthright membership in a church, individuals were required to undergo a strenuous and often emotional experience of conversion during which they examined their lives, recognized their own worthlessness and sin, and finally yielded to God's care. Conversion did not end here, but required a lifelong commitment: church attendance, benevolent work, and devotion to the conversion of others.[5] Evangelicals viewed conversion, effected one person at a time, as the solution to the social problems of the age and the road to the redemption of the world.

Another shared belief was in the power of the built environment. In the wake of the Second Great Awakening, their religious beliefs about human nature and behavior increasingly rested on what I term environmental evangelism: the intentional manipulation of space to promote conversion. Williams was deeply influenced by American Charles Grandison Finney, whose popular revivals on both sides of the Atlantic offered the hopeful message that individuals could take an active role in their own conversion and salvation. Embedded in this idea, known as Perfectionism, was the egalitarian notion that humans had the ability to change. Finney believed that the key to salvation lay in a shaped experience. Conversion was technically a gift from God that could not be forced, but Finney, hoping to speed the process of redemption, believed that it could be encouraged. He favored revivals and tent meetings, two techniques of moral suasion that relied upon the influence of environment. If individuals were removed from their everyday surroundings to inside a tent, and placed in the "anxious seat" at the front of the assembly, he believed they could be brought to see the light.[6]

Finney's ideas appealed to antebellum Protestants who turned to architecture and the cultural landscape as a tool of spiritual reform in their camp meeting grounds and Sunday schools (Figure 1.2). As middle-class evangelicals, this spatial way of understanding social relationships was especially

FIGURE 1.1. Young Men's Christian Association headquarters, London, 1854.

FIGURE 1.2. Unidentified camp meeting grounds, illustrated in B. W. Gorham, *Camp Meeting Manual*, 1854.

potent. Compounding and giving particular form to this "moral environmentalism" was the middle-class ideology of separate spheres, developed in the early nineteenth century. This spatial strategy enabled increasingly worldly Christians to reconcile the new rules of industrial-era commerce and consumption with the social mores of their religious culture, which stressed honesty, self-restraint, and delayed gratification. Essential to the conceptualization of an ethical capitalist order, this gendered moral geography spatially separated economic production from social reproduction.

Women, associated with the domestic sphere and religious life, were assigned the role of socialization. Men were exposed to their refining influence in the home and retained those values when they ventured into their own world of commerce, which operated profitably, efficiently, and free from ethical restrictions under the rules of laissez-faire capitalism. This system removed the middle-class home, with its assigned role of child-rearing and consumption, from its pre-industrial proximity to the workplace to distinctly residential districts on the periphery. As the story of the YMCA building in New York confirms, the boundaries between the spheres were never quite as distinct as the prescriptive literature would have us believe. Nonetheless the conceptual preservation of an untainted sphere of influence, the "bourgeois utopia" defined by Robert Fishman, was important both in the development of the middle class and in the reconciliation of Protestant culture with life in the modern industrial era.[7]

Less than a decade later, popular American Congregationalist minister Horace Bushnell developed the idea of environmental evangelism in a different direction in his popular text *Christian Nurture*, published in 1846. He revised Finney's theories of human perfectibility, suggesting that individuals achieved grace not through a revival-induced adult conversion, but as part of their growing process. Influenced by the associationist strands of commonsense Scottish Enlightenment philosophy, Bushnell suggested religion was taught not by doctrine, nor by adult conversion, but by long-term experience in the proper environment. Thus a child's soul was not inherently depraved, but a lump of clay to be formed by his parents and the religious atmosphere of his home. It was but a small leap to extend this concept outside of the domestic sphere, where its implications could be applied to society at large.[8]

Williams's notion of an association for urban young men housed in "rooms" accorded well with these already established patterns of thought in American evangelicalism. It also met the needs of a growing "class" of young men, who, like their English counterparts, experienced social and spiritual dislocation in their migration to large cities, long working hours, and poor living conditions. Celebrated in American literature and art of the period, the country boy in search of fame and fortune in the big city was a distinct archetype. As portrayed in Thomas Hovenden's famously popular and nostalgic canvas *Breaking Home Ties*, the putative YMCA member was rural born and young, often only fifteen years old (Figure 1.3). He left the comfort and guidance of mother and agricultural community life for the possibilities and perils of urban life.

In the antebellum period, clerical work was an avenue for mobility into proprietorship. The path was well defined, but success depended on initiative, ability, and, to some degree, luck. Preparation was minimal. The entrance requirements were competency in arithmetic, spelling, grammar, punctuation, and composition, as well as neat handwriting. Usually this meant grammar school until the age of fifteen or sixteen. From there, young men left home and boarded with their employers. Whether a farm boy or the son of a shopkeeper, a new clerk in a shop or office was often assigned manual labor. Traditionally, clerks started by sweeping the store and starting the fires. Once deemed trustworthy, they moved up to carrying the goods, then copying letters, copying accounts, and keeping accounts. With hard work

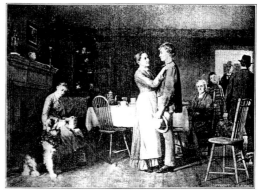

FIGURE 1.3. Fundraising pamphlet for the Tulsa, Oklahoma, YMCA, ca. 1909. This ad, designed to raise funds for a new building, reproduces an iconic image for the YMCA: Thomas Hovenden's well-known 1890 painting, *Breaking Home Ties*. Featuring a tender scene of a young man bidding farewell to his mother and country boyhood to make his way in the big city, this image reminded Tulsa citizens of the needs of young migrants. Reproductions of the painting hung in YMCA buildings around the country at the turn of the century.

and luck a boy could ascend steadily through the ranks to partnership and great wealth.

If it were possible for a young man to attain success, there were also pitfalls that, in the language of the period, could "snare" the young man who was not careful. Without family or friends in the city to provide supervision or an escape from these conditions, a young man floated freely within a permissive, anonymous, and increasingly attractive environment. Few respectable outlets, conceptual or material, existed to meet his needs once he arrived. Although he may have boarded with his employer's family in the 1830s or 1840s, by the time the YMCA arrived in the United States in the mid 1850s the practice of direct responsibility for and oversight of clerks within a domestic structure was quickly being replaced by a more distant relationship, especially in large cities. The expansion of stores and offices meant an increase in paperwork and accounting, and the corresponding number of employees required made it difficult, if not impossible, to house them en famille.[9]

Employers, seeking respite from the growing, crowded city, separated their countinghouses and shops from their living quarters, building homes away from the commercial center. No longer part of their employer's extended family, young clerks often lodged in boardinghouses, where the accommodations, food, and social life were often inadequate. The boardinghouses of New York were poorly heated, lighted, and furnished, and they often placed young men in a dubious moral environment. Thomas Butler Gunn, in an amusing exposé, described the arrangements of a cheap boardinghouse:

> It comprises two tenements which have been stately mansions in their day, but, like the neighborhood, have gone down in the world. . . . Their spacious rooms have been divided and subdivided into so many apartments, that the place resembles a penitentiary, a hive, or barrack.[10]

Verranus Morse, a rural migrant and later a historian of the YMCA, described the sleeping rooms:

> The rooms, unreached by gas pipes or furnace flues, are cold, dimly lighted, scantily furnished and badly cared for; and as they contain two or three or more beds, and the occupants have no choice in the selection of their fellow occupants, it often happens that young men brought up in comfort and refinement are compelled to lodge with those whose systems are saturated with whiskey, tobacco juice, and foul diseases, and whose minds are still more impure than their bodies.[11]

To many reformers and observers, the practice of boarding—however common—was not an acceptable substitute for the home environment. It transformed domesticity—linked in the ideology of separate spheres to the transmission of morality untainted by the market—into a service commodity.[12] The landlady of the lodging house, ostensibly responsible for supervising her lodgers, was often unwilling or unable to do so, and young men were encouraged to seek out a social life elsewhere. Few could afford to marry on their small salaries, and thus they were excluded from the sociability and feminine influence of the domestic sphere. Freed from the structure of separate spheres, young men were adrift in an increasingly large and anonymous urban environment. This particular "class" of young men, as the YMCA termed it, sought fellowship and identity in a warm, welcoming space. For the unmarried, aspiring middle-class young man there were two paths to follow in search of a place to spend his free time: sporting culture and evangelical culture.

Sporting Men and Christian Gentlemen

First emerging in the early nineteenth century amid the longshoremen and sailors in the vice districts on city wharves, a masculine, urban, bachelor subculture emphasized forms of sport associated with gambling: prizefighting, horseracing, and cockfighting, as well as prostitution. This gendered life cut across class lines, attracting both working-class men and slumming gentlemen, who built a shared sense of masculinity in their rejection of traditional middle-class values of self-control, delayed gratification, and hard work. Leisure, not work, defined the "fancy" men, "b'hoys" (or Bowery boys), and dandies of all backgrounds. By the 1830s and 1840s, however, sporting culture was increasingly attractive to youthful clerks and other middle-class young men shut out of the domestic world in which they had been reared.[13] Recognizing this, as well as the opportunity to cash in on a flush economy, canny entrepreneurs introduced more elaborate versions of sporting activities. George G. Foster, in his exposé-guidebook *New York by Gas-Light,* noted the increasing sophistication of drinking establishments in the city:

> Our billiard-"rooms" and ten-pin-"alleys" have been transformed into "saloons"—our oyster "cellars" and drinking shops have emulated their example; and as to a good old-fashioned barber's shop, there is not such a thing to be found within the circumference of the city. To what extent this saloon-mania will spread, it is impossible to calculate.[14]

Newly introduced during the 1850s was the wildly successful concert-saloon. With its pretty "waiter-girls," informal musical performances, and bar, the concert-saloon amalgamated the most powerful vices: prostitution, alcohol, and theater. Another sporting attraction in New York was Kit Burns's Rat Pit, which encouraged gambling (Figure 1.4).

The appeal and peril of these establishments, and the sporting life more generally, for young men fresh from the country was vividly portrayed in the

FIGURE 1.4. "A Dogfight at Kit Burns's," in Edward Winslow Martin, *The Secrets of the Great City*, 1868.

frontispiece of Edward Winslow Martin's voyeuristic guidebook, *The Secrets of the Great City*. Compressing the stages of debasement portrayed in William Hogarth's *The Rake's Progress* (1732–33) in a single image, it details the steady decline and ultimate death of an unwary young man at the hands of disreputable men and loose women in the dens of New York (Figure 1.5). The dangers to young men, though perhaps exaggerated to increase book sales, were real enough. In New York and other cities young men, often under the age of twenty, were seduced by drink or vice, which dashed their ambitions or ruined their health.

For those who felt the pull of home ties, sporting culture and commercial entertainment may have been fascinating, but also frightening. The pious, the ambitious, and those seeking to avoid the "man-traps" of the city turned to the more familiar evangelical culture of New England as their leisure-time resource. Some young migrants to the city sought spiritual succor, self-improvement, and the social ties they enjoyed through church-related activities at home. These connections were not only important for their immediate personal happiness, but also to help guide them through the increasingly torturous path to career success, financial stability, and marriage.

It was, however, difficult for "strangers" without money or family to

FIGURE 1.5. Frontispiece, Edward Winslow Martin, *The Secrets of the Great City,* 1868.

THE FATE OF HUNDREDS OF YOUNG MEN.

1. LEAVING HOME FOR NEW YORK. 2. IN A FASHIONABLE SALOON AMONGST THE WAITER GIRLS—THE ROAD TO RUIN. 3. DRINKING WITH "THE FANCY"—IN THE HANDS OF GAMBLERS. 4. MURDERED AND ROBBED BY HIS "FANCY" COMPANIONS. 5. HIS BODY FOUND BY THE HARBOR POLICE.

establish themselves in the increasingly status-conscious elite Protestant congregations of the age. Throughout the 1850s wealthy congregations erected elaborate Gothic revival buildings that served as much as social clubs as houses of worship.[15] Church membership in the established Presbyterian, Congregational, and Methodist churches required the rental of a pew, and attendance in a Broadway congregation on Sunday morning, as one observer noted, required a prosperous appearance: "if you wore a suit of fashionably cut black; your boots fit neatly; your gloves are fresh . . . you have the odor of jasmine on your person: you can enter unquestioned and sanctified."[16] If, however, a young man showed up in a threadbare suit, he would be ignored. Functioning primarily as arenas for status display and self-identification, churches did not reach out to the marginal young men who strayed into their sanctuaries, nor did they know what to do with them once there.[17] Although there were some complaints about the lack of social feeling and sympathy with young men among evangelicals, little was done to find a place for them.

One exception was the Sunday school. Popular since the eighteenth century, these schools ministered to the children of the working poor, offering instruction in reading and writing in return for the opportunity to teach the Bible and inculcate middle-class values. Standing at the head of the class, the teachers enjoyed a position of power and virtue in relationship to their charges. The role of teacher in Sunday school opened an avenue for a young man (and in some cases, a woman) to participate in religious life, develop social connections, and fulfill a role of civic and spiritual responsibility that was central to his evangelical identity and the role of the "Christian gentleman."[18] In every way the antithesis to the sporting man, the Christian gentleman, a strictly middle-class archetype, defined himself through hard work and philanthropy in the interest of the public good. Through good works he balanced his material success and his ethics, and in the process reduced class conflicts and tensions. Many successful Christian gentlemen, including department store magnate (and YMCA leader) John Wanamaker of Philadelphia, taught Sunday school in their salad days, and went on to endow and build them after they had achieved success. Sunday school teaching was an indication to the world, and to employers, of one's conformity to established values.

The YMCA, with its focus on productive and respectable leisure activities, occupied a site at the intersection of the Sunday school and the saloon, acknowledging a gray area that emerged for young men in the 1850s. It appealed to those young men still in flux, who had not yet reached the height of their careers: a deputy customs collector, a clerk, a broker, the editor of a religious paper, a dry-goods dealer, and a hatter.[19] Organized and run by young men for young men, it acknowledged the temptations of sporting culture and offered an alternative structure for leisure time, a religious reinterpretation of an elite men's club, with its masculine yet domestic comforts.

Membership was a path to friendship and fellowship, but also a way of maintaining home values, and a way to broadcast reliability to potential employers, who listed jobs with the YMCA's employment bureau. In the parlor of the YMCA, a young man, a "stranger" unwelcome in the home of his employer, could find a warm welcome and practice the genteel manners and skills necessary to success and marriage. Bible study, lectures on "Early Business Days of Successful Men" and "Christian Manliness," access to the latest papers, and evangelical work filled his free time.[20]

The success of the YMCA expanded tremendously in the wake of the financial panic of 1857. A sudden downturn in the American economy, linked to losses by land speculators and a lack of confidence in government specie, led to the failure of more than five thousand businesses, shaking the national business community, which had been enjoying a period of great prosperity and expansion. Many individuals, whose material prosperity had allowed them to marry and establish middle-class lives and homes, lost their livelihoods suddenly. In this uncertain business atmosphere and faced with catastrophic reverses, many businessmen were attracted to special noontime revival meetings organized for them by the YMCA in the business districts of New York, Boston, and other cities. Thousands underwent conversion and joined the YMCA and evangelical churches.

The success of the revival and the enthusiasm of new members sparked many associations to shift their emphasis from work dedicated specifically to the social and spiritual needs of young men to more general interdenominational missionary work: tent revivals, tract distribution, and relief for the poor. The Chicago YMCA, led by prominent evangelist Dwight Moody, was in the forefront of this activity, serving as a community-wide distributor of poor relief and supervising the North Market Mission Sunday School. Most YMCAs became clearinghouses for pious young men interested in pursuing general evangelical duties, rather than a program of leisure activities. With rare exceptions, little direct effort was made for the conversion of young men.[21] The rented rooms of the associations became venues for revival meetings and committee work where not only men of all ages but even women were welcomed in the effort to redeem the world.

The Effect of the Civil War: New Leadership and a New Mission

Within a few years another national catastrophe, the Civil War, refocused the organization's attention and work on the particular needs of young men, separated from home and facing mortal danger. The war made young men highly visible and concentrated anxieties about them throughout the North. In addition to mustering special "Christian" regiments from among its members, the YMCA organized the Christian Commission in 1861. Founded and headquartered in New York City, its structure was similar to the United States Sanitary Commission, with local chapters sending donations to serve the spiritual needs of their young men far from home. The Christian

Commission printed and distributed hymnals, Bibles, writing paper, pens, postage, and delicacies. Its more than five thousand volunteers, including Chicago YMCA leader Moody, wrote letters for the wounded, held Bible study and prayer meetings, and generally served as chaplains, working in field hospitals and even on battlegrounds.[22] Ladies' auxiliaries raised more than $3 million. This active service placed the YMCA in the spotlight once again, at the same time that the special needs of young men, in this case soldiers, were the center of attention.

As the New York YMCA emerged from the war years, it attracted the attention of supporters who could see the potential of a coordinated national organization for young men in the industrial America that grew out of the theater of war. By 1864 the leadership, its directors and officers, turned over completely, changing the direction and mission of the organization. Inspired by the active role the Y played in ministering to young soldiers, William E. Dodge Jr. and several of his cousins and friends effected a bloodless coup and took over the organization with visionary ideas about the role the Association could play in shaping and defining modern culture.

This wartime change in leadership was a remarkable transformation, bringing a wealthy, influential, and homogeneous group of businessmen into power. Before the war the directors of the Association were mostly reform-minded civic leaders, educators, doctors, and small-scale businessmen. Norman A. Calkins, the assistant superintendent of schools, was a director, as was distinguished mathematician and textbook author John F. Stoddard, minister Stephen Tyng, and artist Vincent Colyer. There were some merchants and businessmen on the board, but, with a few exceptions, they were not well established. The story of Nason B. Collins, a director in 1862, is suggestive of the relatively uncertain status of the YMCA's business leaders during wartime. Collins's fortunes as a flour broker and commission agent were checkered by periods of boom and bust. According to R. G. Dun's credit agency, in the 1850s he had trouble paying creditors, was "ruined" in the panic of 1857, and had to operate under his wife's name for a short period. His YMCA membership helped him maintain his reputation for "good character" throughout these difficult times. He recovered to some extent in the 1860s by selling goods to the Union Army and took on a leadership role in the Y, but his position in mercantile society remained marginal, and he dropped from the YMCA's board in 1864.[23]

By contrast, the new directors brought with them family and professional connections to the city's most prominent bankers, merchants, and manufacturers. Born Connecticut Yankees, they shared an evangelical upbringing and a deep commitment to the future of the industrial economy, including investment banking, large-scale manufacture, railroads, and corporate enterprises. These men knew one another through family connections, through business, through the Union League Club, and, perhaps most important, through church membership in the city's elite evangelical congregations: the Fifth Avenue Presbyterian Church, Madison Square Presbyterian Church,

Church of the Ascension (Protestant Episcopal), St. George's Episcopal Church, and St. Paul's Episcopal Church.

The group was dominated by men in their thirties who had come of age during the Civil War. Some inherited their wealth, like William Harman Brown, William E. Dodge Jr., and James Stokes Jr. At the time they joined the board Brown was a son of the Brown Brothers banking house, and Dodge and Stokes, cousins, were heirs to Phelps, Dodge, and Co. mercantile house. This firm, founded in the 1840s, began as an import-export company and began to specialize in the acquisition of metals, including copper, tin, iron, and zinc, for which they exchanged American cotton. They refined and manufactured these materials into a variety of goods essential to the industrial development of the United States, including clocks, rivets, and the copper wire used in the first transcontinental telegraph wire, completed in 1861. They were also heavily invested in railroads, including the Delaware, Lackawanna, and Western.[24] Other young members of wealthy evangelical families committed themselves to the YMCA, including Percy R. Pyne, son-in-law of prominent merchant Moses Taylor, and Stephen D. Hatch, an architect and the son of one of the city's most prominent financiers, Alfrederick Smith Hatch. Another new leader, J. P. Morgan, born into merchant money, was in the process of making his own fortune in the bonanza economy by financing the war and speculating in gold.

Sprinkled amid these young heirs was a group of self-made men, like Jacob Wyckoff, who began life as a humble clerk, started his own hides and leather firm in 1862, and amassed a fortune of $150,000 just two years later, selling boots to the army.[25] Another director, John S. Kennedy, who began his career as an Irish immigrant, made his money by financing and supplying western railroad construction, including the Illinois Central and the Northern Pacific. Although they lacked the background of the other men, they had followed the Yankee aristocracy's path of hard work and subscribed to the gospel of success that had made the Dodges, Stokes, Browns, and other families rich. They were also intimately involved in the same enterprises of railroads, banking, and manufacturing.

At the time these men took over the YMCA, capitalism was changing rapidly. When their fathers had come of age in the era of entrepreneurial producer capitalism, young men could still rise quickly from being a clerk to a wealthy merchant. As they came of age, fundamental shifts in the structure and function of economic enterprise, begun in the 1840s, accelerated, culminating in what historian Alan Trachtenberg has called the "incorporation of America." In the years approaching the Civil War, the economy grew and diversified, mercantile enterprises became more complex, and YMCA leaders, their friends, and families were at the center of change. Henry Adams noted that "the generation between 1865 and 1895 was already mortgaged to the railways and no one knew it better than the generation itself."[26] The YMCA men developed the insurance industry as well as transportation and communication systems that transformed the scale of business enterprise and its methods, including the first transatlantic cable. By the Civil War more than 30,000 miles of rail track had been laid, and the construction of the Union Pacific Railroad, beginning in 1863, heralded the beginning of a new interregional society and an increasingly integrated economy that linked West to East and small communities to large.[27] The effect of the railroads on business practices in this period is well documented; they laid the groundwork for twentieth-century big business. Railroads were the first to develop companies with many centers of operation and complex managerial hierarchies, the first to be regulated by both state and federal governments, the first to have great armies of stockholders and bondholders, and the first to deal with public relations and problems of community welfare. The new leaders of the YMCA shared success and involvement in a business revolution that was to transform the lives of white-collar men and reshape the social and economic landscape of the United States.

William E. Dodge Jr. and J. P. Morgan

The personal histories of two of these leaders, William E. Dodge Jr. and J. P. Morgan, suggest some of the contrasting interests and motivations that drove them to take on the leadership of the Young Men's Christian Association. Dodge, one of the most energetic and ambitious new leaders of the Y, was viewed as an upstanding young member of the Yankee business community, the very embodiment of the evangelical masculine ideal: the Christian gentleman (Figure 1.6). A junior partner in his father's well-established mercantile company by the age of sixteen, he helped the business survive the panic of 1857 and went on to transform their business as cotton jobbers into a diversified national corporation involved in the mining, processing, and production of lumber, metals, and copper and brass products from New Jersey to California.

FIGURE 1.6. Portrait of William E. Dodge Jr. in the early 1860s.

Even at a young age Dodge's potential was widely recognized. Diarist George Templeton Strong raved that

> Dodge is certainly among the best men we have. He must spend nearly all his time in undertakings for the public good, in which he is most useful without the least self-seeking or ostentation, keeping himself always in the background as far as may be. His manners are refined and attractive. He is likely to become a very prominent man.[28]

His good works were extensive for one so young, and focused on the needs of young men and employees. By age nineteen he had founded churches for his company's employees at the Bozrah mill in Connecticut and for his lumbermen in Tioga County, Pennsylvania, and had already served as an active member of the Fourteenth Street Presbyterian Church. During the war he took an active role in the Christian Commission and started an allotment savings program for soldiers, encouraging them to bank their pay.

Dodge's particular interest in the YMCA as a cause may well have been sparked by the checkered career of his brother, Anson G. P. Dodge, who did not succeed in the terms of manhood and Christianity established by his family. If Will, as he was known, was a bit of a throwback, a Christian gentleman who symbolized the old values, Anson was the perfect image of a sporting man. He fell into bad company at school and displayed an unwillingness to work hard and delay gratification. Hoping to reform Anson's character, his father, William E. Dodge Sr., removed him from the temptations of his comfortable life to a remote village in the family's vast timber holdings. From there the son moved constantly, investing money in unsuccessful business schemes in Baltimore and Canada that ultimately culminated in bankruptcy. He was a potent example of young men's need for moral guidance and training in their business enterprises.

Like Anson Dodge, Morgan was comfortable testing the elasticity of his moral heritage, if more successfully. A bit younger than Will Dodge, and with a more modest set of fashionable sideburns, Morgan was thirty years old in 1864, with his days as a robber baron still ahead of him (Figure 1.7). At this point he was still under the shadow of his father, a highly successful evangelical Yankee merchant. Like Dodge, Morgan had a Connecticut background, and spent quite a bit of his childhood with his grandmother, who attended church all day on Sunday.[29] Pierpont, as he was known, had been educated in Europe, and returned to the United States in the panic year of 1857. He spent the early 1860s in a junior clerkship arranged by his father at Duncan, Sherman and Company and enjoyed an active status as man about town, attending social functions and perhaps enjoying some of the attractions of the sporting life. By 1864 he had set up his own firm, Dabney, Morgan, and Company, to supply capital for railroad development and soon became a partner in Drexel and Company, establishing himself in the newly developing field of investment banking.[30] The fluid practices of these enterprises, still evolving at this point into the modern corporate business system, frustrated him.[31] He was eager to establish systems and procedures to govern the new business ways, and the YMCA may well have appealed to him as a new and efficient way to educate and socialize white-collar men for the new middle-management roles emerging in corporate America.

The personal history of these two very differ-

FIGURE 1.7. Portrait of J. P. Morgan in the late 1860s.

ent men led them to the YMCA. For Dodge, the YMCA was an extension of his interest in the spiritual lives of young men. For Morgan, it may have been a means to regulate and structure the new world he was involved in shaping. They were also attracted to the Y by common interests that transcended their individual circumstances. This was, at the most basic level, a cause they could call their own. Their fathers, uncles, and employers not only were leaders in their churches, but also took an active role in organizing and funding antebellum reform organizations like the American Bible Society, tract and missionary societies, and denominational Sunday schools. They bequeathed to these young leaders a commitment to religious reform. The YMCA offered them a way of defining their class and masculine identity as evangelical philanthropists while distinguishing them from their fathers' generation. Thus, this kind of good-neighborliness was not an entirely selfless activity, but an attempt to consolidate their class status and authority and to redefine their masculinity.

On the surface, the YMCA offered them a chance to work with and assist men less fortunate, who had to seek out a position in the business world, rather than inheriting one as they had. The 1864 annual report, the first produced by the new Board of Directors, emphasized this rationale by pointing out that "young men educated in New York, with happy surroundings, and knowing its dangers, have a responsibility towards the vast number of friendless strangers coming here, which they cannot throw off."[32] They knew firsthand how difficult it could be to make it in a world of flux, as the apprenticeship system that had made their fathers wealthy slowly disappeared without any clear path of success to replace it.[33] In the growing fields of life insurance, banking, and civil service, the clerk in the countinghouse was increasingly replaced by armies of white-collar workers housed in new purpose-built office buildings and processing the increasing paperwork these enterprises produced. The chance of building a business, or even entering into upper-level management through clerical work, was increasingly minimal. The war brought about an enlargement of federal government and bureaucracy, further transforming the old mercantile economy to a national corporate entity. The subdivision and stratification of tasks, especially in record keeping and communication, increasingly meant that clerkship was no longer an apprenticeship for an executive position.

Clerkship meant stagnation, or even downward mobility, and the job was increasingly assigned to women. As soldiers returned from the battlefield they moved from one kind of army to another. Those interested in white collars increasingly traded in their blue uniforms for a new kind of job in the fields of life insurance, banking, and civil service, especially in large cities like New York, Philadelphia, and Chicago. Eventually a college education would replace apprenticeship as the entrée to business success. In the meantime, the YMCA helped aspiring young men negotiate the change for themselves in their leisure time.

The YMCA and the Culture of White-Collar Work

Helping the less fortunate help themselves was certainly a good deed, in keeping with the philanthropic traditions of the YMCA leaders' evangelical heritage, but it was also a way to cushion the social dislocation brought about by the war and these business changes. The masculine identity these leaders had inherited from their fathers, the role of the Christian gentleman, was in flux. As Olivier Zunz has noted, the new businessman "had a fundamentally different outlook than the small merchants, professional men of learning, expounders of religion or aristocratic country gentlemen of the antebellum world."[34] Threats to the social and economic authority of male Yankee evangelicals, from women, freedmen, and labor, already emerging before the Civil War, intensified during the 1860s.

Middle-class women left their home sphere in large numbers to raise money and nurse the wounded. Unpaid household work became public and political.[35] Although evangelical women were already involved in public charitable work in the antebellum period, the leadership role assumed by women during the war, both at home and in the field, was unprecedented. The exigencies of the war required that the separation of spheres be breached, at least temporarily. The moral capitalist order forged in the antebellum period was crumbling, upsetting the carefully negotiated spatial and gender boundaries between religion and business.

The position of white evangelicals vis-à-vis black men during the war and after emancipation was fundamentally challenged despite (or perhaps because of) their typically abolitionist views. With memories of the New York City Draft Riots still fresh in their minds, New York Y leaders, who had bought their way out of enlistment in the Union Army, were no doubt quite concerned about the repercussions of the growing class divisions within American society. Labor-capital relationships were not the only source of anxiety, however. The increasing divisions within and between the middle and upper classes were also of concern. The new corporate structure fundamentally altered republican notions of individuality and mobility, defining a static managerial middle-class identity for many men. This "change in business ways" meant the hardening of boundaries, a growing impersonality in the relationship between employer and employee. Before the war, office clerks were closer to their employers in dress, status, and prospects than they were to factory workers. After the war, this was not the case.

The leaders of the Y noted the beginnings of this development in their 1867 annual report and cautioned readers about the emotional consequences of such a shift:

> With the change in city ways during the last few years, those employed in our offices and warehouses, and living in cheerless boarding houses,

are rapidly forming a class by themselves. They must be absorbed in our Christian life and activity, or they will become demoralized, disheartened, and disillusioned.[36]

In this state of disillusionment, they were more easily tempted by the attractions offered by a new leisure culture. As Gail Bederman has pointed out, the proliferation of "consumer pleasures and commercial leisure promised men more palpable rewards than Christian self-denial and hard work."[37] To the business community, young men represented the future. If they remained in the clutches of the saloon, the only lessons they would learn would be greed and self-indulgence.

Another threat to the morals of aspiring Protestant businessmen was the rise of a new, morally dubious code of ethics attendant to the formation of large corporations and trusts.[38] The carefully brokered antebellum marriage of market relations to religion was taxed to the breaking point by the rise of big business. The structure of the modern corporation allowed businessmen to divorce themselves personally from unethical behavior, offering an immoral role model for young men. Employers, fearful of the "disillusionment" of this new "class" of workers, needed to promote the allegiance, productivity, and compliance of this middling group with the new corporate order. They also needed a means of training young men whom they no longer directly oversaw.[39] New bourgeois elites like Dodge and Morgan sought new means to organize a disciplined, virtuous citizenry and a dynamic market economy.

The YMCA must have been appealing to Dodge, Morgan, and their friends for a range of reasons. The success of this new generation of financiers, manufacturers, lawyers, and real-estate moguls rested upon the value system of their pious, country-born, self-made fathers. Fearful of the future of the urbanizing nation, they strove to maintain the Protestant value system that might produce success in the next generation of aspiring businessmen: their employees. With an inborn entrepreneurial spirit, they recognized the need for a new kind of agency to guide the conscience of urban young men, an institution to take up the moralizing role of the home and to teach young men how to reconcile Christian morals with the aggressive tactics of modern business. Existing evangelical methods of reform, including benevolent associations, tract distribution, and missions, were no longer sufficient to smooth the rough edges of laissez-faire capitalism, now severely tested by war, immigration, economic depression, and astounding growth. The social and economic conditions of Reconstruction cast the YMCA in a newly attractive light.[40] Commenting on the need for modern methods of social reform, Dodge later said, "Men are of no use who study to do exactly as was done before, who can never understand that today is a new day."[41]

Some of the new leaders knew the organization firsthand and had been early members. As abolitionists they had left the organization several years earlier, when the group refused to take a stand on the issue. Now they saw much potential in the original mission to young men to address what they saw as a growing societal need: a modern urban institution designed to provide a moral framework for the emerging corporate, consumer culture. Although Bederman dates the beginning of this activity to the 1880s I would argue that the Y provides evidence that this struggle began even earlier.[42] The men who took over the Y in the late 1860s did not have to wait to experience the dislocating effects of corporate capitalism and consumer culture. They were the makers and shapers of this new economy. It was, I would argue, the early and conflicted realization of the social consequences of their economic activities that attracted them to the YMCA. Faced with fundamental changes in the structure of business, growing class divisions and conflict, the increasing presence of women in public life, and challenges to Protestant hegemony by vital commercial and ethnic cultures, these men saw in the YMCA an opportunity to reconstruct the social fabric and their place within it.

Thus they understood and presented the potential of the Y as an important resource not only to young men:

> but also to their employers, their country and the church. . . . To their employers, for it furnishes them with honest, active, intelligent clerks and workmen, instead of careless, stupid, pilfering gambling inebriates. To their country, for it gives it useful citizens, able statesmen and strong defenders, instead of felons and paupers to fill its penitentiaries, eat up its substance, and debase its sons; and to the church to which it gives men of piety and zeal for its prayer meetings, its Sabbath Schools, its mission schools, its tract districts, and all its works of love and charity by which it strives to bring salvation to man and honor to God.[43]

The problem of young men was thus not only the problem of individual young men, but the problem of society at large. The Y's mission was to "develop the working power and increase the capacity for usefulness of every young man."[44]

Reconstructing the YMCA

In planning for this move the reinvigorated YMCA became a new kind of urban institution, one designed not only to shape the character and spirituality of individual young men, but to shape big business: to regularize it, to sanction it, to reconcile individual ideas and official behavior regulated through corporate culture and roles. The YMCA sought to offer an outline of modern white-collar manhood and its place in the emerging national corporate culture.

In its prewar iteration as a voluntary organization, the YMCA could not meet this goal. It needed to be rethought and reorganized to meet the needs of the new business culture of incorporation. More aggressive, more secular, and more businesslike tactics, a broadening of the audience, and, most important, a building were all central to the new leadership's vision of the modern YMCA. In a period of five years they undertook fundamental changes. Each year their work, claimed the 1868 *Annual Report*, became "more systematized, and conducted on truer business principles."[45]

One of the first priorities of this new leadership was the application of contemporary business practices to the YMCA. Their new vision for the Y (as a cultural mechanism) required a shift from the antebellum model of the voluntary association to a model that mirrored the more hierarchical, bureaucratic structures that were transforming the mercantile world of their fathers. One of the first and most important elements of this change was the professionalization of YMCA work. They took the planning and management of YMCA affairs out of the hands of committees of young members and gave them over to Robert McBurney (Figure 1.8). Of Scotch-Irish descent, he had emigrated to this country to make his fortune and started in the world of business in the firm of Brainerd and Manierre, an importers' and traders' insurance company. He was, as Y leader and prominent banker Cephas Brainerd remembered him, gifted with an entrepreneurial spirit and the necessary foresight and executive qualities for business success. Such a notable businessman as Dodge Sr. is quoted as saying that he "would have made a business man of the first rank."[46] Yet McBurney also felt a strong sense of religious mission. Encouraged by his employers, he attended an evangelical church, became involved in the YMCA, and taught a Sunday school class. Like many young men of the era in the early years of his career, he was uncertain of what path to follow, particularly as the paths to success in business grew less and less defined.

FIGURE 1.8. Robert McBurney in 1870.

Drawn to both evangelicalism and business, McBurney struggled to reconcile the morals and teachings of the church with the tenets of commerce. For a brief period in 1862 he thought he might combine the two in paid work for the YMCA, and worked as librarian and janitor in the Bible House rooms. After just a short time, he grew frustrated with the limits of that position and left the city to take a new job in a Philadelphia importing firm. When Dodge Jr. and the new leaders reorganized the Y in 1864, they proposed that he return, this time to a dynamic and creative leadership role. Taking a great personal risk, he accepted, looking forward to an opportunity to minister to the souls of young men, who, like him, had to find their way amid the perils and temptations of the city. With the support of Dodge, Morgan, and others, McBurney took on and defined a new chief executive job of administration and management later termed "general secretary." Combining some of the pastoral duties of a clergyman with businesslike entrepreneurship, McBurney fashioned a new and unusual masculine role that combined the intuitive, the sentimental, and the personal with administrative efficacy.

Under McBurney's leadership the Y made a first effort toward redefinition by opening its libraries to nonmembers and offering free lectures. While this did not attract many young men, it did represent a shift from the Y as a club for the pious to the Y as a larger social service organization. McBurney planned several branches: one for German immigrants in Kleindeutschland (Little Germany), one for colored men, and two reading rooms in the downtown boardinghouse districts on the East and West Sides.[47] These would extend the socialization process beyond the white-collar commercial district and present the Y's vision of a universal, consensual culture based on evangelical Protestantism to the city's working classes. That year also brought two major organizational developments: incorporation, which allowed the Y to hold property, and the introduction of what came to be called the fourfold plan of work, which extended the mission to address the social, mental, spiritual, and *physical* needs of young men, paving the way for a gymnasium and a more liberal attitude toward amusements in general.

The addition of this fourth element to the program was a radical change that addressed the bodily health of young men a decade before the Muscular Christianity movement and collegiate athletics legitimized and linked athletics with religion.[48] Dodge and McBurney presented their decision as a bait-and-switch strategy: the introduction of a gym in the New York Y was at this time primarily a competitive lure designed to attract young men who would then, it was hoped, be drawn to other, more respectable activities.[49] They claimed that within the uplifting environment of the YMCA building athletics were a perfectly respectable pastime: it was neither sport itself, nor the focus on the body that was sinful, but rather the activities and spaces typically associated with sport that were degrading. Despite criticism, the New York YMCA leadership departed from this point of view that sport itself was degrading.

The new leadership's decision to make a gymnasium a "respectable" part of their new clubhouse may well have been influenced by an ethnic German organization: the turnverein. First organized by ardent nationalists in Berlin in 1811, it combined physical training with a strong political mission against French cultural domination. When many fled Germany in the aftermath of the 1848 revolutions, they were quick to set up new organizations in the United States. They brought with them a vision of physical training married to a strong political, cultural, and educational mission.[50]

In New York the Turners first organized in 1850 and in a series of rented rooms in the Lower East Side enclave of Kleindeutschland they provided facilities for a rich program of educational, physical, and social activities, including a gymnasium, a library and reading room stocked with German books and periodicals (including translations of important American classics), a hall with a stage, classrooms, and a bar and restaurant.[51] In addition to its central focus on gymnastics, the turnverein was home to a dramatic club that staged frequent plays and performances, a fencing group, a singing group, and social evenings of discussion and debate on important issues of the day, particularly politics.

These activities, like those of the original Turners in Germany, were intended to support the well-rounded physical and mental development of members and to promote a vision of good citizenship that combined revolutionary fervor and love of freedom with physical preparedness to protect it. This militant citizenship, proven by the active service of thousands of Turners on the Union side in the Civil War, was fused with a desire to preserve the forms of German culture and tradition. As historians like David Gerber and Kathleen Conzen have suggested, such festivities demonstrated to a still Puritanical America how sports could be incorporated into a respectable, family-oriented culture.[52] Along with other German immigrant institutions like the beer garden and the music festival, the turnverein was instrumental in reshaping the way Americans structured and experienced their leisure in the second half of the nineteenth century. Devoting their free time to sports like yachting, baseball, bowling, and billiards, Y leaders themselves were products of this change. Thus it is little wonder that they saw in the turnverein something very valuable to their vision of the Y: a programmatic and spatial model that parlayed uplift, amusement, and group identity for young men into a symbol of cohesion to the community at large.[53]

The New York YMCA's new fourfold mission was, to some, shocking. A gymnasium, although it may have attracted more members, was still perceived by most evangelicals to be too closely associated with the culture of the sporting life.[54] In 1857 the Brooklyn YMCA put forth a proposal to the YMCA national convention for a building that was to include a gymnasium, bowling alleys, and classrooms in addition to the standard reading room and library. It met with resistance, not only among clergy, but even among employers, who forbade their clerks to play baseball or cricket, two time-consuming games that were "declared to be the enemy of business habits."[55]

The response of evangelical clergymen to the idea of amusements and athletics in a Christian building after the war varied. Some hard-liners continued to voice concerns about the respectability of the gymnasium, even publishing defamatory articles in the religious press.[56] More supportive were the pastors of the wealthy Manhattan congregations that served the business elite. Stephen Tyng, rector of the Church of the Holy Trinity and an active member in the YMCA, pragmatically suggested that the way to attract a young man was to "lure them [sic] with amusements and then lead him upward in his search for pleasure, until he sees the folly of his former course."[57]

This split between more orthodox and progressive forces was mirrored within the organization itself. On the one hand were the remnants of the old leadership, like Dr. Verranus Morse, former treasurer. In a speech on "Amusements" he revealed his beliefs on the contentious subject to the Y membership. He said that he "did not think it [could] be judicious to introduce them [amusements] into the family, or the Christian assembly, because they so excite and stimulate the evil passions, and imperil the moral character."[58] Not only could these activities lead to gambling, drink, and promiscuity, he claimed, but they also might affect the honesty of businessmen, who could apply the tricks used in games and sports to their affairs in order to obtain an unfair advantage. Even the influence of the church was not considered holy enough to sanctify card-playing and kindred games.[59]

On the other hand was the new Board of Directors, whose members indulged in every sort of amusement money could buy. The schism is well illustrated by the awkwardness that followed the donation by Mrs. J. P. Morgan of a billiards table for the new YMCA building.[60] Her husband and all his friends played the game, and many of them had a billiards room in their own homes. How was she to know that it was an inappropriate gift? Her lack of awareness underscores the change in the organization's leadership and the role this had in legitimizing leisure as a moral and productive activity. The New York YMCA sought to combine the features of the mercantile library with the club. In effect, the YMCA was an evangelical mission, not to the poor or the heathen, but to migrant young men. The YMCA building reinterpreted the idea of a mission church for young men in the language of leisure.

The other major transformation Dodge and McBurney undertook was a campaign to build a permanent YMCA headquarters. Since its inception in 1852 the New York YMCA had voiced a desire for a building, citing the need for a structure to provide permanence and financial security to the enterprise.[61] The founders conceived of a building as a stable spatial container that would anchor a fledgling enterprise. By the time the Y realized its dream in 1869, the proposed role of the building had grown far beyond the antebellum concept of permanent space. Architecture took on a more instrumental role in the organization, beyond the provision of financial security and status. With rhetoric similar to that of the Masons, they saw themselves as builders, metaphorically connecting their enterprise to that of the supreme architect, God. They were anxious to repair the "divided house," its beams broken during the war years, with an "edifice designed for durability . . . firmly consolidated, rightly adjusted, that the future may reveal only the graceful and well-proportioned to the praise of the Great Master Builder."[62] Both a symbol of a modern, ethical, corporate culture and an efficient tool to produce it, the YMCA building became both the message and the medium through which the group's goals were communicated and achieved. To the Y's young and ambitious leadership a new building was, in fact, the most important item on their agenda.[63] The issues of location, amenities, and design occupied their attention from the time they took control of the YMCA until the day they dedicated the new building.

When Morgan and the new leadership came on board in 1864, the Y was, owing to financial difficulty and greatly reduced membership, renting rooms in the Bible House on Astor Place (Figure 1.9). Owned by the American Bible Society, this enormous building just east of Broadway at Fourth Street not

26 / RECONCILING MORALITY AND MAMMON

BIBLE HOUSE, COOPER INSTITUTE, AND CLINTON HALL.

FIGURE 1.9. Astor Place, New York (Bible House, Cooper Institute, and Clinton Hall). From B. J. Lossing, *Hudson, from the Wilderness to the Sea*, 1866.

only housed the massive printing presses of the Society, but also served as home to more than a dozen of the city's evangelical voluntary associations. The rents were no doubt reasonable and the landlords shared the middle-class values and evangelical agenda of the Y, but the surroundings did not appeal to the Y's prospective membership.

Relocating the YMCA

With persistence and verve, the new leadership regrouped and over the next four years worked to convince their families and the Yankee business community of the relevance and feasibility of their vision.[64] They realized that even if the YMCA could not buy its own building, it certainly needed to fulfill another aspect of McBurney's proposal: to move north from the Bible House. This "improving" location (and relatively cheap rent) was appropriate enough for the Y's old role as an evangelical reform group, but by 1864 it was an increasingly problematic site (Figure 1.10). Home to the Cooper Union (1859), the Astor Library (1854), and the Mercantile Library's rooms in Clinton Hall (formerly the Astor Place Opera House, 1848), the area was once dubbed the "Athenian Quarter." By the 1860s, however, the aura of refinement and self-improvement was being challenged by the encroachment of a landscape of commercial leisure and sporting culture: the Bowery.

New York had always had vice areas near the waterfronts, but by mid century new, more consolidated districts had emerged.[65] During the war years concert-saloons, dance halls, beer gardens, brothels, and dime museums lined the Bowery from Chatham Square to Astor Place. As confidence men plied their trade, peddlers and bands played in the streets every night of the week despite Sunday closing laws. Brightly lit by gas and thronged with pleasure seekers, this increasingly dense landscape of cheap commercial entertainment drew people from across the social spectrum: soldiers and visiting merchants, German families, "slumming" gentlemen, and less than respectable women. Broadway north of Houston was known as a haunt for more elite pleasure seekers, especially at night. As James McCabe noted in his 1869 exposé of New York:

> The street resounds with cheerful voices and merry laughter, over which occasionally rises a drunken howl. Strains of music or bursts of applause float out on the night air from places of amusement. . . .

Gaudily painted transparencies allure the unwary to the vile concert saloons in the cellars below the street. The restaurants and cafes are ablaze with light, and are liberally patronized by the lovers of good living.[66]

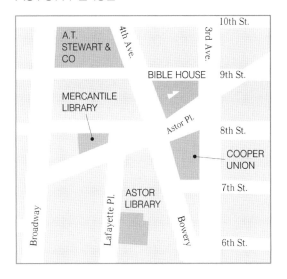

FIGURE 1.10. Astor Place map, 1865–70.

Beyond the obvious objections to sinful activity, the mixture of classes, nationalities, and men and women in common pursuit of pleasure and spectacle challenged established evangelical hierarchies and values and the mercantile vision of an orderly and productive society. Along with legitimate theater owners, who had a vested interest in maintaining the respectability of the stage, pastors and prominent and powerful members of the Society for the Reformation of Juvenile Delinquents attempted to regulate public amusements and proscribe behavior in the Bowery with the Concert Hall Act of 1862. The stated goal of the largely unsuccessful bill was to "preserve the peace and order in the public places of the City of New York" by prohibiting the sale of liquor in theaters.[67] Although this had an initial dampening effect on the concert-saloon business, it became clear that the law would not be enforced and was largely ignored.

The failure of the Concert Hall Act forced the new leaders of the YMCA to accept the inability of the YMCA to compete with the culture of the Bowery in their fusty Bible House rooms. Rather than reforming downtown or engaging directly with sporting culture, they proposed to provide an alternative so that the men handling the paperwork of the nation's new capitalist machinery could maintain their masculinity and their morality at the same time.

One of Morgan's first acts as treasurer was to find space that would help attract more members.[68] Along with the rest of genteel society, he looked uptown. In the fall of 1864 the Y found and furnished temporary rooms in a house at Fifth Avenue and Twenty-second Street, across the street from the prestigious Fifth Avenue Hotel and a stone's throw from Madison Square.

Landscape of Consumption and Leisure

The location selected by Morgan and his colleagues was the city's and the nation's most spectacular commercial district, now known as the Ladies' Mile. This district had, in the antebellum period, been an elite residential neighborhood dotted with church spires. The explosion of commercial activity had removed or subsumed the physical evidence of religion in the landscape. In the bonanza economy of the Civil War the area exploded with commercial development. The elite residential district moved north along Fifth Avenue, and the churches followed. The remaining sanctuaries were demolished or converted to commercial use. Several church buildings were reused as stables, as was the case with a structure just a few blocks from the YMCA on Twenty-third Street near Sixth Avenue. The Church of the

FIGURE 1.11. View to the north along Broadway at Tenth Street, New York, showing A. T. Stewart & Co. in the foreground and Grace Church in the background.

Messiah, on Broadway opposite the New York Hotel, was converted into a theater.[69] A few prominent congregations stayed put, notably Grace Church, which had chosen the site at Broadway and Tenth when it was a suburb. By the 1850s the church was jostling for attention with the cast-iron palazzo façade of the adjacent "Cast Iron Palace," A. T. Stewart's second department store (Figure 1.11). The strong architectural contrast between these two institutions embodied the tension inherent in the mercantile community between Mammon and morality.

Grace Church was a lone reminder of restraint in a landscape devoted to bourgeois consumption and amusement. Stretching from Stewart's Cast Iron Palace at Tenth and Broadway up to Madison Square, the Ladies' Mile derived its name from the concentration of early department stores located in the district. A. T. Stewart's, McCreery's, and Lord and Taylor, as well as specialty shops that carried everything from pianos to silver, attracted elite women from the nearby residential districts, who often promenaded up and down the street. The high visibility of respectable women in public was unusual, hence the appellation traditionally associated with this district. Despite this gendered characterization the district was a center of interest and activity for middle-class women *and* men, as consumers of goods and entertainment. Bounded and distinct both from the financial and industrial world to its south and from the domestic environment to its north, this hybrid public landscape confounded the traditional middle-class moral geography of the separate spheres, fusing elements of public and domestic life. Men and women promenaded together along the streets in a social display, shopped, and ate in restaurants.

Both sexes were drawn to the numerous cultural attractions, which included the first Metropolitan Museum of Art, Steinway Hall, the National Academy of Design, photographic parlors, and legitimate theaters like Booth's and Wallack's. The Ladies' Mile was also, ironically, home to many spaces in which a lady would have felt distinctly uncomfortable. The area was a center of entertainment for wealthy men who patronized a host of elaborate restaurants, including Delmonico's, clubs (including the Union Club, the Union League Club, and the Masonic Hall), elegant bars (including the Hoffman House), and some "cheap" theaters. More plebeian tastes were catered to at the numerous saloons, beer gardens, and oyster houses on Fourteenth Street, as well as houses of assignation and "Temples of Love" that dotted the neighborhood (Figure 1.12).[70]

The attraction and novelty of the Ladies' Mile lay not only in the geographical concentration of diverse and pleasurable leisure activities, but also in the elaborately designed buildings that housed them. In this protean environment, architecture was used to structure and commodify leisure, transforming the process of shopping, eating, drinking, and entertainment into a staged event. Although full-fledged department stores did not appear until the 1880s, during the 1850s and 1860s the small, badly lit dry-goods stores with limited stock began to be transformed into large, airy spaces lit by plate-glass windows, central rotundas, and an increasing profusion of merchandise. Architects like John Kellum and Griffith Thomas applied the most fashionable Italian Renaissance and Second Empire styles to the exteriors, transforming the humble storefront of the dry-goods shops into some of the city's most elaborate architectural adornments. At A. T. Stewart's Cast Iron Palace and Lord and Taylor's 1869 building, the free use of color and elaborate displays of goods, the provision of rest rooms and restaurants, and the implementation of the single-price system (rather than bargaining with the clerk) turned shopping into a highly pleasurable and status-enhancing leisure experience rather than a chore.

Hotels underwent a similar transformation, albeit a bit earlier, replacing taverns and inns with elegantly decorated and technologically advanced multistory structures. Beginning in 1836 with the construction of the Astor House hotel, and followed by larger and even more elaborate newcomers in the 1850s (including the preeminent Fifth Avenue Hotel), hotels offered New Yorkers of both sexes a hybrid kind of social space that provided both temporary and semi-permanent living arrangements as well as a series of elegant public parlors, dining rooms, barbershops, bars, and other facilities adorned with marble statuary, elaborate mirrors, and plush furnishings. Dubbed "people's palaces" by the press, both the hotel and the department store offered patrons something previously unthinkable: a spatial framework of consumption and leisure for the establishment of middle-class identity.

The neighborhood was also home to many elite men's clubs. Modeled on British examples, the clubs of New York were founded to structure leisure time and define the status and identity of the city's wealthiest men. Described by one observer as "anti-matrimonial and anti-domestic havens," the clubs—including the Union Club (1836), the New York Yacht Club (1844), the Century Association (1847), and the Union League Club (1863)—challenged the female-dominated home as the appropriate retreat from the rough-and-tumble world of business both geographically and programatically.[71]

FIGURE 1.12.
Geography of
New York
YMCA map.

MAP LEGEND

1. A. T. Stewart's Department Store, 1862–1870
2. Academy of Music, 1854
3. Aitken Son and Company Dry Goods, 1875
4. Albermarle House Hotel, 1860
5. All Souls Unitarian Church, 1853–1855
6. American Jockey Club, 1866
7. Arnold Constable Dry Goods, 1869
8. Astor Library, 1854–1859
9. Berckmann Lager Beer Saloon
10. **Bible House, YMCA Rooms, 1860–1865**
11. Bigot's Restaurant Oyster and Company
12. Booth's Theatre, 1867–1869
13. Café Morette
14. Calvary Baptist Church, 1854
15. Carol's and Regan's Ladies and Gents Oyster Parlors and Ice Cream
16. Century Club, 1857–1890
17. Clarendon Residential Hotel, 1843
18. Cooper Union, 1859
19. Dean's Confectionery, 1860s
20. Decker Pianos, 1870
21. Delmonico's Restaurant, 1861
22. Delmonico's Restaurant, 1876
23. Domestic Sewing Machine Company, 1872
24. Everett House Hotel, 1853
25. Fifth Avenue Hotel, 1859
26. George Huber's Prospect Garden and Oyster House
27. **German Branch YMCA, 1884**
28. Grace Church, 1845
29. H. Fahrenhor's Lager Beer Saloon
30. Hoffman House Hotel, 1864
31. Irving Hall
32. J. Slattery's Coffee and Lunch Room
33. John Gallant's Oyster and Lunch Room
34. Knickerbocker Club, 1872
35. L. D. Able's Eating House, 1860s
36. Lager Beer and Lunch Room
37. Lauch's and Cooper's Confectionery, 1860s
38. Lord and Taylor, 1869
39. Madison Square Hotel
40. Madison Square Presbyterian, 1853
41. Manhattan Club
42. Masonic Temple, 1870
43. McCreery's Dry Goods, 1868
44. **Mercantile Library, YMCA Rooms, 1854–1855**
45. National Academy of Design, 1863–1865
46. New York and Harlem Railroad Depot/ Barnum Hippodrome, 1871
47. New York Circus, 1869
48. New York Club
49. New York Society Library, 1856
50. Pursell's Ladies Restaurant
51. Racquet Court Club, 1876
52. Spingler Building, 1878
53. St. George's Church, 1846–1848
54. St. Germain Hotel, 1856
55. St. Paul's Methodist Episcopal Church, 1859
56. Steinway Hall, 1866
57. Tammany Hall, 1868
58. Tenth Street Studios, 1857
59. Tiffany's, 1869
60. Trinity Chapel, 1851–1870s
61. **Twenty-third Street YMCA**
62. Union Club, 1854
63. Union League Club, occupied 1868
64. **University Building, YMCA Rooms, 1855–1859**
65. W. Witz's "Rapid Transit" Lager Beer Saloon
66. Wallack's Theatre, 1861
67. Westmoreland Hotel, 1868
68. **YMCA Rooms, 1866–1868**

Housed in mansions abandoned by the elite as commerce encroached on Union and Madison Squares, the clubs presented a masculine domestic image within the shopping and entertainment districts of the city. In 1868 the Union League Club purchased a house at Madison Square and Twenty-sixth Street, near the heart of the Ladies' Mile. The Union Club moved to Fifth Avenue and Twenty-first Street at about the same time. This adaptive re-use of the existing housing stock for men's clubs was not only a pragmatic real-estate move, but also a symbolic assertion of a homosocial world. By choosing a domestic model situated within the country's most commercial landscape, the Union League and other clubs collapsed the traditional separation of spheres. This radical spatial practice extended to the amenities and programs offered in these buildings, which in many ways mirrored the services traditionally provided by wives and mothers in the home setting. Members could eat all their meals in the dining room, relax with friends, consult books and the latest papers in the library, attend lectures and receptions, and view art.[72] These activities were important elements in the socialization of the elite, who depended on the clubs to help them define their status and identity through appropriate pastimes and companions. As club members, elite men, especially bachelors, could live a comfortable, urbane, and sociable life, almost entirely free of the company (and oversight) of women and the home.

It was in this context that the new directors wanted to situate the Young Men's Christian Association. Madison Square, with hotels, restaurants, shopping, and clubs, was convenient both for the directors, who lived in a concentrated cluster within a few minutes' walk north on Fifth Avenue, and for the potential members, who lived in the boardinghouse district to the south and east.[73] Day and night this area was home to a variety of new and exciting sensory and spatial experiences.[74] Light, color, and large new buildings with impressive public spaces created a beguiling atmosphere and provided an impressive stage for status display and self-definition among the city's wealthiest men and women, as well as those who aspired to wealth.

A special building in this neighborhood was central to these men's vision of a larger cultural role for the YMCA within the changing social and economic fabric of the city. The presence of the Y in this district was intended to diffuse the tension between moral and commercial values by representing a new, more secular vision of religion that worked within the vocabulary of the modern landscape.

Cognizant of the need to compete with the surrounding attractions, yet also ruled by the desire for thrift, Y leaders called upon up-and-coming architect and member Stephen D. Hatch to superintend the furnishing of the rented rooms at Fifth Avenue and Twenty-second Street. His participation ensured a certain stylishness and also a 15 to 20 percent professional discount on the bookcases, painting, carpets, tables, and fixtures they purchased. Even so they spent more than $2,200 furnishing the rooms, and the Committee on Rooms and Attractions outlined more changes to be carried out, including better signage on the street. One idea was the use of transparencies lit by gas lamps, typically used by theaters, to advertise their program on the sidewalks. In a further attempt to compete with theatrical entertainments, a new, special committee on attractions purchased a grand piano and scheduled twelve free readings for members that year by well-respected and legitimate actors George Vandenhoff, James Edward Murdoch, and Edwin Booth.

Although the cost of moving to this neighborhood was high, within a year the relocation and the new attractions and activities offered in the rooms paid off in the form of increased membership.[75] Encouraged, Morgan, Dodge, and the other leaders began a building campaign with the goal of purchasing a site in the same vicinity. The size of their budget reveals their ambition: $250,000.[76]

Funding

In 1866 Robert McBurney and the board agreed that the time was at last right to approach the business community for financial support for the construction of a building. They had taken a moribund organization, reorganized it along business lines with an act of incorporation, redefined its mission to include the improvement of the physical as well as the spiritual, mental, and social conditions of young men, changed its location to increase its appeal, and proven the wisdom of these innovations through an increased membership of more than three hundred young men, a figure that rose to five hundred in the following year.[77] The cost of construction and future maintenance of the building and its programs far exceeded the monies commercial leaders had previously provided to the Y. In order to garner support, the Y needed to convince businessmen of the new building type's feasibility and their responsibility to young men.

The new YMCA was still focused on clerks, and many of its activities continued to be religious in tone, but in its appeals for financial support there was less emphasis on the souls of individual young men, and more on the production of a large and reliable labor supply. The failure of bourgeois evangelical society to address institutionally the decline of apprenticeship jeopardized the smooth functioning of commercial enterprise and, by extension, the larger society. The means for accomplishing this "development" of young men was the provision of an attractive, well-equipped headquarters that offered potential members, especially newcomers to the city, a respectable option for their leisure time and an opportunity to acquire and display the values, behavior, and connections that would equip them to succeed in a changing world of business.

McBurney coordinated an appeal to the clergy and lay supporters, issuing a pamphlet titled *A Memorandum Respecting New York as a Field for Moral and Christian Effort Among Young Men: The Present Neglected Condition; and the Fitness of the New York Young Men's Christian Association as Principal Agency for*

Its Due Cultivation.[78] This nuts-and-bolts document, designed like a business prospectus, interpreted the formerly spiritual process of saving souls on a commercial basis. It reported the results of an investigation of the urban landscape inhabited by young men conducted by members of the building committee.[79] It offered hard data to support the assertion that the building was a good (and necessary) investment.

The report presented statistics gathered on every aspect of young men's lives in New York, outlining the immoral and unsupervised nature of their existence. First it documented the decline of the apprenticeship system and the lack of a replacement. It noted that 46 percent of the male population was under thirty and most lived alone in poorly heated, cheap boardinghouses without appropriate supervision. There were few attractive yet appropriate places to spend their spare time. The Astor Library and the Cooper Union were two of the rare exceptions. Even these, it was suggested, did not fill the role the YMCA proposed. Both primarily educational institutions, they simply could not compete with thousands of licensed and unlicensed dens of iniquity.[80]

Citing the millions of dollars invested in saloons, houses of prostitution, and low theaters, the pamphlet implied that more money and competitive tactics were required to control the behavior of young men. A more acceptable leisure institution would be a pragmatic response to vice in the city, and a good investment. The payoff, it was implied, was a safe, clean city, a healthy, reliable workforce, and the satisfaction of saving souls. The new building was justified, not simply as a place for young men to go, but as a public need and responsibility.

To tempt the reader, the pamphlet offered a description of a new kind of building that combined the functions of a library, club, and school, including a lecture room, reading room, circulating library, reference library, conversation rooms, an "unexceptionable gymnasium," and suitable accommodation for religious, literary, and recreational activities as well as committee work. The text went so far as to specify the general location of the building, close to public transportation, and the provision of rental stores on the ground floor to provide an income for the Association. This last feature was intended to suggest that the Y would require no further funds from contributors, but could function efficiently as part of the commercial landscape of the city.

The response of the New York press to the *Memorandum* and the other appeals was overwhelmingly positive. *The Nation*'s editorial in March 1866 is typical: "The movement has the very strongest claims for support on every employer in the city. No man carrying on business in a Christian community today can possibly rid himself of all responsibility for either the moral or physical condition of those who earn their bread by doing his work."[81]

To support and interpret the document McBurney called on progressive clergy. A specially devoted week of prayer was held in elite churches for the support of the YMCA, and lectures and talks were delivered in the rooms of the YMCA and the homes of its directors. Although changes to business practice had altered the direct relationship between employer and employee, these requests were couched in the familiar language of Christian stewardship, still powerful to the older generation. A lecture titled "The Duty of Christian People to Those in Their Employ," by the Reverend William Adams, offered a religious justification for a building.[82] Citing the Bible's regulations regarding the treatment of fellow men, it exhorted employers to accept responsibility for both the well-being and morality of their employees. Support of the YMCA, Adams suggested, was the proper and appropriate way to do this in the modern world. Building on the stewardship theme, yet another lecture emphasized the contradiction between Protestant-based ethics of self-denial, thrift, and individual responsibility and the cultural shift toward instant gratification and display that was the source of social status and often the foundation of the wealth of the businessman whom the pamphlet addressed. As the pamphlet asked rhetorically, "Shall immense sums be expended for personal and family gratification and decoration and almost nothing be attempted to provide attractions of an elevating and ennobling character?"[83]

Businessmen apparently were convinced, donating more than $400,000. This was an astounding amount of money for the time, especially considering that the nearby Union Club's 1854 clubhouse, considered extravagant in its day, cost only $25,000.[84] Amounts ranging from $10,000 to $25,000 came from members of the board, including William Dodge Jr., Morris Jesup, and banker James Brown. Other large donors included department store baron A. T. Stewart and financier Frederick Marquand. Major firms, including Ball, Black, and Company, Low, Harriman and Company, and Fisk and Hatch pledged several thousand dollars each. Personal donations came in from members of the Colgate, Phelps, Stokes, Brown, and Dodge families, as well as prominent individuals like merchant-philanthropist Peter Cooper; railroad executive John Crerar; merchant, streetcar magnate, and promoter of the first Atlantic cable Cyrus W. Field; James Lenox, real-estate mogul and founder of the Lenox Library; and William H. Aspinwall, a merchant and railroad promoter.[85]

The support of these men suggests that two generations of evangelical Protestants contributed to this renewed vision of the YMCA: the young turks and the older, established evangelicals. As a group, contributors represented the cream of the Yankee-bred, New York–based, American mercantile and financial aristocracy. Most of the members of the just-forming boards of the Metropolitan Museum of Art and the American Museum of Natural History were represented, as were the elders of the most prominent churches, the superintendents of the largest Sunday schools, and officers and leaders of the Presbyterian Hospital, Union Theological Seminary, and the College of New Jersey (now Princeton University). Perhaps most significantly, the membership of the Union League Club came out in force for the new vision of the YMCA, which they understood as a junior version of their own establishment. Even though the opportunities for great wealth and advancement were diminishing greatly with the centralization of big business, members of the Yankee business elite continued to believe in the relevance of the values that had contributed to their own success, and sought to instill those values in the minions who would serve them.

The YMCA had convinced the Yankee business community in New York that a building devoted to self-improvement was a necessary institution in the modern city. At a time of fundamental and, to some, threatening transformations in the social and economic organization of American *work* the new vision of the YMCA as a Christian clubhouse was a way to represent the ethical dimension of corporate culture and productively shape the consumption of *leisure* as a middle-class socializing tool.

2
INVENTING THE YMCA BUILDING

On December 2, 1869, the New York Young Men's Christian Association dedicated its magnificent new headquarters on the corner of Twenty-third Street and Fourth Avenue, on the edge of the bustling new shopping and entertainment district known as the Ladies' Mile (Figure 2.1). It was one of the most ambitious additions to the city's fabric since the Civil War, a fact noted by art critic Clarence Cook. He claimed that it ranked "in extent, original conception, and design as one of our finest *modern* erections."[1] Designed by fashionable architect James Renwick Jr., the five-story building physically and programmatically combined religion, leisure, and commerce in an unprecedented way. Behind an elegant Second Empire façade, complex paths of access and circulation connected public and private spaces on five floors, including ground-level stores, club rooms, a library, a gymnasium, classrooms, a large lecture hall, an art gallery, and artists' studios (see Plate 2).

None of these features was, in itself, unique; it was their combination and arrangement in a single half-million-dollar structure near Madison Square that distinguished this building in the eyes of contemporary observers. Speaking at the ceremony for laying the cornerstone, William Adams, pastor of the nearby Madison Square Presbyterian Church, focused on the revolutionary quality of the building's program. Searching in vain for an architectural precedent, he presented this typological fusion of religious and secular functions as a fundamental break with the past:

> The edifice which was to rise upon that spot was not an eleemosynary institution; it was not a charity, not a hospital, not a college, not

FIGURE 2.1. New York YMCA building, Twenty-third Street and Fourth Avenue, in *Harper's Weekly*, October 23, 1869.

a church and yet it combined almost all the ideas which were represented by such buildings. It was not to be a hotel or a clubhouse; but it was a building that would represent before the public the social element of religion.[2]

The Reverend Joseph P. Thompson of the Broadway Tabernacle concurred, identifying this new kind of building as the latest in a long line of Christian structures adapted to the needs of their time: the basilica, the monastery, the cathedral, and the meeting house. What distinguished the YMCA from its predecessors and made it modern, he found, was its pragmatic embrace of worldly features for religious purposes. To him the building was

> an embodiment of a phase of Christianity, which is one of the most hopeful features of our times; a Christianity which is at once practical and refining, which believes in work, yet provides for recreation and cultivates taste, and which, keeping ever uppermost the spiritual

culture of the heart, appropriates whatever is useful and beautiful in the world without, for the glory of Christ and the advantage of mankind.[3]

As these clerical assessments suggest, the significance of this "practical," "refining," and "spiritual" building extended beyond its solution to the problems of urban young men. Ostensibly designed to save souls and socialize the city's growing population of clerks, this "Christian clubhouse" was a significant element in the foundation of a new corporate, consumer culture that emerged at the end of the Civil War.

As Laurence Moore has suggested, pious evangelicals have been creatively involved in a dialectical relationship with commerce since the 1820s, appropriating commercial techniques to "sell God" and in turn shaping commercial culture, but in the years before the Civil War many evangelicals still maintained a conflicted relationship with the material world.[4] Unlike their fathers and the antebellum leaders of the YMCA, who separated morals and religion physically as well as spatially from commerce, William E. Dodge Jr. and the rest of this younger generation of business leaders believed that the tension between Mammon and morality could be profitably resolved *within* the commercial landscape. Attempts to create a moral public sphere, like Central Park, sidestepped the issue of religion and created a utopian landscape separate from the world of business. The leaders of the YMCA enjoyed the fruits of their wealth and took a more pragmatic and, in many ways, more radical approach to reform by incorporating religious, or at least moral, elements *into* the corporate structure they were actively building.[5]

The realization of constructive, Christian leisure in built form required adjustments to established concepts of moral geography and architectural propriety. Such a building, in a district like the Ladies' Mile, transcended the ideal division of life into two spheres: home and work. It broke up the polarized worldview of the Protestant evangelical into a more complicated landscape of moral vectors by suggesting that a male environment devoted to leisure and physical culture could be a respectable, temporary haven for young men.

Contested by conservative evangelicals and other naysayers, these cultural and architectural changes were worked out incrementally throughout all the stages of the building process: conception, financing, siting, design, programming, and reception. The result was the carving out of a new and essential component in the emerging classed and gendered landscape of leisure and consumption in urban America.

Finding a Site

With more than $400,000 pledged, YMCA leaders began to plan their new building. First on their agenda was the selection of the perfect location.

They were already in agreement that it should be in the shopping and entertainment district around Madison Square. After some searching in the immediate vicinity of Broadway and Fifth the organization eventually purchased the large rectangular lot on the southwest corner of Twenty-third Street and Fourth Avenue, across from the National Academy of Design (Figure 2.2). Access to streetcar lines on Fourth Avenue and two blocks away on Broadway made the site easy to reach, although not quite in the center of the action. This site admirably balanced the need to compete with commercial attractions and the desire to associate this religious organization with the uplifting and elite associations of the residential areas to the east.

In this prominent corner location the YMCA could function as a hinge between religious and commercial culture. In the mid 1860s, when the building was being planned, the site occupied a liminal space between two districts (see Figure 2.3). To the east and south lay Gramercy Square, a still exclusive residential enclave and the site of several Protestant evangelical congregations. The YMCA was at the northern limits of that neighborhood. From its windows one could look down Fourth Avenue to Fourth Avenue Presbyterian Church and Calvary Episcopal Church. Madison Square, just to its north, was home to many wealthy YMCA donors and most of the city's elite men's clubs, including the Union League, to which Dodge Jr., Pyne, and several other key leaders belonged. West of the Square, across Twenty-

FIGURE 2.2. YMCA and Academy of Design, corner of Twenty-third Street and Fourth Avenue, New York.

third Street to Broadway and Fifth Avenue, was the heart of the Ladies' Mile, with its hotels, restaurants, and shops. This location was perfect for an institution that did not clearly occupy either the public, commercial world or the private, domestic, religious one, but fused elements of both together in one space.

In September 1867, with the ideal site in hand, the Building Committee issued invitations to Leopold Eidlitz, Edward Potter, Stephen D. Hatch, James Renwick Jr., and George Hawthorne to enter a competition for the design.[6] They chose Renwick, who had just finished building the suburban Riverdale home of Dodge Jr. Even without this personal connection, Renwick's experience made him a very attractive choice to create this ambitious new type of building. In Renwick the YMCA found an architect who understood both their desire for efficiency and practicality *and* the need for architectural character. He had always been interested in stylistic and technical developments, new materials, mechanical devices, and structural systems. His experience in

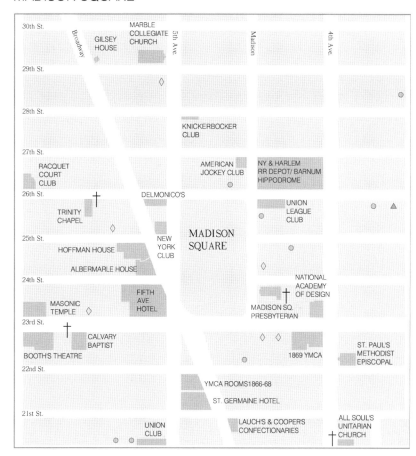

FIGURE 2.3. Map of Madison Square, New York, 1865–70.

architectural reform projects, including hospitals and asylums and Randall's and Ward's Islands off Manhattan, further added to his attractiveness. After this extensive experience in philanthropic architecture he would be entrusted with the commission for a free medical clinic, the Northwestern Dispensary (1869). He was also active in the design of educational facilities, including the Free Academy and a competition entry for the Astor Library.

Renwick experimented with other specialized building types in the design of hotels, commercial buildings, and theaters. His experience designing the Corcoran Gallery of Art in Washington and a home gallery for his father-in-law William Aspinwall (a YMCA contributor) must have especially recommended him to the YMCA, who were committed to including studios and a gallery space in their new building (Figure 2.4).[7] Further distinguishing him from the other competitors was his role as the architect of the Smithsonian (1847–55). The publicity that surrounded the Smithsonian commission, as well as the prominence of Renwick's work in Robert Dale Owen's *Hints on*

FIGURE 2.4. Art gallery for William Aspinwall, New York, by James Renwick Jr., in *Harper's Weekly*, February 26, 1859.

Public Architecture (1848), established him as the leading architect in the United States.

The precise lines between the responsibility of the architect, James Renwick, and the clients, Robert McBurney, William Dodge Jr., and the Building Committee, for the conceptualization and design of the YMCA building remain murky. The record of the building process does not provide a complete accounting of who was responsible for what, yet it is clear that Renwick did not bear the full burden. The development of most modern building types involves a fusion between the imperatives of commerce, science, technology, reform, and the practice of architecture. In the case of the YMCA the clients did more than simply work with their architect: they sought to give form to a new social reality through building. The merchant community possessed what historian Jon Amsden has termed spatial imagination, "the ability and propensity to understand society as it is arranged geographically."⁸ In confronting the bewildering and threatening changes of the industrial age, these businessmen became the architects, both literally and metaphorically, of a new urban middle-class society. They did not, and could not, limit themselves to the conceptualization of a new society and leave the issue of design to those trained in the Vitruvian values of commodity, firmness, and delight. Such a division would have been impossible for men whose ideas were articulated spatially.

In YMCA lore McBurney, the architect of the fourfold plan of work and secretary of the Building Committee, has been credited with much that is unique in the design. Dodge Jr., also a member of the Building Committee, remembered it this way:

> This building speaks to some of us very touchingly of McBurney. There is not a room or a corner of it but he designed. It was absolutely a new thing in those days. Every part of it was thought out so kindly and thoroughly that, although finer buildings and grander ones have been built in other places, not one of them was put up without having for its principal arrangement those plans which he devised and which have stood the test of time.[9]

Similarly, Dodge has also been given credit. L. L. Doggett, a member and historian of the YMCA, wrote that "It might with almost equal justice be said that Mr. Dodge was himself the builder of this building."[10] Doggett follows his comment about Dodge's role with the intriguing suggestion that the building process "was really an evolution—the work of the secretary [McBurney], the committee, the board, and the architects."[11] The YMCA leaders had already spent years developing the idea of this building, and they were unusually active participants in the design process. They knew what they wanted the building to include and how it should function. They also had very specific ideas about its identity in relation to other institutions.

Morgan, Dodge Jr., and the other leaders had already drawn up a list of features the new building should include for their fund-raising campaign: a large, cheery reception room; a commodious, well-fitted reading room; a large and well-selected library; a biblical reference library; an attractive lecture room to seat twelve hundred people; classrooms; rooms for social, religious, and devotional meetings; a music room with piano and organ; and a good, "unexceptionable" gymnasium. The goal was to provide "everything to make the building an attractive and safe evening resort for young men," as well as artists' studios and stores on the ground level to provide income.[12]

If the YMCA leaders knew what they wanted the building to include, the question remained, what form should it take? How should they arrange the many different spaces in relationship to one another? How could they distinguish between public and membership spaces in the limited rectangular dimensions of the site? And what would be the architectural character of the two street fronts? What style should they use to communicate the building's new identity to passersby?

American evangelicals had traditionally shunned elaborate architecture and were not known for their aesthetics or stylistic patronage. The older leaders of the Y, influenced by Puritanical conceptions of art and a strong sense of thrift, valued the functional and comfortable workings of the interior over the external appearance. As leader Frank Ballard noted in 1864, "brownstone veneerings are of small account compared with the inside arrangements of the building."[13] The new generation of business leaders had, however, fully accepted and understood the symbolic value of good design in the new commercial landscape of postwar New York. Dodge Jr., chair of the Building Committee, later explained their attitude toward architectural adornment:

> When we put up our beautiful building in New York a great many people said it was very extravagant, and that it was a very wrong thing to spend so much money for such a purpose. But we did not think so. There were two theatres put up in the blocks adjoining our building about the same time, each of which cost two hundred thousand dollars more than our building, and we considered that our place, which was consecrated to such good purposes, should try to vie with the theatres in inducing young men to enter, and we did not think the money wasted when used for architectural adornments.[14]

In short, this younger generation of leaders embraced architectural ornament as a major statement of the building's intended role.

Their main concern was not over whether the building should have style, but what style it should have: High Victorian Gothic or Second Empire? Their dilemma reflects the conflicting ideas about religion, commerce, and public life that had to be resolved in the building's design. Renwick's winning entry (now lost) was in the High Victorian Gothic style—distinguished by polychromy, pointed arches, asymmetry, and naturalized ornament. Popular for churches, this British style, with its emphasis on the exterior expression of the building's function, was also adaptable to the variety of new building types introduced in the nineteenth century. Heavily promoted by John Ruskin in *The Stones of Venice* (1853), it was believed to have moral associations and was thus favored by religious, educational, cultural, and institutional clients. Just a few years earlier Peter Bonnett Wight had used the style for the Brooklyn Mercantile Library, a similar, though not religious institution just across the East River. This building was an especially appropriate model, for it shared many programmatic elements with the YMCA (including the general reading room, a tall, two-story library with alcoves all around) as well as its religious character, notably its stained-glass clerestory, open-timbered ceiling, painted ornament, and specially designed furniture inspired by the publications of A. W. N. Pugin and Owen Jones. The combination of these elements made for a building with very explicit connections to church architecture.[15]

The other architects seemed to share Renwick's idea that Gothic was the appropriate style for the building, except for George Hawthorne, who submitted a hybrid Gothic–Second Empire design, distinguished by a mansard roof and pointed arches (Figure 2.5). It seems that Hawthorne was ultimately correct about the Building Committee's intentions. Although it awarded Renwick the commission on the basis of the Gothic elevation, it

FIGURE 2.5. New York YMCA competition entry by George Hawthorne, 1868.

changed course shortly after he submitted completed designs for the façade. Instead, they demanded he design a Second Empire building like the one he had done for Booth's Theatre. The explanation for the sudden about-face was vague, suggesting that Second Empire was "more practical and capable of being finished in a more substantial manner."[16] What they seem to have meant really was that the imported style served their mission to build a modern Christian clubhouse better than an overtly religious style. Despite their desire to provide a moral anchor for the development of a new leisure culture, they did not want their building to be mistaken for a church by passersby and potential members. The midstream change in style for the YMCA building indicates a sophisticated awareness of these stylistic nuances on the part of the YMCA's board and Building Committee.

The choice also confirms the committee's acute awareness of a new landscape of Second Empire palaces that emerged in the Ladies' Mile and in the downtown financial district between 1867 and 1872. Most major dry-goods stores, including McCreery's, Lord and Taylor, and Arnold, Constable & Co., all constructed new buildings using this style (Figure 2.6). The most elaborate new government building in the city, Alfred B. Mullett's downtown Courts and Post Office building, adopted the style with a vengeance. Fashionable hotels and the most elegant theaters in the city were designed in the French manner, as were the new office buildings, the first skyscrapers in Manhattan.

Between 1862 and 1870, this stylistic revolution also transformed the landscape of white-collar work in lower Manhattan. Bankers and life insurance companies were building the nation's first corporate headquarters, and

46 / INVENTING THE YMCA BUILDING

FIGURE 2.6. Arnold, Constable & Co. store, Broadway and Nineteenth Street, New York, by Griffith Thomas, 1869. Published in *King's Handbook of New York City*, 1893.

were beginning to understand the potential of a building to have a positive impact on both the public image of a company and the culture of its employees.[17] Like the YMCA, these companies also toyed with the possibility that High Victorian Gothic, with its ecclesiastical connotations, might be able to convince clients of the legitimacy and stability of their enterprises.[18] Wight proposed High Victorian Gothic buildings in competitions for the Mutual Life Insurance Company (1863) and the National Park Bank (1866). In the end, the clients rejected the religious and increasingly dated connotations of the pointed arches and bands of polychromy for the palatial implications of a Second Empire design by Griffith Thomas (Figures 2.7 and 2.8).

The meaning of this choice is currently under dispute. David Scobey has suggested that the Second Empire style, with its distinctive mansard roof and dominance over surrounding buildings and the street, was an "aesthetic of dominance and display, a fetish of the individual edifice quite different than the more republican merchant palazzo." He has described the style as a cloak thrown over the naked profit motive. Angel Kwolek-Folland has recently argued that the Second Empire, with its paternalistic and regal associations, not only communicated the status of owners and users, but also helped to communicate the responsibility, legitimacy, and stability of commercial enterprises. "The hints of (admittedly palatial) domestic architecture . . . subsumed the notions of old families and old money, financial security, the stewardship of monarchy, and the image of corporations as merely larger, and therefore more stable, versions of the precorporate family." It seems that

FIGURE 2.7. National Park Bank: Competition Design Drawing, by Peter Bonnett Wight, ca. 1866. Ink and watercolor on paper, 40 cm × 24 cm.

FIGURE 2.8. The National Park Bank building, Broadway and Fulton Street, by Griffith Thomas, 1866–68.

YMCA leaders, directly involved as clients in the construction of the new skyscrapers, were comfortable enough with the latter explanation to shift away from the explicitly religious Gothic style. The Second Empire allowed male patrons of architecture to appropriate the moral and cultural connotations of domesticity within a masculine, public framework by referencing the domestic and the paternal.[19]

Responding to the board's directive, Renwick submitted a new perspective of the YMCA to the Building Committee by February 1868.[20] The result

FIGURE 2.9. YMCA building, Twenty-third Street and Fourth Avenue, 1869.

was a Second Empire building with just enough Gothic detail to appease any traditionalists uncomfortable with the complete identification of the Y with commerce. Five stories tall, the building sported mansard roofs, a central entrance and dome, and vestigial pavilions. It extended 300 feet down Twenty-third Street. The massing and fenestration suggested a Second Empire building, but several key elements betrayed a Gothic flavor, notably its polychromatic façade of purple Belleville and buff Ohio stone and colored roof slates (Figure 2.9). The almost grid-like symmetry of the Second Empire façade was broken by closely set windows on the western half of the façade. In proper Gothic style this honestly revealed the function of the most public space in the building, the auditorium, to passersby. Horizontal bands on the lower floors, medieval designs in the window trim, and the use of cast iron for the pillars and lintels separating the storefronts on the ground level further added to the building's hybrid identity.[21] The name of the Association was inscribed on the entrance arch, and the arms of the Association, a cross and a prayer book, were executed in bas-relief in the cornice of the second-story tower window. Despite these remnants of the original design, the contrast between the Y and the Fourth Avenue Presbyterian Church next door makes clear the secular identity of the building. The decision to blend the Second Empire and Victorian Gothic together seems to have been a negotiation between the progressive and conservative elements of the YMCA leadership, between a more traditional religious conception of the YMCA's public identity and one intended to situate it more firmly within the commercial world.

Character, Program, Plan, and Precedents

In addition to the style of the building, Renwick, McBurney, and Dodge Jr. had to determine its architectural "character," or identity. Clearly it was to be a prominent building, neither public nor private, that encompassed a variety of functions. In developing the building's program and plan, the YMCA and Renwick were influenced by the wave of experimentation with hybrid buildings in New York's booming real-estate market: notably the Cooper Union, a design for the Union League Club, and Booth's Theatre.

Cooper Union

The Cooper Union was founded in 1859 by industrialist, entrepreneur, and self-made man Peter Cooper. His intention was to provide free technical and scientific education to workingmen, giving them the opportunity to develop their talents and contribute to society. He spent more than $800,000 constructing a new kind of scientific and artistic educational facility (Figure 2.10). Six stories tall, with more than 24,000 square feet of space, this massive building stood prominently on Astor Place, just across the street from the old rooms of the YMCA in the Bible House. Its exterior, an Italianate brownstone design by Frederick A. Peterson, employed a dignified classical vocabulary that identified it as a substantial public institution. Its cast-iron interior was divided into two parts. The first three floors were public and devoted to rental space: stores, meeting rooms, and a nine-hundred-seat Great Hall. The revenue from these floors supported the educational programs of the Union. On the building's upper floors its functions became increasingly private: the domain of the men and women studying photography, engraving, typewriting, and shorthand.[22] For them there was a free reading room and picture gallery, studios, classrooms, and a reference library.

YMCA leaders were certainly aware of the building and its mission. Their move from Astor Place was in part inspired by the competition it posed for the leisure time of young men. Free from membership costs and from religious rhetoric, the Union was part of the reason it was difficult for the Y to enroll more members in its old location. Y leaders acknowledged its importance, but distinguished between the Cooper Union's democratic mission to mechanics and workingmen and its own religious, white-collar emphasis. Nonetheless, the Cooper Union provided an architectural model to follow with its creative fusion of functions and combination of public meeting spaces and educational facilities tied together neatly and skillfully in an impressive shell.

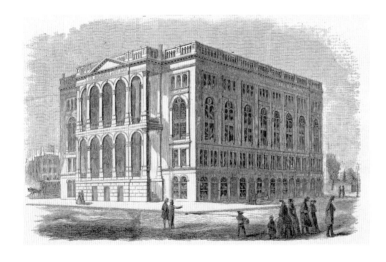

FIGURE 2.10. Cooper Union, Astor Place, New York, rendering by architect Frederick A. Peterson, 1854, in *Harper's Weekly Magazine*, March 30, 1861.

FIGURE 2.11. Union League Club proposal, by Richard Morris Hunt, 1867.

Union League Club

Another important influence on the design of the Y building was a more elite organization: the men's club. In 1867, the Union League, bastion of Republican politics and favored club of YMCA families, decided to move from an old rented house on Twenty-first Street to finer quarters. Richard Morris Hunt, a member and preeminent architect, drew up a proposal to erect a purpose-built clubhouse on the then-empty lot at Twenty-third Street and Fourth Avenue (Figure 2.11).

In devising the scheme for this, the first clubhouse to be built in New York since the brownstone palazzo put up by the Union Club in 1854, Hunt sketched a startling structure that broke with precedent stylistically and typologically. Rejecting Charles Barry's influential use of the Italian Renaissance in his famous London clubhouses, Hunt chose the highly fashionable Second Empire style. Hunt was intimately familiar with the style, having studied with and worked for Hector-Martin Lefuel during the period of the Louvre's construction. His design for the Union League is a creditable interpretation of that model, with a large, projecting central pavilion crowned by a mansard roof. Embellished with wrought-iron balconies and decorated with statues of prominent Union generals, it was to have been an elaborate and elegant, if pioneering, use of what was, in New York, primarily a commercial and civic vocabulary.

Hunt's innovative proposal for the Union League acknowledged both the organization's avowed interest in the arts and the exigencies of the real-estate market in New York by providing income that would offset the high cost of land purchase and construction. Unlike existing American club buildings, Hunt's proposal for the Union League was to have stores on the ground floor and artists' studios and a gallery in the mansard roof, with the rooms of the club occupying the second and third floors.[23] This radical proposal, although never realized, was to strongly influence the conceptualization and design of the New York YMCA.

The choice to build studios for income was astute and practical.[24] Hunt's own Tenth Street Studio building, completed in the 1850s, was the only building of its kind in New York. With just twenty-five studios, it was insufficient to meet the needs of the artistic community. Artists, forced to find space in commercial buildings and rooming houses, were hungry for a similar environment that allowed for privacy and camaraderie as well as group exhibitions. The Union League was willing, even eager, to provide shelter for artists. From its beginnings on Union Square, the club was interested in fostering an atmosphere supportive to the art world. It offered "artistic" memberships, which allowed dues to be paid in paintings. Albert Bierstadt, Thomas Nast, and Jasper Cropsey all became members in this manner. In 1869 Union League members, including Dodge Jr., president of the YMCA, were instrumental in the founding of the Metropolitan Museum of Art.[25] This kind of activity rendered Hunt's suggestion that the club incorporate artists' studios into its clubhouse more than an economic decision. It was, essentially, an extension of the club's own activities.

The same could not be said for the presence of the shops on the street level of Hunt's design. These clearly put the clubhouse in the commercial realm, giving the building the profile of a building block—the multipurpose commercial building that was a precursor to the tall office building. This development strategy was not unusual in New York; many nonprofit organizations, particularly religious ones like the Bible House and the Methodist Publishing and Missions Building, farther up Broadway, relied on rental income within their buildings to keep them located within the city center. Hunt's proposal, however, adapted it to an elite men's club, a rather bold challenge to the previously domestic, elite character of club architecture in New York.[26]

Dodge Jr., as a member of the Union League Club, would have been involved in the approval and fund-raising for Hunt's design, and although it was never built it seems to have gripped his imagination as he took responsibility for developing the plans for the YMCA in more detail.[27] In 1866 plans for the Y building simply noted the need for some sort of income-producing element to support their regular operations.[28] Soon after the Union League proposal was presented and rejected, the YMCA began to specify artists' studios and ground-level shops as the appropriate solution to their cash-flow requirements. While shops were a typical solution, the YMCA's choice of artists' studios betrays a direct link to the Union League plan (as well as to the Cooper Union).

The organization's own relationship to artists was also very strong. From

1855 to 1859 it had occupied rooms alongside the artists' studios in the University Building on Waverly Place, and again in the Bible House during the Civil War. Many artists exhibited their works in the YMCA rooms, and the organization enjoyed a cordial relationship with the National Academy of Design, which often invited Y members to its receptions. Some of the YMCA building's biggest financial supporters, including J. P. Morgan and John T. Johnston, were prominent collectors, and were well acquainted with the artistic life of the city. They knew that the studios would provide not only income, more than $11,000 annually, but cachet and education for young men aspiring to a better place in the business world.[29] They not only believed that art had a moral quality, but they also knew that involvement in, knowledge about, and acquisition of art was perceived as a sign of refinement. In addition to philanthropic work, involvement in the world of art, especially art collecting, was one of the key markers of arrival into the bourgeoisie.[30] Young men who sought financial success could, in the new YMCA building, absorb not only proper business ethics, but also the culture and refinement of Y supporters like Aspinwall, who had a gallery attached to his house and invited public visits.[31] The inclusion of a gallery and studios as an income-producing feature was a canny way to derive social and educational value from the rule of real estate on Manhattan Island.

Booth's Theatre

The closest geographical and conceptual influence on the YMCA was undoubtedly Booth's Theatre, designed by Renwick for famous Shakespearean actor Edwin Booth in 1867 and completed in 1869 (Figure 2.12). Constructed in granite in an ornate Second Empire style, Booth's Theatre was located a few blocks west of the YMCA on a similarly sized corner site. Its façade was

FIGURE 2.12. Booth's Theatre, Twenty-third Street and Sixth Avenue, by James Renwick Jr., 1867–69.

a faithful rendition of the style, with sophisticated sculptural decoration. Attached to the west end of the theater itself was a less elaborate five-story wing, the ground floor of which was for shops, with three floors above for actors' rehearsal studios and offices. The top floor was reserved for Mr. Booth's own private apartment. It was, at the time of its construction, the best and most glamorous legitimate theater in the city, and perhaps the country. Single-handedly Booth had raised the sophistication and the moral tenor of the theatrical experience in the United States. George Templeton Strong felt that the theater had the potential to be "a humanizing and educating influence."[32]

The connections between the two buildings were strong, linked definitively through the office of Renwick, who designed the YMCA as the theater was under construction. Although the YMCA building was not nearly as elaborately designed as the theater, there are distinct similarities in everything from the program of the building to the shape of the windows. The very obvious alignment of the YMCA with the concept and appearance of a Second Empire theater and shops was a most startling departure from their antebellum identities.

Inside the building, elements of all three precedents joined together into one program: school, club, art gallery, stores, theater. Five stories tall, the building was a series of public, semipublic, and private spaces for YMCA members and leaders, shoppers and shopkeepers, artists and their patrons, and the audiences for public entertainments. These were organized in a series of interlocking volumes, tied together by a series of staircases that both

FIGURE 2.13. Vertical circulation diagram, New York YMCA building, 1869. Three separate staircases and an elevator were key components of control and access to the multiple functions of this innovative "building block." They carried members to the YMCA rooms, artists and patrons to the studio and gallery on the fourth and fifth floors, and the public to the large hall for lectures and performances.

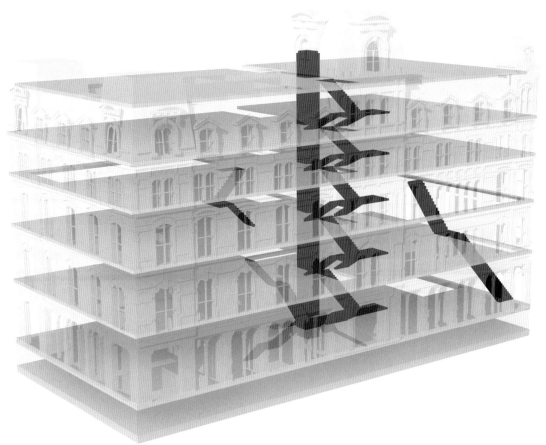

promoted circulation and controlled access throughout the building (Plate 2 and Figure 2.13).

To the passersby on Twenty-third Street and Fourth Avenue, the building was a row of street-level stores, whose glass storefronts tempted them to enter and buy a pair of eyeglasses, a suit, or a hat. The large central entrance served the artists whose studios occupied the fourth and fifth floors, or visitors to the central gallery space, where exhibitions of the artists' work were on display. Ticket holders to a public lecture on temperance or an organ concert might ascend the main central stair or enter by a small, dedicated entrance to the large hall, a fitting amalgam of church and theater for this new kind of Christian leisure institution. The hall's long, rectangular plan, with side galleries and raised dais, is reminiscent of a sanctuary, but its "box" overlooking the stage, individual seats, and lavishly decorated ceiling lend a dramatic flavor to the religious space. The hall was, as one source called it, the finest in the city, "charming in the extreme, and possessing all the luxuries possible" (Figure 2.14). It was adorned with "beautifully decorated panels and exquisite cast-iron supporting columns," and luxurious upholstered chairs for 1,400 people; the plan assured the audience of easy entrance and egress.[33]

FIGURE 2.14. Association Hall, New York YMCA building.

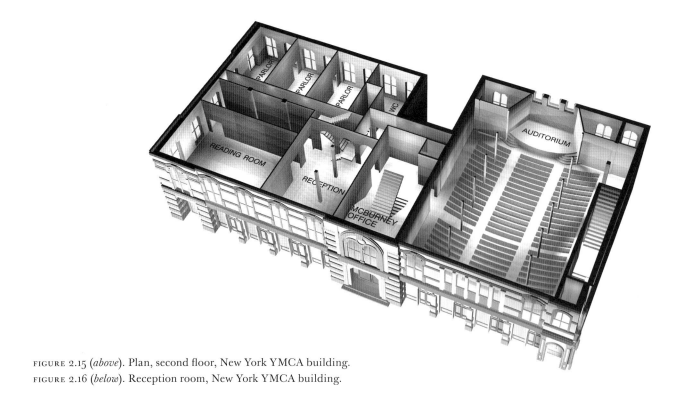

FIGURE 2.15 (*above*). Plan, second floor, New York YMCA building.
FIGURE 2.16 (*below*). Reception room, New York YMCA building.

FIGURE 2.17. Reading room, New York YMCA building.

A young man, "a stranger," entering the building for any of these purposes would encounter the YMCA rooms, accessed off the main staircase on the second floor (Figure 2.15). From there he entered a large reception room divided by columns and decorated in dark wood with oil paintings, marble sculpture, and hunting trophies mounted on the walls (Figure 2.16). At the center stood a desk, with a welcoming employee to greet him and inquire about his situation. As period photographs taken for advertisements show, young men were expected to comport themselves in a genteel manner. Members and guests stood carefully and formally upright, welcoming newcomers and chatting companionably in small groups, each individual in his own bubble of space, situated at a discreet distance from others.

From there our young stranger might be invited to proceed to the large reading room, whose wide doors, racks of local and national papers, and well-lit interior beckoned. Young men perused newspapers in wooden chairs, or aligned in neat rows at reading desks, productively spending their free time studying papers in much the same manner, and in the same posture, that governed their work life as clerks (Figure 2.17).

If our visitor was persuaded to join the YMCA, he could move beyond

FIGURE 2.18. Parlor, New York YMCA building.

the reception and reading rooms to a suite of parlors for a congenial evening of conversation, music, and, on occasion, prayer, with friends (Figure 2.18). The walls were covered with dark wood wainscoting and rich wallpaper, the windows screened by patterned curtains, and the floor covered with fine carpet. A baby grand piano occupied a corner of the room, and the furniture, including the elaborate Renaissance Revival table at left and the plush velvet conversation piece in the center of the room, was of high quality and the latest style. Brass chandeliers and wall sconces lit the rooms, and reproductions of religious paintings and sculpture decorated them. One of the finest features was the elaborate fireplace that stretched from floor to ceiling. Adorned with cast-iron andirons, tile work, and a frieze of what appears to be a loose interpretation of the Horsemen in the procession on the Ionic frieze on the north side of the Parthenon, it lent a distinctly masculine yet refined presence to the room that contrasted with the mirrored walls, cheap chromolithographs, and raucous atmosphere of the saloons.

An ambitious member might prefer to read an improving book, or consult a reference work. In that case he would have ascended the staircase to the third floor, where the large double-story library offered one of the finest collections in the city, arranged in bookshelves lining the room (Figures 2.19 and 2.20).[34] Here and in the auditorium the walls were decorated with frescoes by decorative painter Louis H. Cohn, described by one reviewer as "in extreme good taste."[35]

Classrooms adjoining the library were the site of courses in languages, bookkeeping, and other edifying and useful subjects. The YMCA offered a

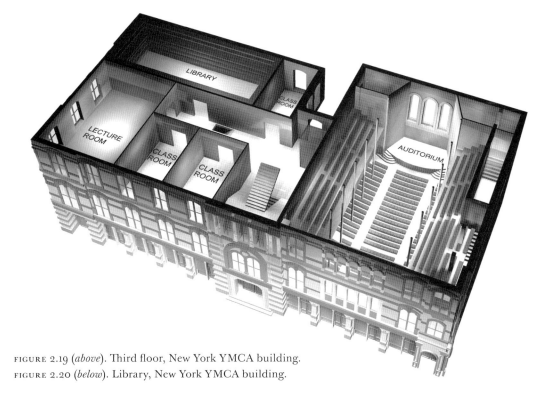

FIGURE 2.19 (*above*). Third floor, New York YMCA building.
FIGURE 2.20 (*below*). Library, New York YMCA building.

FIGURE 2.21. Gymnasium, New York YMCA building.

curriculum similar to those being introduced in new "business colleges" that had begun to appear in American cities, inflected with a veneer of refinement and culture. Although young men did enroll in these courses in large numbers, it is more likely that once a member checked in at the reception room he would descend yet another set of stairs to the basement, which offered young men the features they found most attractive: bowling alleys and a large gymnasium (Figure 2.21).

Located directly under the hall, the gym—equipped with parallel bars, a horse, and flying rings—was at first supervised by a committee of lay members. This element of the building was, McBurney and others admitted, the most challenging to oversee, largely because it was so unprecedented. At first circus gymnasts were hired to teach acrobatics. By the late 1870s professional physical directors implemented more systematic work, based on German and Swedish gymnastics, to provide complementary tutelage to that offered upstairs in the classrooms.[36] Lined up in rows, performing repetitive motions in synchronization, young men followed the directions of the leader in a form of gymnastics that emphasized the role of the individual within a coordinated system of exertion.

Control and Surveillance

In a creative collaboration between the client and the architect, Renwick was ultimately responsible for tying together all the functions of the building into an efficient and accessible structure that fit into the irregular rectangular site. This was a difficult job that required the resolution of tensions between practical issues, such as access and circulation, and conceptual issues of propriety and control. Staircases occupied a large portion of the building's volume, unifying its central, public core, but also defining paths of access to the rooms reserved for members and the individual storage rooms for each store on the ground level. Much attention was devoted to the design of stairs; the ascent from the second to the third floor of the YMCA rooms was, for instance, given pride of place in the reception room and framed ceremonially by a raised platform and archways.

This attention to a point of transition was part of an overall attempt by the designers to negotiate between the public and private functions of the building. As was typical in Victorian homes, the overall plan and flow of the highly segmented space is not transparent; hallways, doors, arches, stairways, and other connections between spaces were highly articulated and motion carefully choreographed (Figure 2.22). Unlike a private home, or even a men's club, however, the space was more than a place to relax and display one's identity. It was also intended to facilitate control and surveillance. Somehow the rooms had to fulfill a dual and sometimes contradictory mission: to attract young men *and* shape their characters. The interior design had to be attractive yet dignified as well as efficient and discreet in its socializing purpose.

How could the YMCA get young men to submit to supervision of their

FIGURE 2.22. "Ghosted" view from the lecture hall, across the stair landing, into the New York YMCA reception room. On the second-floor landing of the New York YMCA building, members and potential members, known as "strangers," could enter the YMCA reception room, the point of access to the rest of the "Christian clubhouse." Contemporary digital imaging allows for the interpretation of the discrete, divided Victorian rooms on the second floor, and the staircase to the third, to be viewed and understood as conceived: a series of linked spaces designed for controlled access and visual surveillance.

private lives when there were many options for their free time? The building itself was something of a velvet glove sheathing an iron fist: a combination of a club and an institution of social control. Renwick, McBurney, and Dodge Jr. combined elements of elite masculine spaces, like the library, with design features intended to encourage and reinforce desirable behavior. Drawing upon an upper-crust model of paternalistic oversight, they used the parlor, the library, and other facilities to create a moral, male, and middle-class world.

The Parlor

Set back from the street, down the hall from the public entry to the Association rooms, was the YMCA's parlor. This feature, usually associated with femininity, was an essential element in the YMCA's claim of masculine morality and middle-class respectability. The centrality of the parlor to middle-class genteel identity has been well-established by scholars. This carefully decorated ceremonial room was the connection between the public sphere and the privacy of the home. In this space, suffused with moral associations, women received their guests, educated their children, and displayed their good taste.

The inclusion of a parlor in a public building was not, in and of itself, a departure in New York. By mid century many of the new buildings on the Ladies' Mile, including hotels, department stores, and photographic parlors, included parlors to lend moral ballast to a new landscape dedicated to leisure and consumption.[37] The Fifth Avenue Hotel, owned by YMCA supporter Amos R. Eno, had one of the most elegant in town. Although men were welcome in these exquisitely decorated rooms, they were expected to be on their best "home" behavior (Figure 2.23). Contrasting with this protected domain

FIGURE 2.23. Ladies' drawing room, Fifth Avenue Hotel, Fifth Avenue and Twenty-third Street, New York, in *Harper's Weekly,* October 1, 1859.

FIGURE 2.24. The reading room of the Fifth Avenue Hotel, Fifth Avenue and Twenty-third Street, New York, in *Every Saturday,* 1871.

of genteel women was the men's reading room, on the opposite end of the hotel's ground floor. Male guests and passersby lounged there comfortably, kept their hats on, and smoked to their heart's content (Figure 2.24). Under one roof, in one establishment, the hotel offered distinctly gendered male and female space.[38] Buildings equipped with such spaces attracted both middle-class men and women and maintained, to some degree, the separation of spheres within a new hybrid landscape of blurred boundaries.

The YMCA inclusion of a parlor proposed an alternative model to the separate but equal facilities of the hotel. The YMCA parlor was a masculine space. Women might have visited from time to time, but the primary inhabitants of the room were to be men. This departure from traditionally understood social practices can be comprehended through the lens of class: elite families framed the parlor differently from the aspiring middle-class. Growing up as members of the Yankee aristocracy, the YMCA's young leaders understood the parlor as a setting for the enactment of male authority, success, and stability. This masculine conception of the parlor is presented in a series of paintings, *The Blodgett Family* (1864), *The Brown Family* (1869), and *The Hatch Family* (1870–71), all commissioned by Y leaders from Eastman Johnson, one of the preeminent genre painters of the 1850s and 1860s.

These paintings of people in parlors were more than simple representations of the family physiognomy. Their scale and arrangement of space on the canvas, the costumes, and the distant treatment of personal features

64 / INVENTING THE YMCA BUILDING

SOCIAL HEADQUARTERS.

FIGURE 2.25. Parlor with library reading table, New York YMCA building. This library table is nearly identical to the one depicted in Eastman Johnson's *The Hatch Family* (see Plate 3).

suggest an abstraction, a generalization of mother, father, child, that draws both from the tradition of portraiture and from genre painting.[39] The paintings, all displayed at the National Academy of Design, were intended by artist and patron to serve as models of family life and behavior, fulfilling the moral duty of genre painting to instruct a public audience. The message was clear: the home was a stabilizing force in society for both men and women, and the ideal to which the young men were to strive. In a bold and risky move, the YMCA redefined the middle-class parlor on the model of elite homes: as a dynastic space for both men *and* women.

The most famous of these paintings is *The Hatch Family,* which includes several generations that represent the continuance of the traditions and values of the past into the future (see Plate 3). The whole family of Alfrederick Smith Hatch, a partner in Fisk and Hatch and financier of the Civil War, from the grandfather to the newest baby, is grouped in their red-draped parlor. Architect Stephen Hatch, who had helped decorate the Fifth Avenue YMCA rooms, stands in shadow by the heavily draped window. The interior, dominated by a Renaissance Revival library table, seems to have been the inspiration for the parlor in the YMCA building, which contained a library table practically identical to the one in the Hatch home (Figure 2.25).

The Library

In a period before public libraries, access to books was privileged, and the design of the YMCA's galleried hall was reminiscent of elite membership libraries like the Boston Athenaeum. Separated by pilasters and crowned by an elaborate cornice, multiple levels of shelves were made accessible by galleries reached by light iron stairs.[40] There was, however, one important distinction. Private libraries included alcoves in the galleries, which screened readers from full view and allowed them to find and enjoy books with a sense of privacy.⁴¹ While this freedom and license might have been allowed elite young men, at the YMCA behavior was more carefully monitored. Whether they sat at long study tables or climbed the stairs to retrieve a book, they were visible, able to see and be seen.

Sermon Pictures

One feature that distinguished the YMCA from the men's club was the dual purpose of the art displayed within the building: it was both decoration and an unobtrusive yet constant source of cultural education, even indoctrination. Its walls were adorned with fine paintings, as at the Union League, the Century Association, and other clubs with art galleries on the premises.⁴² Thanks to the proximity of the National Academy of Design, its studio spaces, and the connections of its leaders, the new YMCA building was adorned with paintings by some of the most prominent artists of the day, including Albert Bierstadt and Thomas Cole.

Many of the works chosen for display—such as Thomas Prichard Rossiter's 1857 painting *The Merchants of New York* (Figure 2.26)—were meant to inspire and motivate young men. This gargantuan work covered an entire wall in the reading room, forcing young men who came to peruse the day's newspaper to confront a portrayal of upstanding, pious, and successful role models of the previous generation. Included in the portrait were manufacturer Peter Cooper, real-estate mogul John Jacob Astor, department store owner

FIGURE 2.26. *The Merchants of New York,* by Thomas Prichard Rossiter, 1857.

A. T. Stewart, and financiers Albert Gallatin and Stephen Girard, many of them country boys made good. This painting, a sermon in oil paint, silently but firmly offered the young men proof of the viability of the now-outdated model of the successful Christian gentleman proposed by the YMCA and supported by the building and its programs.

YMCA leaders did not always rely upon young men to construct the proper meaning for a work, as they did with the Rossiter painting, but provided an interpretation. Members and visitors received pamphlets detailing the message communicated by one of the most famous paintings in the New York YMCA, Thomas Cole's series titled *The Cross and the World*. There are two paths in life, the text explained, taken by two different pilgrims; one the path through the World, the other the often more difficult, but more rewarding, path of God (see Plate 4).[43]

Reception Room

The exhortation to take the "correct" path was also communicated subtly, and more mechanically, by the physical arrangement of the rooms. An examination of the building's plan, reconstructed from written descriptions, reveals an arrangement designed to facilitate efficient supervision. For members, all entrances, exits, and stairways to the social rooms, parlors, and gymnasium passed through the reception room. Richard C. Morse explained the importance of the plan in the conception of the building:

> This may justifiably be termed the structural center, about which both the edifice and the work are reared. It corresponds to the bar, the gambling table, or other focal point of interest in the various demoralizing resorts with which young men are familiar.[44]

This design was indebted, at least conceptually, to Jeremy Bentham's Panopticon. Conceived in 1791 and widely publicized on both sides of the Atlantic, the Panopticon was influential in the design of prisons, libraries, company towns, hospitals, and factories throughout the late eighteenth and nineteenth centuries. In Bentham's ideal diagram a circular space was under the potential scrutiny of a centrally located jailer, librarian, or manager.[45] Those under surveillance did not require constant attention or physical force to control their actions. The architecture itself encouraged compliance with the established order. Michel Foucault has described the process:

> He who is subjected to a field of visibility, and who knows it, assumes responsibility for the constraints of power, he makes them play spontaneously upon himself; he inscribes in himself the power relation in which he simultaneously plays both roles; he becomes the principle of his own subjection.[46]

The YMCA was, of course, not a strict interpretation of Bentham's original plan, which had a more rigid arrangement with complete control over the population in individual rooms. But as a later diagram, intended to present a conceptual image of the 1869 building, shows, the panoptic principle was clearly in the mind of Renwick, designer of asylums and hospitals (Figure 2.27).

The Panopticon was also quite familiar to Y leaders, many of whom had had firsthand experience with this architectural concept in a recent and widely publicized "Akron Plan" for Sunday schools. In 1867 Lewis Miller, the inventor of the Buckeye mower and reaper and the superintendent of the Sunday school of the First Methodist Episcopal Church of Akron, Ohio, devised this improved plan.[47] Instead of arranging semicircular benches within a square or rectangular room, Miller advocated that the room itself be semicircular, divided like a pie with partitions to form classrooms for different age groups. At the center of the semicircle, the superintendent, seated on the platform, could efficiently monitor everyone without disturbing schoolwork. Published widely in the religious press, the semipanoptic Akron Plan was adopted by Sunday schools around the country. The YMCA was no doubt aware of this widespread development, since its members, patrons, and even staff were active in the Sunday school movement.[48] YMCA leaders, including New York YMCA secretary McBurney, were involved in Sunday school work. The YMCA's modified use of the panoptic plan, filtered through the religious experience of the Sunday school, was intended to provide an efficient and modern means of surveillance, reducing the necessity for paid staff and allowing young men to enjoy a sense of freedom while under the caring and watchful eye of Christian leaders.

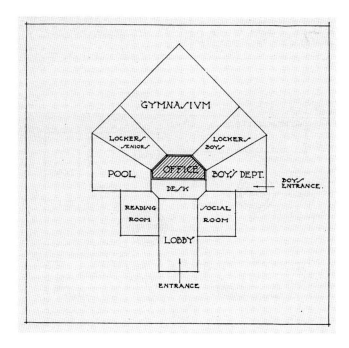

FIGURE 2.27. Diagrammatic plan of ideal supervision by Louis Jallade, in *The Association Building*, 1915.

McBurney's Domain

The power and control of the building's director and superintendent, McBurney, over members and visitors was consolidated in the design of the building's central vertical core. The main staircase, extending from the ground floor up to a private room under the mansard dome, was his domain. On the second floor of the stair hall, with windows facing Twenty-third Street, McBurney located his own private office, which offered access to both the reception room on the east side and the hall on the west (Figure 2.28). From there he had visual control over the various functions, users, and points of access in the building. McBurney, seated at his rolltop desk in this central office, could observe the staircase and the street below. Three stories above

68 / INVENTING THE YMCA BUILDING

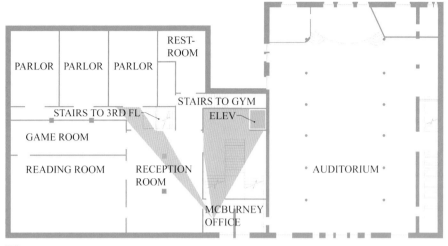

FIGURE 2.28. Diagram of the line of vision from Robert McBurney's office in the New York YMCA building. From his office overlooking the stairwell and adjacent to the reception room and the auditorium, Robert McBurney was able to efficiently administer entrance, egress, and circulation throughout his domain.

his office, in the attic, McBurney reserved a dwelling space for himself, a monastic, collegiate attic room, much like Edwin Booth's apartments on the top floor of Booth's Theatre. It was decorated carefully with bric-a-brac and furnishings that represented its masculine, yet moral, inhabitant: a center parlor table, floral carpet, grandfather clock, velvet divan, hunting trophy, an oddly "popish" sculpted crucifix, and prints of foreign places, including the Piazza San Marco (Figure 2.29). There he lived and received, as special guests, young members who required additional guidance and personal attention.

New York City could now offer young men a respectable place to spend their free time, if they were willing to relinquish their autonomy. The design of the building, Y leaders hoped, would offer preventative, continuous, automatic, economical, and mechanical production of character to the public and respectable leisure activity to the young man. The efficient design of this "manhood factory" was essential to their ambitious attempt to define and mass-produce a new kind of man: an efficient, competitive, yet moral upholder of the industrial social order.[49]

Reception of the Building

When the building was completed, the press praised it as a major addition to the architectural fabric of the city. One anonymous review, republished by the YMCA, glorified the design of the building in the context of the period:

> Time was when New York consisted of nothing more than several elongated blocks of what would now be termed second-rate tenement houses, with scarcely an exception to its dull monotony by anything

FIGURE 2.29. Robert McBurney's tower room, New York YMCA building.

that approached somewhat the beautiful. . . . It is gratifying to notice that the more recent of the structures display an originality of design and construction that the others greatly lack.⁵⁰

One acute observer, a reporter for *Harper's Weekly,* identified this religious-secular hybrid building as a new *interpretation* of the clubhouse, saying that "it is, indeed, fairly entitled to be designated the handsomest club-house in the city. Clubhouse we call it, for such in fact it is . . . though consecrated to the cause of good morals, [and] of pure religion."⁵¹

The young men of the city responded immediately to the YMCA's innovation, with membership increasing from two thousand to seven thousand in the year the building opened. In the following years it continued to maintain high membership levels, although admittedly only a small fraction of the city's young male population could afford the annual $5 dues. But what need was the building fulfilling? Did it function the way its creators had hoped? In 1884 the YMCA sent an evaluation form to all the members involved in evening classes or gymnasium instruction. Two questions were asked: "What advantage have you derived from the class you are attending?" and "Of what other advantage has the Association been to you?"

Some replies seemed to indicate great success for this new socioreligious building: "It has kept me from going out at night with young men to theatres, saloons, to play billiards, etc.; when I go out of a night now, I go to the Library and peruse useful books, or magazines," said one respondent, while another reported, "The very atmosphere of the place seems to make you feel that there is something more to work for than earthly gain." The emphasis on the environmental influence of the building was emphasized by one pious young man:

> Joining the Association when my mind was filled with doubts I was drawn into the meetings in the parlor by the singing, and while attending these meetings was led to see the error of my ways, and through this was led to give my heart to Christ.

In these replies there is evidence that some young men welcomed the upright religious atmosphere, but also an indication that this group was in the minority, and often the subject of scorn as effeminate. Another young man confessed that

> I often hooted at the Association and its seeming ridiculous work, but my mind's change even now astonishes me, as I am now one of its best advocates in trying to get friends to become members. I have discovered its very good work and regret deeply that I had not long ago joined it.

Both of these comments, while of dubious authenticity, seem to reflect the YMCA's vision of a young man's experience. Embedded in both these statements, whether wishful products of YMCA public relations or the thoughts of real young men, is the implication that the amenities offered to members outweighed the "ridiculous" religious program.[52]

Even the YMCA admitted that the attraction of the gym was by far the most common reason its members joined. In annual reports, articles, and committee minutes the organization questioned how to strengthen the religious work and how to infuse spirituality into the gymnasium program, indirectly acknowledging that access to the gymnasium, library, evening classes, and free concerts and lectures were what attracted young men. The majority of replies to the survey, indeed the phrasing of the questions themselves, position the YMCA as a service agency. Members noted improved skills in bookkeeping and language, assistance in finding employment, and improvements in health and increased energy. Others emphasized the social benefits: "It has been a second home to me in the city," and "It is one of the most sociable societies I have the honor to be a member of."[53]

Although it may have served a genuinely religious purpose for a small group of men, the New York YMCA was most successful in the secular activity of self-definition. Aimed at the middle class, the YMCA's facilities and programs offered self-improvement, status definition—and the use of a gym. The panoptic reception room was not only a site of surveillance, but a place to see and be seen by fellow aspirants to middle-class status. This reception room functioned to some degree as a men's club would have: a space in which members could identify successful role models and to assume that position themselves.

The introduction of the New York YMCA building acknowledged the blurring of boundaries—conceptual, geographical, and architectural—between morality and commerce.[54] There had already been some blurring of those boundaries in hotels, clubs, banks, office buildings, and public parlors. The YMCA muddied the distinctions prescribed by the gendered middle-class ideology of separate spheres, which dictated that religion and morality be spatially and conceptually separated from the male world of work into a cloistered feminine domestic environment.

Conclusion

This new building represents an important turning point not only for the New York Association, but also in the general history of the YMCA. It reflects the metamorphosis of the relatively primitive antebellum concept of environmental evangelism into a bold, proactive vision of the YMCA as a formative, competitive element in the urban landscape, rather than a refuge from it. The present-day conception of the YMCA as a building, rather than a social-service organization, can be traced directly back to the New York YMCA's pioneering headquarters. Its leaders viewed architectural form as integral to the identity of the organization. The New York Association claimed its role in urban society based upon the unique function and design of its new building.

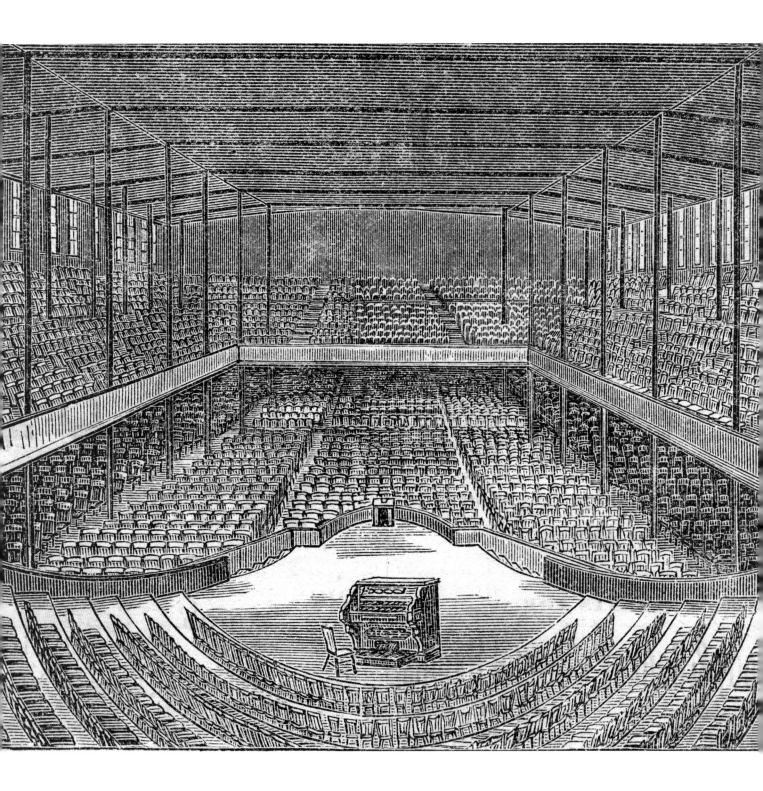

3
ACCEPTING THE CALL TO BUILD
Architectural Evangelism on Main Street

AFTER THE COMPLETION of their impressive new building in 1869, the young leaders of the New York YMCA and their allies focused their efforts on a larger and even more ambitious task: the placement of a similar structure on every Main Street in the United States. Fusing their evangelical missionary heritage, their Republican politics, and their role as the pioneers of modern corporate structures, they envisioned a national network of Ys as important unifying elements of an increasingly modern, urban, and unified public culture. As David Scobey has written, in this period of reconstruction "nationhood in the United States was remade by linked processes of capitalist, cultural, [and] territorial . . . expansion and unification."[1] The YMCA's "call to build," issued from Manhattan to every corner of the country, was an important part of this remaking of the nation.

From its headquarters in the country's first Christian clubhouse, the New York–based Central (later the International) Committee promoted its architectural experiment throughout the growing country, especially in the South and the West. At the beginning of this effort most YMCAs were still tenants of "halls used at times for other purposes, business offices, generally contracted and not always cleanly, rooms in out of the way buildings."[2] The New Yorkers' hoped-for transition from a collection of obscure rented rooms to a network of new, elaborate buildings on the New York model would require not only architectural effort, but conceptual change. Symbolically and practically, the YMCA building converted the organization overnight from one of the age's many ephemeral volunteer associations into an institution of higher purpose, an arbiter of morals with the power to enforce them. The financial support required for such a large-scale building program forced the YMCA, already a religious organization with strong ties to the business community, to fuse its interests and methods even more closely with those of the leaders of the commercial economy.

The means and the method of their promotional campaign, based on new forms of communication and transportation technology, including railroads, journals, and postcards, was an early, prescient, and remarkably successful attempt to use the tools of an emerging mass culture to shape a nation in the image of New York. Responses to the YMCA project varied from place to place and from region to region as locals sought to reconcile it with their established ideas about gender, religion, architectural propriety, and urban form. The YMCA filled in the map of the United States in bursts and starts, with periods of growth tied to economic trends and national events like the Chicago 1893 World's Fair (see Figure I.2). By 1915, urbanized America had answered the YMCA's "call to build."

New York and the Nation

Although the New York YMCA was, in many ways, a local product of individuals and circumstances, in the years during and after the Civil War its influence and power extended far beyond the Hudson River. New Yorkers understood their city as an incubator for the nation, a place for the development of new ideas as well as a center of business, banking, and communication. The YMCA building, like Central Park and other experiments in urban design and public culture, was understood by a broad variety of observers to serve as a proving ground for the expanding urban culture.[3]

This image of New York as the capital of the United States was produced and disseminated through a new medium of persuasion: *Harper's Weekly*. Beginning in the 1850s this quarto-sized, self-proclaimed "journal of civilization" covered politics and published belles lettres. By 1865, aided by the continuing expansion of new railroad systems, the journal had a circulation of more than one hundred thousand for each issue, and was one of the leading illustrated newspapers in the country. Its readership was especially strong in the West, where Anthony Trollope found the paper in even the most rudimentary settlements.[4] During the Civil War illustrations increased in number until they comprised nearly half of its pages. Artist Thomas Nast joined the staff, and his scathing political cartoons joined pictures of everything from natural disasters to political meetings, parades, battles, and horses.

Clearly identifiable among this wealth of imagery was a group I characterize as the "architectural portrait." Combining descriptive text with detailed perspective views, this genre portrayed, in serial form, the new American urban landscape of the bonanza economy.[5] Every issue included at least one example, often on the front page under the masthead: the new Post Office building in Boston, the City Hall in Baltimore, Crosby's Opera House in

Chicago, and the Mercantile Libraries in Philadelphia and San Francisco are but a handful. Although national in its coverage, *Harper's* focus was clearly on Gotham. A survey of the illustrations included in the years 1867 to 1869 indicates that its new buildings were represented in the pages of *Harper's* more completely than any other American city. Frequently designed in the highly fashionable, ornate French Renaissance style, this collection of buildings presented a prescriptive and visually unified image of the American city as shaped by the cultural aspirations of the increasingly wealthy commercial class. As Scobey has suggested, *Harper's* constituted "a new kind of public sphere where middle- and upper-class Americans of all regions consumed increasingly standardized . . . visual and narrative representations of themselves as a public."[6]

For many middle-class Americans outside of New York, the first introduction to the idea of a "Christian clubhouse" came in the pages of *Harper's*. In November 1868 and in October and December 1869 its readers were presented with reports of the novel building project of the New York YMCA, with illustrations and text that delineated its unusual combination of features and marked the stages of its construction and completion (Figure 3.1).[7] In November 1868 the magazine featured a half-page depiction of the ceremony of laying the cornerstone, with a description of the amenities to be included in the building. A year later, as the YMCA was nearing completion, a view of the building's façade portrayed its size and Second Empire splendor against the background of a street bustling with pedestrians and horse-drawn carriages. Finally, just as the building was set to be opened, *Harper's* introduced its interior with an article and a set of three images: the library, the reading room, and the lecture room. Together they offered readers a view of this new kind of gendered, respectable, middle-class space for young men. The library, lined with bookshelves on several levels from floor to ceiling, is populated by earnest and formally posed young men. Women appear on the margins of the reading room, literally guided on a tour that readers enjoy vicariously in the images and text. The furnishings of the rooms, especially the upright stands for journals and newspapers in the reading room, mimic the members' upright posture, reinforcing the discipline and increasingly serial and repetitive nature of their workplaces and tasks in the white-collar office. Only in the semipublic space of the lecture hall do fashionably dressed women and men appear together, making introductions, conversing comfortably, and seating themselves for an event.

Missing from the images is the gymnasium, the most controversial feature of the new building. This had, perhaps, been omitted by *Harper's* for an article meant to sell the idea to more conservative audiences outside of New York. As presented, the YMCA appears as a more elaborate version of the mercantile library, but dedicated to a Christian cause. Clearly outlined in print media, in a forum that reached beyond New York to hundreds of thousands of Americans in the newly reunited Union, was the spatial transformation of what had been the dowdy, ad hoc quarters of a voluntary evangelical

HARPER'S WEEKLY.

A JOURNAL OF CIVILIZATION.

VOL. XIII.—No. 676.] NEW YORK, SATURDAY, DECEMBER 11, 1869. [SINGLE COPIES, TEN CENTS. $4.00 PER YEAR IN ADVANCE.

Entered according to Act of Congress, in the Year 1869, by Harper & Brothers, in the Clerk's Office of the District Court of the United States, for the Southern District of New York.

THE NEW YORK YOUNG MEN'S CHRISTIAN ASSOCIATION.

THE LIBRARY.

THE READING-ROOM.

It was a noble conception, that of him who first formed the idea of employing the instrumentality of a club in the work of Christ. It has been, thus far, nobly realized in the new building of the New York Young Men's Christian Association.

For years this Association has been carrying on its work without any adequate means. It has undertaken to provide for the moral, intellectual, and social improvement of the young men of the great metropolis. To this work it has strictly confined itself. Other similar organizations have added to the sphere of their labors. They have organized mission-schools, tenement-house prayer-meetings, temporal charities. That in New York has found as much as it could do in its single self-chosen mission. It has had between one and two hundred thousand young men to provide for. Over seventy-five thousand of these, as nearly as can be ascertained, are homeless and almost friendless. Some are penniless. Those who have money are more to be pitied than those who have not. Their danger is just in the ratio of their means. The allurements to vice are numerous and attractive. Without discussing the much-vexed question of amusements, it is certain that the theatre, the billiard-room, the café, are in a large majority of instances, and to a large majority of young men, open doors to ruin. The dance is little or no better. We speak not of what they might be, but of what they now actually are. Until the recent excise law Broadway was lined with brightly-lighted halls, where women employed their arts to add to the enticements of music, drink, and dancing. Attention to business does by no means always serve to counteract the influences of vice, which are erroneously supposed to captivate only the idle. Business often demands of the young salesman, as a part of his professional duties, that he accompany his customer to these dens of iniquity, and show him the pollutions of the great city. Every now and then some great defalcation, some atrocious swindle, startling the

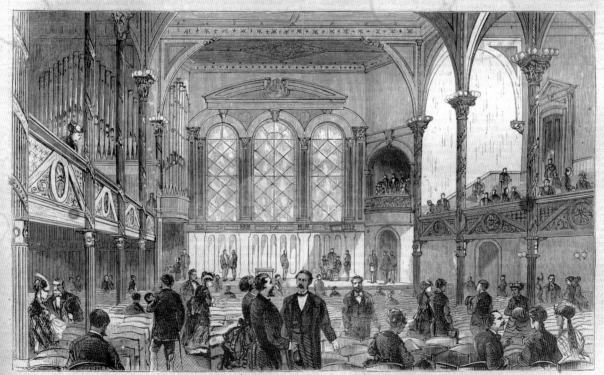

THE LECTURE-ROOM.—[SKETCHED BY STANLEY FOX.]

organization for men and women into a lavish building that communicated the organization's central place in a modern landscape.

Most provincial *Harper's* readers would have already been familiar with the Y before the appearance of these articles. In the antebellum period hundreds, if not thousands, of cities and towns in the North, South, and throughout the expanding Midwest organized Young Men's Christian Associations. Housed in rented "rooms" above stores, most YMCAs focused exclusively on Bible study and evangelical activities. Many had been formed in response to the so-called "businessmen's revival" of 1857, but few survived the Civil War. The presence of the daring New York YMCA building on the cover of *Harper's* marked the reemergence and redefinition of the organization on what was, perhaps, the most visible national stage.

The editorial decision to feature the New York YMCA building was in keeping with *Harper's* larger goals to represent the bourgeois public sphere to its readers. This concentration on the building boom of the YMCA may have had to do with the pious yet commercial interests of the publishers, the Harper Brothers. Ardent Methodists, they sought throughout their varied publishing interests to use commercial strategies to further their interest in promoting character, including the publication of attractive Bibles.[8] The YMCA's pragmatic, competitive use of amusements to win men to Christ would have appealed to them. Even more attractive, however, was the Y's proposed vision of a Republican nation with New York as its capital. Nonetheless, to have three separate features on the same building was unprecedented for the newspaper. Even more notable was the choice to publish accounts of two additional Y buildings constructed in Washington and San Francisco. Although the Harper Brothers did not directly provide financial support to the building of the New York YMCA, they nonetheless were instrumental in its promotion to a national audience.[9]

The *Harper's* campaign presented to the American public a vision of public urban culture that required the integration of a new institution into the urban fabric. The YMCA was an architectural symbol of progressive modernity that helped bridge the transition from autonomous, local, traditional values to a national, corporate system that accommodated and depended upon geographical, if not social, mobility, heterogeneity, and urbanization.

Regional Resistance to New York: Chicago's Farwell Hall

In the 1870s the idea of the YMCA presented in the New York building, with its fourfold program that included emphasis on the physical well-being of young men, was too radical, especially for many of the new, more religiously conservative organizations in the West. Before 1880 Dwight Moody, the famous evangelist, directed the Chicago YMCA in a program of missionary activities for the entire population: revival meetings, Bible study, and a well-attended daily prayer meeting each noon. Its members engaged in relief work for the poor, taught Sunday-school classes, and visited the jails.[10]

FIGURE 3.1. The New York YMCA, illustrated in *Harper's Weekly*, December 11, 1869.

FIGURE 3.2. Dwight Moody, in *The Watchman*, July 1876.

Moody, a former shoe salesman, is well known for his embrace of modern methods, including advertising, to attract people to his meetings, but, unlike New York Y leaders, he remained focused on the spiritual conversion of individuals (Figure 3.2). Moody applied business methods to his promotion of religion, while the New Yorkers appropriated religion to facilitate the smooth operation of business. The Chicago YMCA, influential in its region, challenged the New Yorkers' national vision of modern bourgeois culture. Both organizations were interested in a pragmatic solution to resolving the conflict between business and religion in modern urban life, but they took different paths.

Perhaps this competition with Chicago for leadership of the YMCA accounts for the fact that its very large and impressive, but evangelically oriented building, Farwell Hall, was never featured in *Harper's*. Another reason for its omission may have been its short life span. Dedicated in late September 1867, it was destroyed by fire in early 1868 and the organization lost its replacement in the Great Fire of 1871. Only a few images and some written descriptions remain of the original buildings (Figure 3.3).

The building Moody envisioned reveals his particular cultural fusion of business and religion. Designed by prominent architect W. W. Boyington, it was one of the largest and most impressive buildings in the city. Five stories tall, with mansard roofs and classical detailing, it was named for dry-goods magnate John F. Farwell. Like the New York building, it was a building block, intended to be self-supporting through the rental of store and office space to the city departments of police, fire, and health. In addition to space for commercial tenants, rooms were to be rented, as they were in the Bible House in New York, by kindred missionary, tract, and temperance societies, making the building a center of evangelical culture. Located in the heart of the downtown at Madison and LaSalle, on a site donated by Farwell, the building could command good rents. Rather than seeking donors, Moody developed a joint-stock plan, with investors receiving a 6 percent return on their money through the rental of space. He cleverly applied for a charter from the state for the organization even before the money was raised for the building, exempting this profit-making real-estate venture from taxation.

The architectural identity of Farwell Hall as a building block with ground-level stores, and a parlor, library, and reading room above, linked it to the new building erected by the New York Y. The characterization of the building as a "hall," however, indicates a slightly different programmatic emphasis. Its auditorium, with seating for 3,500 people, was one of the largest public gathering spaces in the city at the time. Unlike the Renwick building in New York, which integrated the 1,400-seat hall as part of a multifunctional clubhouse, Boyington's design for the YMCA articulated the auditorium as a separate volume that occupied the rear of the site. Screened from the street, it stood apart awkwardly from the rest of the building and was linked to it only by a narrow hallway. Sometimes referred to as Moody's Hall, this space

FIGURE 3.3. Farwell Hall, Madison Street, between Clark and LaSalle, Chicago, 1868.

was a frequent platform for his large public revival meetings, an annex or extension to his Tabernacle building just a few blocks away (Figure 3.4). Although there were some facilities for members, and even a primitive gymnasium rented by the Metropolitan Gymnastic Club, located up on the fifth floor, Farwell Hall was primarily known to the public as a site for revival meetings rather than an innovative leisure center for young men, as was the New York building.[11]

Further distinguishing Farwell Hall from the New York model was the fact that Farwell Hall was open to women as well as men. The Chicago YMCA's 1863 constitution openly challenged the specifically masculine function of the organization, claiming that its mission was the "spiritual, intellectual, and social improvement of *all* within its reach, irrespective of age, sex, or condition."[12] This policy remained unchanged for thirty years, much to the dismay of New Yorkers. To them, the Christian clubhouse was intended as a homosocial world in which an upright, principled manliness would be cultivated through contact with other men. The role of women was strictly auxiliary: arranging flowers, fund-raising, helping with furnishings. This limited role for women was not warmly received in the West and Midwestern com-

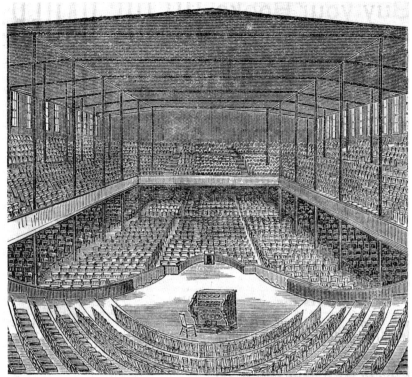
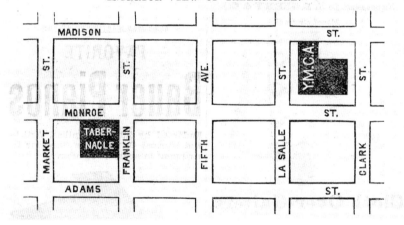

FIGURE 3.4. Moody's Tabernacle and the YMCA, in *The Watchman*, July 1876.

munities, where men significantly outnumbered women. In Chicago's sphere of influence many YMCAs understood their rooms as a place to find a mate, rather than a place to assuage the anxiety of the modern work world. The Midwest ideal of manliness diverged from that of the urban East Coast. With its frontier, agrarian base, the proving ground of manhood was not in business or political leadership, but continued in the traditional role of a paternal figure in the household.[13] It took more than fifteen years to convince Chicagoans, who supported Moody's more religious mission, to accept the New Yorkers' architectural vision of a homosocial space for the shaping of a modern national culture. In the late 1880s the Chicago Association, led by a new generation, including Cyrus McCormick Jr. and Marshall Field, rejected Moody's leadership. In 1888 they refocused their efforts on young men, discontinued women's memberships, and, in a feat of architectural one-upmanship, built a new building that contained all the latest features of a modern Y, including a gymnasium and swimming pool.

New York's Cultural Satellites: Philadelphia, San Francisco, and Omaha

Despite Chicago's powerful and influential resistance, the New York vision of the YMCA found traction in pockets across the country in the 1870s: northern coastal cities; the urban Great Lakes; Omaha, Nebraska; and San Francisco. These far-flung communities, connected by economic and social links to New York, were outposts of a Yankee landscape held together by urban, Republican, evangelical values. Most receptive were the large East Coast cities like Philadelphia and Baltimore, as well as the areas affected by the central westward trajectory of New England Yankees as they moved across

Ohio and Indiana. Large urban centers in the Northeast and Midwest—notably Cincinnati, Cleveland, and Indianapolis—responded relatively quickly to the call from New York for a national YMCA building movement, buying or constructing major structures in the early 1870s, before financial panic hit and brought architectural development of the YMCA to a virtual standstill (see Figure I.2). First Indianapolis and Cleveland (1871), then Poughkeepsie (1872), Boston (1873), and Cincinnati (1874) purchased and converted buildings. Montreal (1873), Philadelphia (1876), and Baltimore (1877) soon followed, erecting large, expensive buildings according to the fourfold plan introduced by Robert McBurney and William E. Dodge Jr.

Philadelphia's building, costing a half-million dollars, emulated the New York building quite directly (Figure 3.5). At Fifteenth and Chestnut streets, the building occupied a prominent corner site not far from City Hall. The program, drawn up with the advice of the New Yorkers, included a hall, two-story reading room and library, parlor, classrooms, employment bureau, gymnasium, and bowling alley—together embodying the secular leisure center advanced by the New Yorkers. It also called for stores on the ground level to provide income for the Association. Following New York's example, the Building Committee chose a secular rather than a religious style for its new building, rejecting a churchy Gothic design with a corner spire by David Gendell in favor of Addison Hutton's hybrid, polychromatic Second Empire elevation. Despite a YMCA reviewer's contention that in the Philadelphia building "there has been less effort to copy or follow any given example than to adapt a fitting exterior to the internal requirements," it is quite clear that Hutton modeled his design directly on New York's example, going beyond stylistic kinship to mimic its massing and the exterior articulation of functions.[14]

FIGURE 3.5. The Philadelphia YMCA, Fifteenth and Chestnut streets, by Addison Hutton, in *American Architect and Building News*, August 23, 1877.

Both buildings were five stories tall with a central stair tower. Hutton drew direct inspiration from Renwick's round-arched portal, which occupied a central position on the façade. This feature was intended in both designs to draw the attention of the pedestrian away from the ground-level shops to the YMCA as a whole. Also familiar is the irregular fenestration on the south side of the façade, revealing the presence of the auditorium to passersby. Even Renwick's irregular, smaller tower, meant to provide a separate entrance for the hall in New York, is present in Hutton's design. The only major departures from Renwick's building are Hutton's use of Gothic rather than classical detailing on the windows, and his substitution of a central tower for the small dome used to cap the central stair tower in the New York building.

The other major Yankee building of the period was located on the West Coast, about as far away from New York as possible, in San Francisco. Despite this distance, the two cities were linked and united by commerce and trade. San Francisco shared connections with New York that dated to the Gold Rush of 1849, even before the Union Pacific linked them physically in 1870. William H. Aspinwall, co-owner of the Pacific Mail Steamship Company and supporter of the YMCA, linked them quite literally through shipping and transportation. In the 1850s the city attracted adventurous Yankee sons and relatives of eastern merchant houses seeking mobility and quick money. The lack of an ordered social hierarchy inspired these men and a few genteel women to found mercantile voluntary associations like the Chamber of Commerce and the YMCA to regularize and control behavior.[15]

Although completed just a few weeks before the Renwick building opened in 1869, the YMCA building in San Francisco was a copy or an emulation of the New York building, which had been designed first (Figure 3.6). In a fusion of High Victorian Gothic and the French Renaissance, the San Francisco YMCA housed clubhouse space, a gymnasium, and an auditorium. Income for the Association was produced by the rents from stores at ground level and artists' studios in the mansard roofs. San Francisco's allegiance to Gotham extended beyond style to program as well, confirming the centrality of the New Yorkers in the emergence of a national vision of urban culture. The appearance of the San Francisco building, and its publication in *Harper's*, affirmed New York as the capital of America's culture, able to extend its provincial domain all the way to the Pacific.

Halfway between the two, almost directly in the center of the country, sat a third outpost of the YMCA's Yankee landscape. Although Nebraska was technically closer to Chicago than New York, Omaha's strategic position on the Union Pacific Railroad linked it more closely to Wall Street than to the Loop. A small Missouri River town before the Civil War, by 1865 Omaha had a population of seven thousand and was poised for enormous growth as a central depot and servicing and jobbing point on the soon-to-be-completed Union Pacific Railroad. "Train Town," as some called it, was an important linchpin in New York's vision of a national system. It was a logical place for a YMCA to appear, especially since New York YMCA leaders and building donors like George Opdyke and J.D.F. Lanier were key financiers and builders of the Union Pacific.

The Omaha YMCA was founded in 1866 by George Frost, a purchasing agent for the Credit Mobilier Corporation, the arm of the Union Pacific responsible for the actual construction of the railroad. His job involved the funneling of materiel from east to west, ensuring the provision of an enormous range of supplies furnished by New Yorkers, including Morris Jesup and William E. Dodge Jr.: iron castings for cars, copper and pig lead, picks and axes, as well as groceries and provisions to feed the workers. Frost expended $6 million in 1868 alone and was responsible for the more than thirty acres of supply houses, repair shops, sheds, and lumber piles that spread

FIGURE 3.6. The San Francisco YMCA, 232 Sutter Street, in *Harper's Weekly*, February 6, 1869.

HARPER'S WEEKLY.

A JOURNAL OF CIVILIZATION

VOL. XIII.—No. 632.] NEW YORK, SATURDAY, FEBRUARY 6, 1869. SINGLE COPIES, TEN CENTS. $4.00 PER YEAR IN ADVANCE.

Entered according to Act of Congress, in the Year 1869, by Harper & Brothers, in the Clerk's Office of the District Court of the United States, for the Southern District of New York.

THE Y. M. C. A. BUILDING, SAN FRANCISCO.

This elegant and commodious building, of which we give an illustration on this page, has been recently erected for the use of the Young Men's Christian Association in San Francisco. It is located on Sattee Street, and has a frontage of 54 feet with 120 feet depth. It consists of a basement and two stories, with a Mansard roof overlooked by a tower, and contains a reading-room, lecture-hall, a library, and lodging and bath rooms. There is also a gymnasium connected with the building. The front is built of blue sandstone wrought after the Venetian style. The building and lot cost $75,000.

"THE LONG SLEEP."

On first glancing at this touching picture—and only at the first glance—some uncertainty may be felt as to M. Rivière's intention, so ambiguous is the title (though, of course, on reflection, it must appear most significant and happy), and such excellent taste has the artist evinced in avoiding any of the more painful indications of death. For that the awful and mysterious counterpart of sleep—that sleep from which the soul only awakes, "the long sleep" of death—is represented, admits not of a moment's doubt. Death, in the welcome guise of tranquil, customary sleep, has come at last, as Friend and Liberator, to that aged shepherd in his chair. Every thing intimates the peaceful, not untimely, close of a long life spent in a monotonous round of humble duty with little to cheer, and none left to solace, or even now to mourn its ending, save the mute creatures, sole sharers of his cares and hearth. Perhaps the poor shepherd passed the village church-yard last evening, faint, worn, and infirm, and thought of death in sure and certain hope as he gazed wistfully toward the grave of her who had followed the dear ones gone before, or had alone remained to him after their probably enforced departure to tend flocks on wide Australian plains or prairies of the Far West—she who had perhaps till lately welcomed him, constant as sundown, with blazing hearth and boiling kettle. Alas! since then he has had himself to prepare the eventide meal, however fatigued with watching or recovering the lost sheep of his flock. At length came the preparations for a meal of which he was never to partake. The fire burned up briskly, the kettle sang cheerfully, as usual, and the tired shepherd composed himself for a short nap while yet he should have to wait. But now the fire is gray and dead and cold, like him who put to it the living spark; the kettle has boiled out, its contents have vanished like his expired breath; and it has fallen on its side. The night stole on, and the dogs slunk to their corner without their wonted feed and caress. The night wore away without sound or sign from the sleeper. The life-giving, awakening rays of a new-born sun pour in at the casement, but they do not vivify or rouse the late slumberer. Yet—so gentle was the stroke of Death, so quietly did the spirit pass away—they reveal no change in his attitude: save, perhaps, that the head has sunk a little lower; the chest propping the jaw, which would have fallen. With instinctive apprehension the dumb animals try, by licking face or hands, and by uneasy, mournful whine, to waken their master. But in vain—in vain! The Night has come and enveloped him within its shadows. He is sleeping "the long sleep." His waiting and watching are forever ended. He will never more call those faithful companions of his solitude to the pastures on hill or plain; never more will they hear his voice—never more do his bidding. His sheep are left without a shepherd; he himself is gathered to the fold of the Good Shepherd.

THE COLORED CONVENTION.

The object of the National Convention of colored men, recently in session at Washington, was to inquire into the actual condition of the negro race in this country, and to consider the political and social problems which that race has to encounter as the result of emancipation. At the close of the Convention, on the morning of January 19, the Convention sent a committee of twelve to call upon General Grant. Mr. Langton, the Chairman, addressed the General as follows:

General Grant:—In the name of 4,000,000 of American citizens; in the name of 700,000 electors of African descent—electors who braved threats, who defied intimidation, whose numbers have been reduced by assassination and murder in their efforts in the exercise of a franchise guaranteed by American law to every one clothed in the full livery of American citizenship, to secure in the late Presidential canvass the election of the nominee of the National Republican party to the high places to which they were named, we, the accredited delegates of the National Convention of Colored Men, the sessions of which in this city have just closed, come to present to you our congratulations upon your election to the Presidency of the United States. Permit us, General, to express, in this connection, our confidence in your ability and determination to so execute the laws already enacted by our National Congress as to conserve and protect the life, the liberty, and the rights, no less of the humblest subject of the Government than those of the most exalted and influential. Called as you are to fill the Chair of State, your duties will be arduous and trying, and (especially since in this reconstruction period of the Government, removing the rubbish, the accretions of the now dead slaveholding oligarchy) you will administer the government according to the principles of morals and law announced by the fathers. In advance we bring to you, General, as a pledge of our devotion to our common country and Government, the liveliest sympathy of the colored people of the nation, and in their name we express the hope that all things connected with the administration of the Government, upon which you are so soon to enter as our Chief Magistrate, may be, under Providence, so ordered for the maintenance of law and the conservation of freedom, that your name, written high on the scroll of honor and fame, may go down to posterity, glorious and immortal, associated with the names of your illustrious predecessors in the Great Chair of State—Washington and Lincoln. Again, General, we express our congratulations.

To this address General Grant replied:

I thank the Convention, of which you are the representative, for the confidence they have expressed, and I hope sincerely that the colored people of the Nation may receive every protection which the laws give to them. They shall have my efforts to secure such protection. They should prove by their acts, their advancement, prosperity, and obedience to the laws, worthy of all privileges the Government has bestowed upon them; and by their future conduct prove themselves deserving of all they now claim.

THE YOUNG MEN'S CHRISTIAN ASSOCIATION BUILDING, SAN FRANCISCO, CALIFORNIA.

84 / ACCEPTING THE CALL TO BUILD

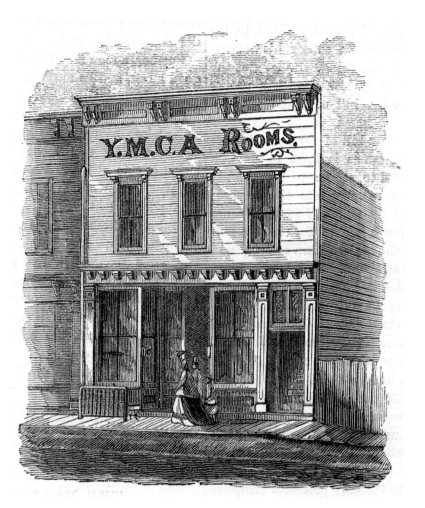

FIGURE 3.7. The Omaha YMCA building, located in the Wholesale District, 1869.

along and dominated the once quiet Omaha riverfront.[16] He was an active member of the territorial legislature, continuing to serve after statehood in 1870. The quintessential urban booster, he took great interest in the urban development of Omaha, investing in real estate, promoting the development of the Omaha Horse Railway in 1867, and serving as a director in the incorporation of the Omaha and Southwestern Railroad in 1869.

Frost, perhaps through the persuasive efforts of his employers, believed that a YMCA was an important part of city-building along the western railroad: a required element along with churches, schools, and hotels. In 1869, the year the transcontinental line was completed and Omaha was set to become a hub of the new national transportation system, he managed to erect a YMCA headquarters. It was a very modest structure, particularly in comparison with New York's magnificent headquarters. A simple two-story storefront, which cost $2,600, took its place in the center of the downtown wholesaling district and distinctly resembled the hardware, grocery, dry-goods, and drug stores that surrounded it (Figure 3.7).

The Call to Build

The presence of a purpose-built YMCA, even a simple balloon-frame structure, was encouraging, but it was just one tiny dot on a map that was quickly filling in with settlements and towns. If the YMCA building was to be an established part of the American urban landscape, more systematic and efficient "evangelization" in the cause of architecture was needed. Although presented to the nation under the aegis of the YMCA's national organization, the Central Committee, this was a New York initiative. Not only had the idea originated in New York, but that city's active and influential leaders, including Dodge Jr. and McBurney, aggressively assumed control of national conventions, posing questions and framing debate to advance their new fourfold idea. They lodged the Central Committee in the New York Association Building, and its executive board was dominated by New Yorkers.[17]

They initiated a "continuous effort for the formation of new Associations" that shared their values.[18]

This nationwide project required local support and alignment with the ideas of the New York Association. Because this architectural vision was bold, innovative, and expensive, it required time and persuasive effort. The first job was simply to convince others that a building was necessary. *Harper's* had already begun the work, and the YMCA emulated that journal's pictorial advertisement of the YMCA with its own national publications: *Association Monthly* and *The Watchman*. Like *Harper's*, the front page of each issue was devoted to a recently erected or purchased structure, including a perspective drawing and a detailed written description of the interior.[19] *Association Monthly,* published by the New York YMCA, served as the official mouthpiece for the "fourfold" New York agenda. *The Watchman,* published under the auspices of the more conservative Chicago YMCA, also advocated the construction of purpose-built clubhouses, but put more emphasis on religious matters than its eastern counterpart.[20] The two magazines began publication in 1870 and 1874, respectively, just as the building movement began to take shape. Their primary purpose was to advise and inform incipient or youthful associations as to the purpose and methods of the YMCA.

In June 1870 the *Association Monthly* published an editorial justifying its building fever in terms of Ecclesiastes' injunction: "To every thing there is a season, and a time to every purpose under the heaven." The editorial inaugurated the organization's building age, stressing the inevitability and appropriateness of the YMCA's architectural development: "Societies or Churches, if they are destined to become permanent institutions, must live long enough to reach their building era. They all find out there is 'a time to build.'"[21] Local associations received a clear impression of the status-enhancing power of new buildings from the illustrations in the journals. Although Jesus Christ was called "the chief cornerstone" of their activity, building was promoted as a worldly, but worthy, goal. Articles with titles like "Why Should We Have a New Association Building?" were a common feature. The YMCA periodicals, with their illustrations and wide circulation, were powerful promoters of this new vision of the YMCA.

The power of a national mail system, through which the journals circulated, was enhanced by the increasingly complete coverage of the nation's rail network. Over these rail lines traveled representatives of the New York YMCA to sell the fourfold, building-based vision of the organization. Throughout the 1870s and early 1880s Robert Weidensall and several other field secretaries crisscrossed the country as home missionaries, encouraging existing associations to adopt modern methods and sowing the seeds of new associations on the New York model. Like traveling salesmen, they knew their territory and helped to adapt national ideas to local culture and local interests. They gave illustrated lectures, distributed pamphlets, and helped struggling associations solve financial and organizational problems. They also organized state-based associations in Pennsylvania, Massachusetts,

Illinois, Indiana, Wisconsin, Iowa, and Virginia to provide continuous and up-to-date assistance to local YMCA groups.[22]

In pamphlets, articles, and personal consultations their experts answered three important questions posed by communities: Why should we have a building? How should we go about getting a building? And, finally, what should our building look like? The first question was the easiest and most frequently addressed. Pamphlets suggested that a building was necessary to lend permanence to the institution and garner respect for its mission, to be a proper symbol, to attract young men, and, most of all, to carry out the work properly.[23] In "The First Year's Experience in a New Association Building," and "What Advantages Have Accrued to Work for Young Men as a Result of Securing Association Buildings?," secretaries from Pittsburgh and Newburgh, New York, told of increased membership and attendance, a better class of members, larger contributions, and "home feeling."[24]

The Reverend T.G. Darling's much-republished 1881 tract, "Advantages of a Permanent Home for a Young Men's Christian Association," pointed out that, without a building, the YMCA would not receive the support of the community:

> A peripatetic Association, like a tramp in a limited beat, without a visible home of permanence, sleeping about from barn to barn of a public hall, and counting mournfully its chance of living long enough in one dingy place to get the value of a single coat of whitewash or paint, lacks many elements of impressing the public with that idea of permanence in work which will rally either friends or contributions to its support.[25]

According to Darling, a permanent YMCA building would bridge over times of financial depression, maintaining the institution in the community even when local crops or banks failed. This was the kind of enterprise a businessman could more easily support than a shaky philanthropy in rented rooms.

Underlying this effort to encourage building was an appeal to the values of the small-town (or even big-town) booster. Architecture was the major currency of self-promotion, indicating geographical commitment and permanency. A Y building would be valuable to a town regardless of one's religious beliefs as a sign of public spiritedness and a moral community. Taking a leaf out of the Ruskinian "Lamp of Sacrifice," one pamphlet argued that a handsome building, prominently located, would be a sermon in stone, a visible symbol commensurate with the town's "largeness of love and Christian zeal for young men."[26] Y leaders also presented it as a yardstick by which a community could measure its progress. To that end reproductions of elaborate buildings in other towns were sold by the committee as a set of framed prints or slides, suitable for reproduction in the local newspaper or display in the local church. *The Watchman* developed a magic lantern show with text for narration.[27] Pamphlets were printed for distribution to local merchants and

FIGURE 3.8. YMCA Jubilee Exhibit, Mechanics Hall, Boston, 1901.

prominent citizens touting the benefits of a Y building to the community, often embellished with quotes by political or business heroes.[28] Displays at national conventions gave members and secretaries the opportunity to exchange ideas and hear about the concept of the building in special lectures and displays (Figure 3.8).

The YMCA in the Small-Town Landscape

In tension with the booster ethos and excitement about a YMCA building was a bit of uncertainty about adding a Christian clubhouse to a developing town. Outside of major cities a YMCA building was an ambiguous force in the changing urban landscape. Neither a church, nor strictly a place of business, nor a school, it was something in between all three. Especially in smaller communities, such an institution was a radical social and architectural innovation.

More so than in large cities like New York, where new phenomena like the Ladies' Mile blurred the boundaries of the separate spheres, in smaller places the line between religion and commerce remained very clear geographically after the Civil War. This was the case, for instance, in Omaha at the end of the 1860s. The city was composed of three distinct zones: the industrial riverfront dominated by the Union Pacific and its machine shops and warehouses, a commercial district defined by two- and three-story business blocks and a few hotels, and an institutional and residential area high on a hill with the capitol and courthouse.

In Omaha the YMCA challenged the separation of morality and commerce with a structure devoted to respectable Christian activities located in the center of the commercial district. There were, of course, social spaces for men in the commercial district: general stores, barbershops, and livery stables. These spaces were not specifically designed for a social purpose, but they served as makeshift solutions to the lack of respectable social space for young men. Although not as bad as the saloons, these haunts did not provide what upstanding members of the community would consider an uplifting atmosphere. There men smoked, played cards, traded tall tales and spicy stories, and observed the customers.[29] Claiming men's free time for respectable pursuits, the Omaha YMCA building entered into the commercial district under religious auspices.

Compounding the difficulty of its downtown site was the appearance of the YMCA building in Omaha (see Figure 3.7). Taking the form of a building block, it was indistinguishable from the buildings around it. This precursor to the modern office building had its origins in the ancient combination of shop and residence so prevalent in colonial and early American cities.[30] As cities grew, this form evolved to encompass nonresidential functions as well, growing to as many as five stories atop a plate-glass storefront. Simple brick façades and rectangular windows presented a regular appearance to the street that did not reveal the often complicated subdivided interiors. This kind of anonymity was necessary, since the building block was designed to shelter the ever-changing activities of the American city and produce revenue for its owners. All the different sorts of commercial and associational enterprises—stores, saloons, banks, insurance agencies, newspapers, hotels, opera houses, fraternal lodges, and literary and lecture associations like the YMCA—were located in this type of vernacular structure.

The Omaha YMCA, without a spire and located in the midst of building blocks and warehouses, looked nothing like a church and muddied the previously crystal-clear distinction between church and saloon. This breach of architectural propriety and separate spheres was unsettling. To many clergymen a new YMCA building, supported by the community, was a material acknowledgment that the church could not satisfy all the religious needs of the community. By respectably accommodating the desire for leisure, the YMCA removed the little absolute moral power the church had retained in the urbanizing nation.

Furthermore, its interdenominationalism was troubling to communities clearly divided among competing Protestant churches. Was the YMCA, with its buildings equipped for religious meetings *and* leisure activities, a dangerous new sect that accommodated sinful behavior rather than censuring it?[31] In towns where hard work and practicality were the measure of a genteel middle-class man, loafing of any kind was considered unacceptable.[32] YMCA leaders, dependent on the approval of clergy, acknowledged the prevalence of this misapprehension:

> Many excellent people get the idea that the Association is only a place in which a few young men, too lazy to work for a living, get together and dawdle away time and flatter their vanity by electing each other to office, keeping conscience quiet that they are about the Master's business.[33]

Answering these concerns, Y leaders emphasized that they did not attempt to replace the church, but instead to prod it into adapting to the needs of young men:

> The example of the Association has its legitimate effect, when it stimulates the Churches to the putting on of a more inviting aspect to the stranger. They will undoubtedly respond and lose much of the repellancy which has made it so easy and almost necessary for the young man to wander into the dram shop, the theatre, or the gambling hell. . . . [A] Young Men's Association may become part of the machinery of each Church.[34]

Another justification was the Y's stated mission to attract young men otherwise not involved in religious life and to direct them to the churches. In a YMCA, one apologist noted "the entire absence of any provision for family or household. If the germ of a Church is here, it must be an impossible church of one sex." The YMCA maintained a strong position that it was a foot soldier of the church, guiding its members to a full Christian life.[35]

Despite these reassurances, some persisted in fearing that the YMCA would weaken the church, and with some justification. The claims that the Y was only meant to stimulate the churches and to direct young men to church membership seem disingenuous in light of its building agenda. Fund-raising literature focused on the need for a specialized YMCA building, not an impermanent set of rented rooms in a building block. The Reverend Darling compared the YMCA to other social institutions:

> Every other work, which is carried on, whether religious or secular, has found the need of adjusting its material appliances to its wants. . . . The schoolhouse will not meet the need of the asylum, of the public library, the church building of the Sabbath School classes. For the highest efficiency, the soul of the institution, be it secular or religious, must develop about itself a body fitted for its use.[36]

This claim for a specialized building challenged the architectural landscape of the small town, where new building types like the department store, the library, and the museum had not yet appeared.[37] At a time when hopeful boosters plotted and planned metropolises along the Union Pacific, the construction of a permanent business building, let alone a YMCA building, was a sign of major commitment. Given the largely undifferentiated nature of downtown buildings and the strong dichotomy between commercial and religious or civic buildings, the idea of a specialized structure to cater to the religious and leisure needs of young men was unusual and, perhaps, a bit unsettling, even risqué.

Local communities differed in their interpretation of the central directives on typology and siting as they sought to figure out exactly how the YMCA should fit into the social and architectural fabric of the town.[38] While not recommended in the official YMCA literature, a hybrid building, aligning the Y with the civic or public interests of the town, was certainly both a powerful symbolic gesture and also a practical solution to the difficulties of fund-raising in smaller places. In the case of Wichita Falls, Texas, this problem was solved by literally fusing the Y with the First Methodist Episcopal Church, with separate entrances and a shared, domed auditorium (Figure 3.9).

In Cooperstown, New York, the YMCA was combined with a public library, and in Knoxville, Tennessee, with a firehouse. The most extreme example, where the YMCA was physically combined with the City Hall, Fire Department, and Police Department, was the North Tonawanda, New York, YMCA, constructed in 1892. These combinations of civic and religious functions were an adjustment for some locals. A postcard of the Tonawanda building, sent from Edith Sussman to her daughter, Katherine, aligns the commercial-style building to religion by pointing out that it is "right across the street from the church" (Figure 3.10). This desire to associate the YMCA with the religious forces in the landscape signals some of the tensions these decisions embodied in more conservative communities.[39] Many YMCAs were located in close proximity to churches and were frequently depicted that way in postcards.

FIGURE 3.9. The Wichita Falls YMCA and the First Methodist Episcopal Church, Wichita Falls, Texas.

To many communities the New York vision of the YMCA building *did* present a new kind of faith, a practical Christianity that divorced Protestant virtues like self-discipline from their spiritual context. Not until the late 1880s, when money was flush and new building types appeared in America's urban landscape, would a specialized, distinctive YMCA building arrive on the scene in most cities and towns.[40]

FIGURE 3.10. City Hall and the YMCA, Main and Tremont streets, North Tonawanda, New York.

The Reception and Local Meaning of the YMCA in the New South

From its perch in New York, the Y Central Committee (later the International Committee) did its best to put forth a national vision of the YMCA that would supersede old local and regional differences. Nowhere would this vision be tested more strenuously than in the South, where resistance to Yankee culture and encroachment was entrenched. The issue of abolition had so severely divided the New York YMCA that dozens of members had resigned and the national organization disbanded. The newly formed Central Committee worked hard to bring the men of the New South into its fold. Reconstruction of the Union was an integral part of their political and economic vision of national manhood. For white Southerners, the new, modern YMCA, equipped with a building and situated in the heart of their newly segregated cities and towns, signified both progress toward the future as well as allegiance to the values of the past. During periods of economic boom, first in the 1880s and then again in the first decade of the twentieth century, the elites of the New South embraced the YMCA, building clubhouses that linked their cities to the North and West, effacing regional boundaries in favor of a common vision of modernity.

In the years immediately following the Civil War, the national leadership of the YMCA identified the South as a field for expansion and devoted resources to send traveling secretaries on sales tours. As he had in the West, Robert Weidensall, along with Thomas K. Cree and other Y officials, took extensive trips through the South in the early 1870s to organize new associations. His 1872 fact-finding twenty-city tour of the South revealed that only three or four associations existed.

Despite this discouraging news, the reports that Weidensall and his colleagues sent to New York suggest that these representatives of the New York YMCA were met with enthusiasm everywhere they went. They drafted new leaders, often migrants from the rural South or transplants from the North, and made them welcome at the national conventions. Through the YMCA's dedication to the welfare of young men, at least to white young men, the organization's leaders hoped to weave the South back into the fabric of the Union. In Richmond, Virginia, and Atlanta, Georgia, clubhouses built in the 1880s linked the southern landscape back to the North, with designs that literally connected the places together in a common vision of an efficient, urban future.

Nowhere was this reconciliation more marked than in the former Confederate capital. Despite its partisan past, in 1886 Richmond became one of the first southern cities to build a modern YMCA building. Intensely industrialized since the war, with six railroads, more than fifty tobacco factories, and numerous iron and steel mills, Richmond argued for its continued importance as a capital, this time of the New South. Its new YMCA building, sited in close proximity to the state capitol, emphasized and underscored the organization's embrace of Yankee culture. The building's architectural connection to the Northeast was marked. Instead of hiring a local architect, the local Association chose Cope and Stewardson, a Philadelphia firm, to design the building, probably at the suggestion of Addison Hutton, designer of the Philadelphia YMCA. They would go on to design college campus buildings at Princeton, Bryn Mawr, and the University of Pennsylvania in the collegiate gothic style. For this, their first big commission, however, they employed a Romanesque Revival style popularized by Bostonian Henry Hobson Richardson. With its corner tower, gabled profiles, rusticated stone, and continuous band of round arches, the Richmond YMCA, in the heart of the South, would have been quite at home in New England (Figure 3.11).

FIGURE 3.11. The Richmond YMCA, Seventh and Grace streets, Richmond, Virginia, by Cope and Stewardson, 1886.

Contending with Richmond as the capital of the New South was Atlanta, which was completely rebuilt after the Civil War. The city was shaped by the railroads and northern concepts of modern urban culture, including the YMCA.[41] Atlanta was viewed by many as the most "northern" southern city of the period, with a can-do attitude similar to that of Chicago. The editor of the *Atlanta Constitution*, Henry Grady, had coined the term "New South" in a speech in New York. In contrast with the old, antebellum, agrarian South based on slave labor, the New South was a vision of a forward-looking, industrialized region in sync with the business culture of the North. Its booster elite was not of local origin, but instead was composed of both northern migrants as well as young men from elsewhere in the South. Hoping to project a progressive, modern profile to the world and attract capital from northern financiers, they organized the International Cotton Exposition in Oglethorpe Park in 1881. Its centerpiece was a model cotton factory. In the years immediately after the Exposition a massive building boom changed the landscape of Atlanta. New additions included the construction of an impressive new state capitol, the new Girls' High School, the Georgia School of Technology (now the Georgia Institute of Technology), the Traders' Bank Building, and the YMCA.[42]

Atlanta first organized a YMCA in 1858 in rented rooms, but the organization disappeared during the Civil War. It was reorganized in 1873 at the height of Reconstruction, and a building followed in 1888. Supported by Grady and the *Atlanta Constitution*, building fervor was whipped up by the presence of an International YMCA Convention, and the community raised $75,000. Very much on the model of the New York YMCA building, the Atlanta YMCA building had stores on the first floor to provide income. Its facilities and program were up-to-date. Its gymnasium, "equal to the best in the country," was directed by a superintendent educated at the new YMCA Training School in Springfield, Massachusetts. Its shower and spray rooms, only recently introduced in YMCA buildings, were lined with marble, and young men could rent lockers to store their clothes (Figure 3.12). A parlor, reading room, lecture room, and concert hall were all intended to be "attractions" to young men.

Growing prosperity in the 1880s made the dream of a building a possibility for many of the Southern YMCAs, and by the end of that decade every large southern city had one, including Nashville; Wilmington, North Carolina; New Orleans; Mobile; Charleston, South Carolina; and Savannah. The Y's appeal extended beyond the New South businessmen who paid for the buildings. Despite its Yankee origins, the YMCA met the need of white Southerners, both men and women, to look ahead to the future without relinquishing their heritage and history. As the South's old agrarian economy grew increasingly urbanized, industrialized, and incorporated into a national system, urban Southerners looked to the YMCA as a guide to navigating the cultural dislocations that followed Emancipation.

FIGURE 3.12. The Atlanta YMCA, Pryor and Auburn streets, Atlanta, Georgia, by Willoughby J. Edbrooke and Franklin P. Burnham, 1887.

The YMCA and Segregation

As their northern counterparts had found, Southerners needed an institution to help them negotiate a new kind of white manhood for a corporate world. Although the rhetoric of the self-made man was certainly present in the South, popular imaginings of manhood did not follow the same trajectory that they did in the North. The embrace of the YMCA in southern cities was not only a symbol of reconciliation, reunification, and modernization in the cities of the New South, but also an affirmation of the old chivalric standards of southern manhood. Masculine identity there tied very much into memories of the war. Instead of the Christian gentlemen of Rossiter's *Merchants of New York* or the country boy of Hovenden's *Breaking Home Ties,* modern moral manhood in the South was based on the honorable self-sacrifice of the Confederate soldier. An icon of the South, created largely by southern white women, the soldier was represented in countless statues, monuments, and memorials. These statues, often located in the town square, helped to define collective memory of the past and its particular character and values in an age of "callous and calculating industrial expansion."[43]

In fact, southern YMCA buildings were often sited in relationship to, or represented in juxtaposition with, memorials to fallen soldiers. In Jacksonville, Florida, Savannah, Georgia, and several other southern cities, YMCAs were built as part of civic ensembles, alongside a park that contained recently constructed memorials of soldiers, generals, and other war heroes. In Savannah, the YMCA building was located on Madison Square, home to an 1888 statue of Revolutionary War hero Sergeant William Jasper as well as cannon from the Savannah Armory (Figure 3.13). This site, selected in 1905, suited the unifying role of the YMCA perfectly, honoring the soldier as a self-sacrificing symbol of chivalry but sidestepping the contested history of the Civil War in favor of a common struggle against the British.

This choice of the Revolutionary War hero as icon in Savannah also avoided the difficult legacy of Emancipation faced by the Y. Racial equality posed a challenge to antebellum concepts of manhood in the North and the South. Black men were not welcome in the YMCA, which had always maintained Jim Crow in its rooms. This segregation was not limited to race, but also to class and nationality. Since the 1860s, YMCAs in the North had established independent branches for Germans and Chinese, and later extended their specialized work to Scandinavians, French-Canadians, and American Indians. Beginning in the 1880s the International Committee began to promote the provision of separate but unequal facilities for working-class men, for Negroes, for women, and for railroad workers, uniting individual groups under the same national, Christian rhetoric. The central, downtown YMCA building, ostensibly *the* YMCA building, was intended for white, white-collar, Protestant men.

YMCA leaders, with their strong Republican sympathies and Christian piety, did admit to some discomfort with this arrangement, but argued that

FIGURE 3.13. The William Jasper Monument and the YMCA, Bull Street, Savannah, Georgia.

the Jim Crow approach was necessary to compete successfully for the souls of young white men. Responding to an outcry against the rejection of an "estimable young colored man" into membership, the chairman of the Board of Managers of the Cleveland YMCA claimed that "No one regrets the necessity . . . more than we do, but no other course was open to us. . . . [T]here is a strong prejudice against colored men among those we are particularly anxious to reach, and we cannot ignore it."[44]

Such accommodationist philosophy guided the YMCA throughout the nineteenth and early twentieth centuries, when "colored" YMCAs (to use the parlance of the time) were accepted within the national framework and conventions of the organization, but only within carefully defined spaces. Because each group was responsible for raising its own funds, rooms for blacks were fewer in number and considerably less elaborate than those of their white brethren. In most cases, a colored YMCA building required white sponsorship. In the nineteenth century black YMCAs owned buildings in Norfolk and Richmond, but nowhere else in the South. In response, perhaps, to *Plessy vs. Ferguson,* the landmark 1896 Supreme Court case upholding "separate but equal" segregation, the YMCA began to address the building needs of the black community. With the help of white philanthropists, including George Foster Peabody, John D. Rockefeller Jr., and, most notably, Julius Rosenwald, African-American communities were able to raise enough funds to build their own facilities in the first two decades of the twentieth century. Although these YMCAs were rarely as elaborate as those erected for white men, they included all the standard athletic facilities and clean, respectable dorm rooms, a desperately needed resource for black young men.[45]

The segregated space of the YMCA building was appealing to the new business elite, who, as members of a growing white middle class, sought a means of constructing a usable definition of whiteness in the late nineteenth century. Their authority, once lodged in "the personalized social relations of specific localities," no longer functioned effectively in the emerging national mass culture. Power and identity, once fixed, was now a volatile thing. Throughout the late nineteenth century, local southern elites depended on the official boundaries of segregation to delineate difference and power.[46]

YMCA buildings were part of the shaping of a symbolic, segregated, white Protestant public sphere in southern (and sometimes northern) cities. The Y occupied and helped to define streetscapes that were later, in the 1890s, the site of lynchings and, in the 1960s, the site of lunch-counter sit-ins by civil rights protesters. The YMCA's spatial separation of groups linked regional racial views to national conceptions of progress and modernity.

The YMCA and the City Beautiful

After a hiatus in building construction during the financial depression of the 1890s, the YMCA (like many other public and semipublic organizations) enjoyed another building boom in the South between 1905 and 1915. The organization was the beneficiary of the fever for city planning and grandiose architecture that swept the nation in response to the world's fairs in Chicago and St. Louis. Architects, planners, and boosters throughout the country sought to improve their towns and cities. New buildings, roads, and street architecture operated as symbols of progress in a nationally recognizable architectural language that communicated a city's place in the linked system of urban centers extending beyond its immediate region. Noting a convergence of this trend with their traditional appeals to the local ethos of boosterism, YMCA leaders updated their architecture and their persuasive rhetoric.

At their conventions, in lectures and literature, the YMCA now portrayed their buildings not only as good investments, but also as necessary elements of civic responsibility, a fusion of the civic and public interests of the town with commerce and religion.[47] Progress and membership in the national corporate system required a YMCA building, and the rhetoric appealed to new elites' desire to fit in and operate beyond the boundaries of their city. A series of fund-raising pamphlets from just before World War I chronicled the emerging civic role to be played by buildings in the age of the City Beautiful. With titles like "For a Great and Better City" (Great Falls, Montana), "A Civic Movement to Meet a Civic Need" (Rochester, New York, and New London, Connecticut), and "The Test of a City's Greatness" (Pittsburgh, Pennsylvania), these pamphlets assured loyal citizens that "what Louisville (or Billings, South Bend, or Cincinnati) can do, so can we!" Prominently pictured in each pamphlet were the recently completed buildings of similarly sized cities with the amount of money raised to erect each structure cited.[48] The Association in Minneapolis made its intended role as one of the building blocks of the community very clear with promotional literature that visually compared its building with the new public library, city auditorium, and a church. This conception of the YMCA as part of the "constructive forces" of the city was emphasized by the publishers of *Association Men,* who in 1908 suggestively printed a photograph of an unidentified YMCA building alongside a church and a school.[49]

Between 1900 and 1915 the number of southern YMCAs almost doubled, bringing the organization strongly into Florida, Texas, and emerging centers like Birmingham, Alabama, and Greensboro, North Carolina (Figure 3.14). These new YMCAs, part of a nationwide boom, were designed according to standards developed by the national organization. They definitively anchored the region, not just a few cities, to the rest of the country.

Greensboro is typical of this expansion of the YMCA in the first decade of the twentieth century. Known as the "Gate City," Greensboro, the seat of Guilford County, is located in the heart of the Piedmont region of North Carolina. Beginning in the 1880s the city's economic base extended beyond its immediate boundaries and attracted outsiders like Moses Cone, who established a branch of his Baltimore textile company in a purpose-built

FIGURE 3.14. Young Men's Christian Association, corner of Sycamore and Green streets, Greensboro, North Carolina, by Shattuck and Hussey, 1908.

factory town that housed hundreds of operatives. A sleepy country town with only three thousand residents in 1890, Greensboro had ten times that number by 1900. At the turn of the century it became a major stop and transfer center on YMCA man J. P. Morgan's newly consolidated Southern Railway, linking its antebellum railroad lines to a large network.

In the first decade of the twentieth century, the city moved decisively from its local, regional roots onto the national stage as it grew astoundingly in population and economic diversification. Greensboro was a regional educational magnet, home to North Carolina Agricultural and Technical University, Greensboro Female College, and Guilford College. Within the next fifteen years it would become a leader in the southern insurance industry, and home to several large national companies, including the manufacturer of Vick's VapoRub.

The new Greensboro elite, active in civic reform and wealthy through large-scale manufacturing, finance, and insurance, embraced symbols of modern urban progress. To them, a YMCA was an important and necessary element of city form, especially in the age of the City Beautiful. This civic vision of the YMCA appealed to a local booster in Greensboro, publisher Joseph Stone. He understood how the Y could fit into the changing social, economic, and cultural landscape of this putative metropolis.[50] His goal was not only the revitalization of the Y, but also the assertion of the urban aspirations of this growing city on a regional, even national, scale. These aspirations were shared, he knew, by the city's new and wealthy leaders. In 1908 he judged, rather accurately, that it was at last time for the YMCA to take on an important public, architectural role in the community.

This was not the first effort for a YMCA building in Greensboro. Local Y leaders sought permanent quarters in 1891, when they moved out of their rented rooms into the old Planter's Hotel, using the proceeds of a successful tent revival they had sponsored. The program, focused on Bible study and other religious activities, reflected the traditional mores of established residents rather than the pragmatic fourfold plan promoted by the New Yorkers and, by now, accepted by the Chicagoans. The depression of 1893 struck the Greensboro YMCA hard, and it was unable to sustain payments on its building. The members were forced to return to rented rooms and by 1900, greatly reduced in numbers, they disbanded.

Within ten years the YMCA was housed in its new modern building, reflective of the specific mission to young men and a symbol of the city's modernity and progress. Stone proposed a building campaign in 1909, when he judged that the city's cultural aspirations and desire to outshine its regional competitors had reached its peak. Greensboro had just celebrated its centennial the previous year with much civic pomp, marking the event with a parade some feared the city could not afford.[51] Main Street was embellished not only with the usual banners, but also with a City Beautiful–inspired decorative scheme complete with a triumphal arch and a colonnade that rhythmically marked the cleanly paved and well-lit route. These columns echoed the regular, if less beautiful, presence of telephone poles and streetcar lines, two recent and more permanent signs of the city's modernity and progress.

But more needed to be done. Although there were beautiful churches and fine residences, the urban core needed updating. In 1908 Main Street was still dominated by three-story building blocks constructed in the 1880s (Figure 3.15). The landscape of the commercial district—defined by the 1872 county courthouse, the old Opera House, post office, and railway depot—was undergoing development, signaled by the arrival of the six-story Dixie Fire Insurance Company in 1904 and a new Carnegie Library and an Elks Lodge in 1907.[52] A YMCA would be an equally useful and necessary addition to the city's architectural balance sheet, if only to maintain parity with regional rivals Raleigh, Columbia, Greenville, and Sumter, all in the process of funding or building YMCAs.

In Greensboro the site of the YMCA was carefully chosen to emulate this alignment of the YMCA with public interest. After much consideration, the Building Committee purchased the old home of Mrs. Madison Smith on Sycamore and Green, one block from the main commercial thoroughfare, Elm Street (Figure 3.16). Densely packed with commercial buildings, Elm was the site of entertainment and shopping in Greensboro. The city's hotels lined the street, as did drug stores, cafes, newsstands, and its first movie

FIGURE 3.15. Elm Street, Greensboro, North Carolina, 1908.

theater. Some questioned the remoteness of the chosen site, but Jones had been advised by the North Carolina State Committee and the International Committee to position the Y as a civic rather than a commercial institution.

Siting and representing the Y together with fraternal buildings, the public library, and government buildings—as well as parks and monuments—was a common strategy that presented the inhabitants with a genteel, often gender-segregated but decisively middle-class, Protestant, and white definition of public culture. These civic building groups combining masculinity and public life were constructed in Eau Claire, Wisconsin; Danville, Illinois; Augusta, Maine; Hartford, Connecticut; Grand Junction, Colorado; and Muscatine, Iowa (see Plate 10). These miniature City Beautiful settings included the YMCA in the civic landscape, infusing the civic ideal with religious values and, in some locations, racial identity.

In its new position the Greensboro Y was part of a roughly rectangular grouping of public buildings on the north and south sides of Market Street. At the center of the composition was the Guilford County Courthouse, surrounded by a wide green lawn on all four sides. Across the street and to the north stood the Methodist Episcopal Church and the new Carnegie Library. South of the courthouse to the west was the Episcopal Church. On the east end of the block sat the YMCA building. The position of the building, up

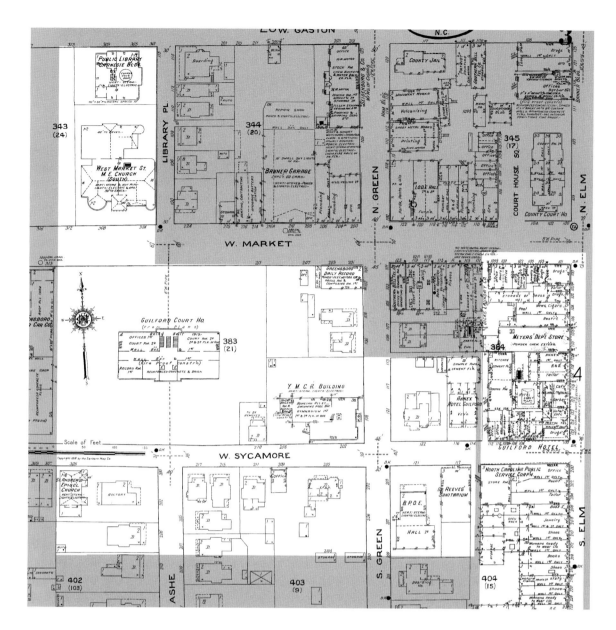

against the street rather than centered in the lot, suggests a vestigial connection to the commercial architecture of Elm Street. Diagonally across the street from the Y was the Elks' new clubhouse. On the north corner stood the *Greensboro Daily Record*'s building. Although it was clearly not planned as an ensemble, this grouping of buildings outlined a civic landscape like those elsewhere in the country, one that aligned religion, middle-class identity, and public life together spatially.

The YMCA building itself also followed national trends closely. Designed by YMCA specialist architects Shattuck and Hussey, and costing $65,000, this building seems commonplace. Three stories tall, on a corner site with separate entrances for boys and men, this minimally detailed brick box was barely distinguishable from the dozens of Y buildings also designed by Shattuck and Hussey (see Plate 1 and Figure 3.14). Although not particularly adventurous architecturally, in Greensboro it was an architectural phenomenon, a major landmark and a most modern building, equipped with

FIGURE 3.16. Sanborn Fire Insurance Map, Greensboro, North Carolina, 1918. By 1918, ten years after the construction of the Greensboro YMCA building, the public landscape of the "Gate City" had consolidated around the commercial zone of Elm Street and the nearby but distinct civic landscape of courthouse, YMCA, library, Elks' Lodge, and churches.

electricity, a heated pool, and stylish furnishings. Its program included bowling alleys, a billiard room, and a gymnasium.[53] Its appearance was intended not to highlight local identity but rather to express conformity to a common ideal and national system. Its similarity, its standardization, was a virtue to Greensboro. With this building, and dozens of others like it, the YMCA participated in a nationwide process of urban development, working with other public and semipublic institutions to define a standardized, respectable, Protestant, white public sphere at the center of the American city.

Postcards: Shaping the Image of the YMCA

The stupendous geographic scope and success of the national vision of the YMCA can be understood through mapping, which displays the increasing presence of Y buildings in the United States from 1870 until the beginning of World War I (see Figure I.2). A more potent and graphic way to understand the success and reception of the YMCA on the local, regional, and national level is through another medium: the postcard. As Alison Isenberg has shown, postcards were an easily manipulated means of representation used by local boosters to express the ideal image of their city.[54] The YMCA postcard operates in a similar fashion, providing everyday people the opportunity to "fix" the image of themselves, their communities, and the YMCA through the production, consumption, and systematic distribution of postcards across region and nation. Representations of Y buildings on postcards not only advertised the organization on a massive scale, but also allowed millions of people the opportunity to comment on and make meaning of its architecture. Postcards constitute an omnipresent, democratic, and highly portable source of architectural representation, for the publisher (who made the decision of how to frame the building in the image), for the sender (who reinterpreted and represented the building to the recipient by selecting the card addressing it, writing a message, affixing the stamp, and posting it), and for the recipient (who in this period frequently chose to collect the cards on the mantel, the vanity, or in an album that resided on the parlor table).[55] This visual and brief form of postal communication shaped popular conceptions of the YMCA and promoted the organization in a highly personal way.

Although it had appeared in the American mail system earlier than 1893, the postcard was, like so many mass-produced products, first popularized in the United States at the Chicago World's Fair. Official cards depicting the buildings of the White City were sold and sent from the grounds in great numbers. This represented a revolution in visual communication. What distinguished the postcard from the other kinds of imagery available at the fair was its systematic and dynamic mobility, and its democracy: its ability to be transported cheaply and quickly across the country. Once selected, written upon, and stamped, these images traveled along a rapidly growing national railway network of postal communication linking distant parts of the nation

PLATE 1. A selection of YMCA buildings by specialists Shattuck and Hussey, 1904–1916.

PLATE 2. Exploded axonometric rendering of the New York YMCA building. The building designed by James Renwick, Robert McBurney, and William E. Dodge Jr. fused a variety of commercial public and private YMCA functions in a tightly composed series of volumes within a rectangular site.

PLATE 3 (*top*). Eastman Johnson, *The Hatch Family*, 1870–71.
PLATE 4 (*bottom*). Thomas Cole, *The Cross and the World: Study for "Two Youths Enter upon a Pilgrimage, One to the Cross and the Other to the World,"* 1848.

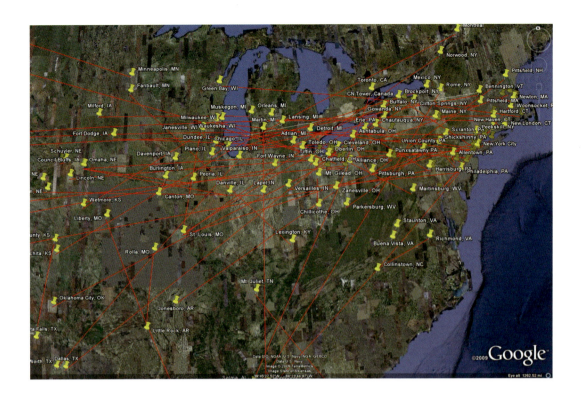

PLATE 5 (*above*). Postcard Exchange Map. Mapping the points of origin and destination of postcards from the Cliff Smith YMCA Postcard Collection shows a widespread pattern of circulation throughout the Eastern and Midwestern United States. Images of the YMCA traveled small distances, within regions, or across the country; from large city to small town, from north to south, and east to west.

PLATE 6 (*left*). "The Big Y": the Brooklyn Central Branch YMCA, Hanson Place, by Trowbridge and Ackerman, 1913.

PLATE 7 (*top*). Billiards room at the Brooklyn Central Branch YMCA, ca. 1914.

PLATE 8 (*bottom*). Hot cabinet baths, Brooklyn Central Branch YMCA, ca. 1915.

PLATE 9. The Chicago YMCA building, LaSalle Street and Arcade Court, by Jenney and Mundie, 1894.

PLATE 10. "Civic Group. Post Office, Masonic Temple, and Y.M.C.A.," Fifth and Rood streets, Grand Junction, Colorado, ca. 1915.

PLATE 11. "His Home over There," propaganda poster designed by Albert Herter for the United War Work Campaign, 1918. During World War I the American YMCA was active in the construction and operation of several thousand standardized YMCA huts for servicemen at home and abroad in cities, camps, and on the front lines. Fund-raising posters garnered support for the immediate needs of soldiers, but also paved the way for a postwar YMCA building boom.

to one another with systematic regularity and relative ease. Universal postal service based on a fixed national grid of numbered addresses began in 1863 in large American cities. The growing railways, especially the transcontinental ones, helped to speed delivery to rail-stop towns in the expanding West. The introduction of rural free delivery routes in 1902 meant that even remote places could be linked to local towns, to small cities, and beyond the state and region, transforming and liberating communication across the entire country.

This type of "unwrapped" missive, combining a mass-produced image with a strangely "public" private message, appealed to a cross-section of the American population as an inexpensive and accessible way to keep in touch quickly in an age before general use of the telephone. Although tourists, then as now, used postcards to display their status and memorialize their travels, postcards were an innovation that was used by everyone from courting couples to traveling salesmen as a quick and easy form of communication. More than 770 million postcards were purchased just in the year 1906. There is an estimate of more than one billion cards purchased in the United States in 1916.[56] Many of them were purchased by collectors, who, in addition to arranging them in scrapbooks, often sent local cards to large networks of pen pals.[57]

To feed the frenzy for cards, hotels, pharmacies, five-and-ten-cent stores, and the YMCA itself sold postcards. The postcard craze even spurred the establishment of specialized postcard shops in most American cities. These shops stocked cards from large enterprises like the Detroit Publishing Co. and Rotograph, which published series of urban views for every city. Such "portraits" of buildings or city streets were hardly new to most Americans, who had been consuming relatively affordable mass-produced images of cities in the form of daguerreotypes, stereographs, and chromolithographs for decades.[58] Thanks to improved European printing technologies, postcards were cheaper than most other kinds of views and of high quality, and, most important, they could be sent easily.

Published by the YMCA, local boosters, and news agencies, as well as by large national companies, individual cards, or, more often, series of local views, documented the appearance of the institutions, streets, parks, homes, and events in American cities and towns with an exhaustive completeness.[59] One publisher in Birmingham, Alabama, William H. Faulkner, produced and stocked more than 120 views of that city, as well as a wide selection from other locations around the world at the Postcard Exchange (1907–17) (Figure 3.17).[60] Displayed in wall racks and cases, and by 1908 on spinning circular racks, the postcards presented a visual categorization of the nation's built environment, placed side by side for the comparison of the customer, encouraging acquisition, classification, and comparison.

In the early twentieth century the modern YMCA building was almost always a part of any collection of urban views. Those who chose to send

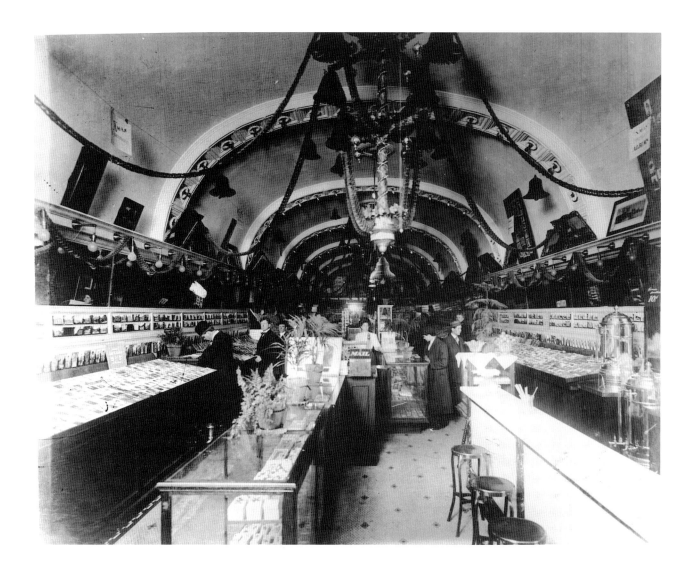

FIGURE 3.17. The Postcard Exchange, Birmingham, Alabama, ca. 1913.

them did so for a variety of reasons not always clear from the brief text on the verso, but common themes emerge in the more than five thousand cards collected by Cliff Smith, a YMCA employee. The pride of local boosters in their YMCA, and the identification of a community with its YMCA building, comes through clearly in postcards exchanged by pen pals. Postcard clubs linked collectors from around the country. A common practice was to introduce oneself with a view from one's hometown, and evidence suggests that the YMCA, often a new building, was one of the subjects used to identify and embody the town to outsiders. In her initial contact with fellow club member Mrs. Cora Lancaster of Wetmore, Kansas, Mrs. William Rodenz, who lived on a rural route in a village outside of the town of Edgerton, Wisconsin, chose to send a card of the "New Y.M.C.A." in the nearby and larger city of Janesville, Wisconsin, describing it as her hometown. Rodenz chose the card no doubt because the Y was a source of great pride for Janesville, which had just replaced its nineteenth-century structure with a modern one. The card depicts the building with an electric streetlamp, modern cars parked out front, and battlement detail that linked the building to the

Lombardesque style that was popular for hotels and clubs and large urban YMCAs of the period (Figure 3.18).

Several cards in the Cliff Smith Collection of YMCA Postcards at Springfield College suggest that individuals, especially tourists and travelers, frequently made judgments about a place on the basis of its YMCA building, as in a card sent from Parkersburg, West Virginia, to Union County, Pennsylvania, in 1916.[61] The inscription "this is the YMCA *here*" (italics mine) implies

FIGURE 3.18. Janesville YMCA Building, 402–404 West Milwaukee Street, Janesville, Wisconsin.

familiarity with YMCA buildings elsewhere. This also seems to be the case for a correspondent in Charles City, Iowa, writing to Elizabeth Stokes in Bridgeton, Rhode Island, asking for her opinion of this "Y building," and a card written to Walter Rightneour of Pottstown, Pennsylvania, inquiring whether the one in nearby Lancaster was "as nice as the one at home." Writing back to friends in Gainesville, Florida, from Jonesboro, Arkansas, on a YMCA card, one woman compared the one there unfavorably to the one back home. Another, writing to a friend on a postcard of the Greenwich, Connecticut, YMCA building, noted that the building was considered to be the finest in the state. These cards helped link boosters to a national system of changing urban culture.

Other groups who commonly used YMCA cards were young migrants, traveling salesmen, and courting couples. For them the Y was not a link to the wider world, but a connection with the one they left behind. In some cases the choice of a YMCA card was a subtle, or sometimes not so subtle, symbolic gesture to assert adherence, to mask resistance, or perhaps even to satirize the traditional moral values and standards of their small-town or rural homes.

Despite their modernity, "manhood factories" were often seen as symbols of traditional Christian values of hard work, delayed gratification, and church attendance. In the Midwest and in smaller towns, as John Gustav-Wrathall has observed, YMCA buildings were generally associated with women, who were often instrumental in fund-raising and programming the Y. In fact, far more women than men sent YMCA postcards, choosing them when on vacation or to communicate regularly with their relatives or friends in other towns. YMCAs were, for many, a symbol of the feminine "home" sphere in the big city, a refuge from vice, corruption, greed, and all that made the city modern and masculine.

FIGURE 3.19. "Ignorance Is Bliss," unidentified cartoon, ca. 1870s.

Thus, when writing home to wife, mother, sister, or sweetheart, men frequently chose YMCA cards. They knew their women would be interested in the Y building, and the choice also signaled an allegiance to the home values symbolized by the building. As far back as the 1870s, the YMCA was perceived by women as a safe place for their men. This view was satirized in a period cartoon, depicting a bartender covering for a customer by telling his wife, "Seen your husband, goin' into the Young Men's Christian Association rooms about two minutes ago, marm" (Figure 3.19). In a like manner, YMCA postcards were frequently used by traveling salesmen as a means of stabilizing and legitimizing their sojourn away from home. Some used the postal service to chart their itineraries and communicate quickly with their wives. Along with providing practical information about comings and goings, writing and sending the card helped the drummer resolve the inherent conflict between the spheres in life on the road. As Timothy Spears has shown, traveling salesmen felt a need to internalize domestic morality through poetry, lyrics, and other kinds of objects, including Gideon Bibles and, it seems, postcards.⁶²

Young migrants from the countryside, the target population of the Y, used postcards in the same way. Some men seemed quite sincere in their affiliation with the YMCA, strongly identifying with the organization, its building, and its mission, even its rhetoric. One young man, writing home to a female friend or relative, chose an interior view of the reception room of the YMCA building in Adrian, Michigan (Figure 3.20). The YMCA's mission of modern, productive manhood is clearly communicated in the image. Young men are carefully posed at the reception desk, on the stairs, and sitting stiffly against a column on the circular bench. They display the refined body language and careful dress of respectability. The author of the card is eager to confirm his association with the image and all it conveyed: "This is where I have had so many good times. I wish you could see all the building."

Even when the Y was not specifically mentioned, the pairing of the card with the message seemed to indicate a reassuring tone. In a YMCA card from Hastings, Nebraska, a young man wrote, "This is a dandy town of about 15,000 and I have good work." Just sending a Y card with your signature could have potential meaning to a mother or sweetheart worrying at home about the moral state of her boy. Some young men, however, turned the image to communicate a less dutiful outlook. One young man in Bennington, Vermont, whose slightly cryptic and slightly cynical message, "Getting no better, fast," to George Sawyer of Dundee, Illinois, seems an implicit critique of the YMCA's goals of improving young men, a form of visual double

FIGURE 3.20. Lobby, Adrian YMCA, Adrian, Michigan.

entendre that twisted the meaning of the image on one side with the writing on the other.

YMCA postcards were also important symbols in the tortuous process of courtship at the turn of the century. Because of the postcard's brevity and transparency, parents and perhaps young people felt it was a "safe" method of communication. This kind of safety was enhanced by the choice of a YMCA card, which signified what appeared to be the proper sentiments for upright young lovers. In November 1910 a young woman named Marie chose a card of the Lansing, Michigan, YMCA to send to Howard Helmer, forty miles away in rural Ionia County. Jokingly, perhaps flirtatiously, she lets Howard know that she's "heard" that he is "stuck on moonlight evenings." Jealous, perhaps, of May, Florence, and Gertrude, whom she asks after, she assures Howard that she will "remember" him before she signs off. The card seems to be a reminder of her, and also, through the choice of the Y as the subject, of proper moral behavior for young men.

Thanks to collectors and travelers this medium was, arguably, a more effective, more comprehensive, and more universally recognized form of public relations and communication than any of the methods the Y itself used. Postcards negotiated shifts in scale, between the macro, national, standardized, YMCA building program and the region, the community, and the individual. As the diverse pairing of the points of origins and the addresses on these cards suggest, postcards linked young migrants to small towns and rural routes; traveling salesmen from their "territory" to their families at home; tourists, travelers, and collectors to friends across the state and across the country (see Plate 5). Mapping the addresses of the sender and recipient of YMCA cards suggests that modernity and national urban culture were not disseminated in a straight line from New York or Chicago to Davenport, Iowa, but instead were diffused through a complex web of correspondents that extended throughout the entire postal system, regionally from smaller cities like Parkersburg, West Virginia, to rural Union County, Pennsylvania, but also nationally, from Baltimore to Houston. Through these cards the YMCA's "Christian clubhouses" came to be understood as a standard part of the American Main Street, a key element of the commercial "center" of the city.

Conclusion

The New York YMCA's coordinated campaign to put a Christian clubhouse in every town across America was an early, creative attempt by men to construct a respectable evangelical public culture for the modern, corporate age. Appropriating methods of traveling salesmanship, advertising, and publicity from business and the emerging mass culture, YMCA secretaries and their supporters promoted a plan that would link young men and their communities to a national system of values through the process of building. In all phases, from fund-raising to construction to the use of the buildings, the YMCA project tied individuals to a specific place, but also to a common experience that crossed local and regional boundaries.

Acceptance of the New York idea required local interpretation and adaptation. Communities throughout the West and the South made their own meaning out of the YMCA building. In the South new elites wanted to put their communities on the national map and signal their participation in a national economy. Other Southerners found the YMCA a useful way to honor their Confederate dead or define their whiteness. As period postcards show, women often supported the Y as a symbol of old home values, an idea at odds with the New Yorkers' vision of the YMCA as a corporate male institution.

Despite these differences many Americans found the YMCA building to be a valuable addition to their urban landscape. By the first years of the twentieth century this male, religious, leisure institution had succeeded in its salesmanship, achieving a place for itself as a standard element in the public sphere of American cities. Joining the school, the library, and the government building, often in close proximity, the YMCA had become a symbol and benchmark of modern life.

4
BEDROOMS, BILLIARDS, AND BASKETBALL
Retooling the YMCA

At the turn of the century YMCA buildings, now an accepted element of the urban landscape, "grew up." Both literally and metaphorically the architecture of the Christian clubhouse developed into a sophisticated, complex, and often monumental structure. Long-established features, remnants of its mercantile evangelical origins, like the street-level stores, the parlor, and the revival hall, made way for dormitories, swimming pools, billiard rooms, lunch counters, and separate facilities for boys. These changes not only required an increase in height and square footage, but they also challenged the identity of the building itself. What had been designed as moral ballast and a beacon nestled within the commercial landscape and the market system became a free-standing civic institution and a purveyor of services to a larger public.

Changes in the building were catalyzed by the rise of a mass culture that challenged the YMCA's vision of a national, genteel, yet modern evangelical public sphere. Communicated through advertisements, movies, and high-circulation newspapers and magazines, mass culture was especially powerful in growing cities. There the streets were increasingly filled with enticements that offered socially and, in some ways, morally legitimate ways to enjoy oneself, through consumption and entertainment. The classless, secular, commercial ethos of mass culture trained Americans to give in to their desires for pleasurable experiences, deemphasizing thrift, self-denial, delayed gratification, and hard work.

The competition for young men's time was fiercer and much better organized than in the past. The Y was forced to respond if it was to remain relevant as an organization. As the editor of *Association Men* noted in 1910,

"If [the YMCA] is to gain the attention and hold the passing crowds of men to-day, it must make more of a social life. Just now it is the moving picture show that draws men by the thousands. This interest may be used to provide a real education as well as popular entertainment."[1] Although not intrinsically part of the commercial sphere, the Y learned much from the tactics of corporate America.

The organization chose to move beyond basic acceptance and accommodation of leisure to fully integrate and legitimize it in their programs and buildings. The result was an increasing secularization of the organization and transformation of the building in a way that would acknowledge mass culture, but still maintain the Protestant values that its leaders continued to see as necessary to the moral function of the corporate economy. By the turn of the century most YMCAs were also remodeling or completely removing their parlors and assembly halls, and introducing in their stead new facilities for boys' work, dormitories, lunch counters, swimming pools, and billiard rooms. In developing the new building for the age of mass culture, the Y drew upon and influenced contemporary building types such as libraries, schools, hotels, fraternity houses, student unions, and movie theaters.

Two buildings, constructed ten years apart, offered varying interpretations of the new, "modern" YMCA: the Chicago YMCA skyscraper in 1893–94 and the "Big Y," the Brooklyn Central YMCA in 1913 (see Figure 4.1 and Plate 6). These buildings, considered the best YMCA buildings in the nation at the time of their construction, provided two alternate models for local associations to emulate, two ways of interpreting the new public role of the organization. The Chicago skyscraper presented the YMCA as a fusion of commercial and public interests. The Brooklyn interpretation was much subtler, cloaking the YMCA's business-sponsored social institution in civic garb.

Chicago's Temple of Practical Christianity

At the time of its construction in 1893–94, the Chicago Association's new skyscraper building ousted New York's venerated 1869 building as "the crowning glory of the building movement of our associations."[2] Daring, original, and well equipped, the fourteen-story building served a dual function: forty thousand square feet of modern office space *and* clubhouse. Using the latest steel-frame construction, Chicago's new building was a reconception of the YMCA in the new physical terms of the changing city. Choosing a skyscraper for the new headquarters was an act of vision in what was still largely a city of five-story buildings. This decision was not only a bold aesthetic move, but a practical one. The YMCA viewed its building as a tool and was prepared to embrace new building technology in order to improve efficiency. The sheer height of the new headquarters would draw the attention of both the real-estate community and the passerby.

FIGURE 4.1. Chicago Central YMCA building, LaSalle Street and Arcade Court, Chicago, by Jenney and Mundie, designed 1894.

At a time when many local associations were moving their central headquarters out of the business district, to the edge of residential neighborhoods, the Chicago Y chose to remain downtown in the heart of the Loop. Moving around the corner from their old quarters on Madison, they purchased a long narrow lot on LaSalle and Arcade Court, close to the Board of Trade, the Rookery, and the Monadnock Building. Thus the new building was part of a landscape of innovative tall buildings shooting up from older five-story building blocks. The cost of this prominent site, almost a million dollars, required that the YMCA follow suit and build a skyscraper that would increase its rental property.[3]

The combination of cultural facility with office space was a familiar idea to Chicago's businessmen. Adler and Sullivan's Auditorium Building, completed five years earlier, had already established the idea of a multipurpose tall building. In addition to its theater, it also housed offices and a hotel. The Board of Managers was no doubt familiar with plans by the Masons, the Women's Christian Temperance Union, and the Odd Fellows to construct new skyscrapers in the Loop.[4] The idea appealed to boosters of the World's Fair City, who were proud to show the world that "Chicago's wealth in brick and mortar is not solely devoted to the purposes of sordid gain."[5]

After some calculation, the board decided upon a fourteen-story "skyscraper." Real-estate experts had advised them that this would provide both the necessary space and prestige for the YMCA's purposes and enough square footage to offset their costs and secure an income for the organization. To design this structure they chose William Le Baron Jenney, architect of the famous steel-framed Home Insurance Building (1883–85) and numerous office blocks. In a letter to the committee he outlined his qualifications: "I am very familiar with buildings of this class, having built the Home Insurance, the Manhattan, the Fair, [and] the Leiter."[6] This choice clearly indicated that the board saw this building, above all, as a modern skyscraper.

Jenney and his partner William Mundie's design for the YMCA building called for a distinctive and currently fashionable roofline: a Romanesque tower, or campanile, as they called it (see Plate 9). This formula had been a popular choice in civic, institutional, and religious buildings throughout the East and Midwest during the 1880s, primarily owing to the influence of Henry Hobson Richardson. The Romanesque tower made the building easily recognizable and different from the surrounding flat-topped buildings, many erected in the 1870s and 1880s before the advent of the steel skyscraper. In its immediate vicinity, only Burnham and Root's Women's Temple, with its sinuous shape and irregular roofline, rivaled the YMCA building's distinctive character. The deliberateness of this architectural gesture is clear when the rear of the building, less noticeable to the public, is viewed. It is a plainer, functional flat-topped office building, for which the tower section serves as a false façade, establishing the building's identity. The tower, or campanile, as Jenney called it, clearly and somewhat uncomfortably communicated the building's dual role: speculative office tower and semipublic institutional headquarters.[7]

The building contained every modern amenity for its office tenants, including elevators, abundant light, and a beautiful mosaic-floored lobby. It also represented the most up-to-date offerings for Y members. Before designing the building Jenney traveled east with Wilbur Messer, the general secretary of the Chicago Y, to Boston, Cambridge, Providence, New Haven, Albany, Detroit, Cleveland, and Rochester. There they inspected the latest, most "modern" Y buildings to ascertain what features should be included, how they should be arranged, and what materials were to be used.

One major observation from their eastern tour was the shrinking role of the revival hall. Whether in a large city or small town, the early YMCA building of the 1870s was first and foremost a place of assembly. The original YMCA building in Chicago, named Farwell Hall after its primary donor, emphasized the central importance of that particular space in the building's architectural identity and in the function of the Association. Intended to provide a permanent meeting place for young men, it was also rentable for public revival meetings and other large gatherings, including public lectures offered by the lyceum circuit. The hall was, until the turn of the century, the site of middle-class public entertainment, framed by the respectability of the YMCA.

By the turn of the century the underused hall had become a liability. As YMCA programs shifted away from large-scale religious meetings, revival halls were used only for the occasional lecture or large celebration. In 1900 new forms of quasi-respectable leisure activities were taking shape in the American city. Nickelodeons, vaudeville theaters, and movies were increasingly available alternative attractions and new sources of large meeting spaces. Some Y secretaries tried to update the organization's programming to use the old hall space more efficiently. In 1913 Halsey Hammond of Minneapolis met one of the biggest new competitors, the movies, head-on by scheduling a series of motion pictures in the YMCA Hall.[8] Other YMCAs encumbered with little-used revival halls transformed them into new kinds of spaces. Holyoke, Massachusetts, carved out a suite of rooms for boys' programs from their old hall; in Providence the hall became a series of classrooms; and Fall River, Massachusetts, converted theirs into dormitories.[9]

Without a doubt the most popular adaptation of the revival hall was into a space for athletics. Despite initial skepticism in some evangelical circles, sports were now generally accepted and even encouraged as part of a larger Protestant nativist movement known as "muscular Christianity." Rebelling against the Victorian image of religion as feminine and genteel, this movement's proponents believed that the modern division of labor had sapped the strength and virility of white-collar men, who were badly needed to maintain and even enlarge the role of evangelical Christianity in an age of immigration. Through sermons, art, and publications, ministers and laymen like

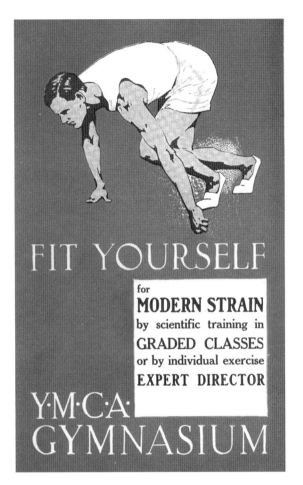

FIGURE 4.2. "Fit Yourself for Modern Strain." YMCA advertisement in *Physical Training*, 1909.

Theodore Roosevelt replaced the traditional image of Jesus as gentle and mild with a more martial image, "a virile hero who might be described as having fought it out on the football field of life."[10] With this sanction the Association repositioned the role of gymnasiums in YMCA work. No longer simply a lure to attract young men, gyms, supervised by increasingly professionally trained directors, became intrinsic elements of the YMCA's character-building program (Figure 4.2). Because uplift was now built into sports, Y officials began to offer special athletic memberships, which attracted hundreds, if not thousands, of men who simply wanted to swim and use the gym.

Springfield, Massachusetts, Bangor, Maine, and Charleston, South Carolina, transformed their halls into gymnasiums, providing a space that would be efficiently used twelve hours a day, six days a week. Throughout the 1880s communities from Louisville to Erie, to New Britain, Connecticut, added a separate, often freestanding gymnasium to their original building (Figure 4.3). The shift from hall to gymnasium was especially marked in the Chicago skyscraper building. A bastion of revival work under Dwight Moody, the Chicago Y underwent a major shift in the 1890s. A new leadership group—including Cyrus McCormick Jr., son of the inventor of the reaper; John Farwell Jr., heir to his father's dry-goods fortune; and banker James L. Houghteling—implemented the fourfold work advocated by the New York Association in the plans for its new building. Accordingly the "hall" was reduced in size from 4,500 to 1,400 seats and renamed the "auditorium," a distinctly more secular term.

FIGURE 4.3. The Louisville YMCA and gymnasium addition, 431 West Walnut Street, Louisville, Kentucky, 1887.

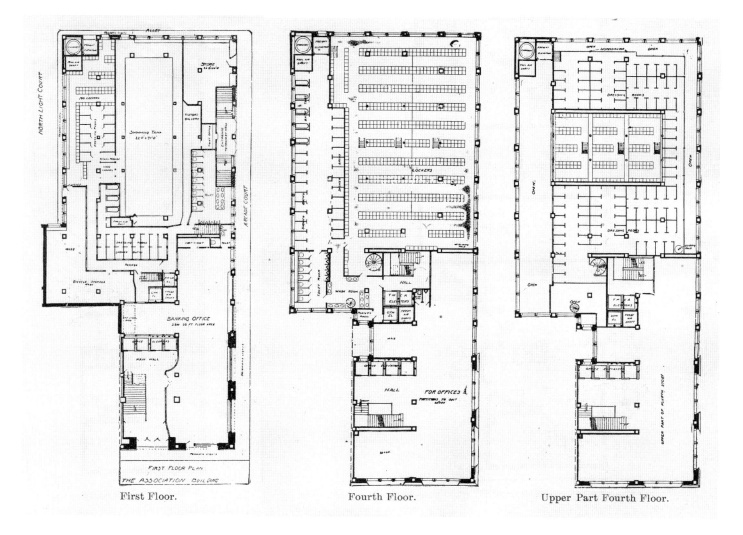

First Floor.   Fourth Floor.   Upper Part Fourth Floor.

While Chicago's Farwell Hall had been dominated by space for assembly and prayer meetings, the new skyscraper building was organized around an astonishing array of recreational facilities, including bowling alleys, a swimming pool, extensive locker rooms, steam baths and showers, dressing rooms, a gymnasium, an indoor running track, a darkroom, woodworking shops, and handball and tennis courts, as well as a small observatory on the roof. The gymnasium, swimming pool, lockers, and showers occupied the lion's share of the members' spaces in the building, extending throughout the rear of the fourth, fifth, and sixth floors (Figure 4.4).

Although central in today's YMCA, the pool played a relatively minor role in the athletic program of the associations at the turn of the century. The first YMCA swimming pool dates from 1885, at the Brooklyn Central building; by 1895 there were more than seventeen pools, sometimes called natatoriums or swimming baths. This nomenclature reflected the uncertainty within the Y and other organizations as to the pool's purpose: bathing, playing, or competitive swimming (Figure 4.5).[11] Most were rather small, located in the basement in a dark, unventilated room. Chicago's pool was only 22 by 70 feet, perhaps a third the size of a modern Olympic tank. It was, nonetheless, one of the few indoor pools in downtown Chicago at the time of its construction.

FIGURE 4.4. Floor plans for the Chicago Central YMCA building, 1894.

FIGURE 4.5. Advertisement for the Cincinnati YMCA gymnasium, in *Physical Training*, 1911.

The gymnasium represented the latest thinking on gym design, a significant improvement on those built in the 1870s. James Renwick's New York gymnasium, understood as the finest in its day, had been a large square room supported by posts that held up the floor of the hall above, but obscured the sight lines of the athletes (see Figure 2.21). Located in the basement, the gym had minimal lighting and ventilation. In many YMCA buildings, like the one at Rockford, Illinois, the gym was little more than a large room with equipment. Thanks to improvements and innovations in the gymnasiums at Boston and Bridgeport, Connecticut, in the late 1880s and early 1890s, the YMCA had evolved a more useful, efficient plan, with unobstructed floor space and a running track encircling the room on a mezzanine level (Figure 4.6).[12] Chicago's gym, with its steel-trussed roof, specially designed lighting, and mezzanine level track, allowed simultaneous use of the gym for individual and group work (Figure 4.7).

More impressive than the pool or the gymnasium were the Chicago skyscraper's locker rooms, which occupied nearly twice as much space as the auditorium. Once simple, smelly, and moldy, locker rooms became important, specially designed facilities for transformation of the body from its street guise to that of a wet, sweaty, and physical being and back again. What had been a simple space for changing and storing clothes evolved into

FIGURE 4.6. The gymnasium of the Bridgeport YMCA, at Main and Gilbert streets, Bridgeport, Connecticut, 1892.

an array of discrete spaces to house two distinct classes of men: men, and, euphemistically speaking, "businessmen," that is, men who were older and more substantial (financially and perhaps physically). YMCAs attempted to attract businessmen with private lockers, showers, club rooms, and, by 1901, Turkish baths.[13] This separation and elaboration of space correlated to the general policy of segregation and distinction by class, race, and gender practiced by the Y since its beginnings.[14]

Regular members had access to one of more than nineteen hundred individual lockers in a large room abutted by twenty-two marble-lined shower stalls (see Figure 4.4). The reliance on the relatively new practice of showering represented a major advancement from the days when a few members could hold up the departure of an entire gymnasium class by lingering in the bathtubs for too long.[15] Ultimately the lockers went the way of the tubs. The provision of permanent space for members became unsustainable as membership levels climbed. In the interest of efficiency most YMCAs adopted the Kansas City tote box system. Members no longer stored their athletic gear and street clothes in individual locked cabinets, but deposited them in wire bins, which were stored under the supervision of an attendant. This not only reduced the amount of floor space devoted to storage, but prevented young men from leaving their gear in small unventilated spaces to accumu-

FIGURE 4.7. The Chicago Central YMCA gymnasium, LaSalle Street and Arcade Court, 1895. An athletic class fully occupies the floor of the Chicago YMCA gymnasium, with members aligned in neat, quasi-military formation. Early gymnastic instruction at the YMCA was a fusion of Swedish and German calisthenics and circus acrobatics. By the turn of the century Y leaders had developed a curriculum that emphasized the importance of individual achievement within a synchronized system, echoing and reinforcing the managerial discipline of corporate culture.

late unpleasant odors. It also had the effect of depersonalizing the space, where members no longer maintained a hold on a specific location or territory. The notion of individuality and ownership was replaced by a more fluid, anonymous process managed and overseen by an attendant, whose role was to maintain order and decorum in the locker room.[16]

These athletic spaces were embedded on several floors within a complex building, zoned for different purposes. Office tenants occupied the thirteen stories in front and eight stories in the rear, served by dedicated stairways and elevators. One floor in front and six in back were dedicated to the activities of young men. This section contained all the athletic, educational, and recreational facilities of a standard Y and more. The two functions met at times, as in the first and fourth floors, where offices and the swimming pool and locker rooms were separated by a wall. Despite these awkward juxtapositions and the need for members to traverse stairways several times to access all of the membership features in one visit, the building was counted a success. A writer for *Harper's Weekly* noted, "From whatever side we approach the magnificent edifice the [Chicago] Young Men's Christian Association has been rearing, we shall find it the most stately temple to the power and prowess of unsectarian Christianity erected in modern times."[17]

Despite its success, the bold choice to lodge YMCA facilities in an office building did not spawn imitations elsewhere. Few places faced the same real-estate imperatives as Chicago's Loop. Also militating against the YMCA skyscraper was a general move away from the commercial associations of the past, toward a building type that fused the features of clubhouse with that of a hotel. In the 1850s the typical YMCA rented a few rooms above a store, and was identifiable only through modest signage (Figure 4.8). By the 1880s the Y was erecting its own building blocks and renting stores for income, but the form continued in the commercial mold, its increasingly complex facilities squeezed into long narrow city lots with party walls and little light (Figure 4.9). With greater acceptance of the organization, the building had less need for ground-floor stores, and this opened up new architectural possibilities. As Nelson Evans of Philadelphia reported at the YMCA Convention of 1887, in building design, "there is not now the same need to consider great prominence and revenue in a building project. The Association is widely known and its work better understood."[18] He suggested that new YMCA buildings should no longer be located in proximity to mercantile houses. Instead, they should be surrounded by residences and clubhouses.[19] Two years later another official argued that street-level shops, which distracted passersby from the building's identity as a YMCA, should be suppressed or removed, and the emphasis placed on the main door.[20] Mt. Vernon, New York's YMCA from the 1880s remains in the center of Main Street amid grocery shops and the optometrist, but is clearly distinguishable from the stores around it, with two lampposts at street level and a short flight of steps leading to an entrance framed by columns.

FIGURE 4.8. Decatur YMCA Rooms, 148 Merchant Street, Decatur, Illinois, 1890.

The distinction between these "clubhouse" YMCAs and their predecessors is quite clear, involving as it did a shift from a vernacular mercantile model toward a high art, civic one. Y leaders came to understand their buildings not simply as sources of revenue, permanency, and prestige, but as explicitly designed spaces in which all the elements, including revenue-producing features, served the needs of members and staff. The earliest buildings were a wedge into commercial culture, an attempt to engage with it on its own

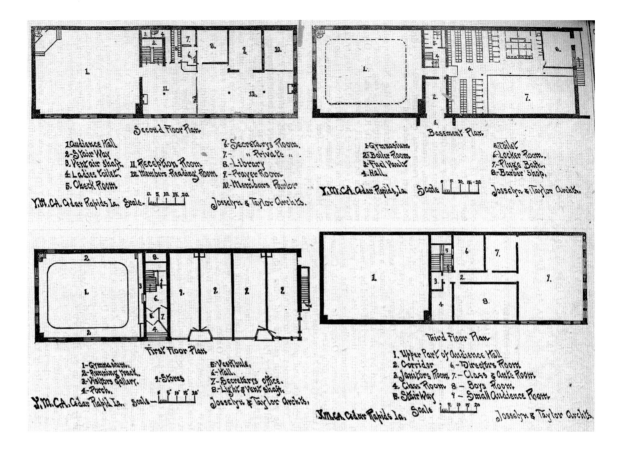

FIGURE 4.9. Plans of the Cedar Rapids YMCA, 310 Third Street Southeast, Cedar Rapids, Iowa.

terms and vocabulary, the building block. This next generation of clubhouse buildings represented an even more radical step: the creation of a new kind of building altogether. This new type was no longer a means to an end, but a more integrated expression of middle-class recreation and leisure.

The "Big Y"

Best exemplifying this new, more civic model is the Brooklyn Central YMCA, built in 1912–13. The "Big Y," as it was dubbed, was the largest and most complex YMCA building in the world at the time of its construction, a major landmark, and a symbol of modernity, a quality highlighted in advertisements by the headlights of an airplane (see Plate 6). Thirteen stories tall, with handball courts located atop the roof, it matched the height of the Chicago YMCA skyscraper, but was spread out over a whole rectangular city block in an envelope of brick with classicizing stone trim, presenting a different aspect to the public. Located near downtown Brooklyn but on the edge of a residential district of Fort Greene, it was an ideal location near the intersection of two subway lines and close to a cultural district that included a Brooklyn Public Library branch, a Masonic Temple, and the Brooklyn Academy of Music.

Although the building was as tall as the Chicago skyscraper, it was not an office building. This building, like most other YMCAs built at this time, moved decisively away from the commercial identity of the skyscraper. Designed by Trowbridge and Ackerman, the massive bulk of this building is similar to large hotels built by Statler and Hilton in the period.[21] The lower levels, sheathed in gray granite, supported a brick block of identical floors divided by stringcourses. Restrained Georgian Revival detailing, including pediments and rustication, mark the entrances, and a heavy cornice caps the roofline. This style had already been used in smaller city YMCAs, like Pittsfield, Massachusetts, and Wilmington, Delaware, but in larger cities like Detroit, Los Angeles, and Louisville the clubhouse model had to be elongated and stretched, sometimes uncomfortably, to fit a whole city block.

Dormitories

The size of the Brooklyn building was largely due to the presence of more than four hundred dormitory rooms on the upper floors. These dormitories, like the offices in the Chicago skyscraper, were meant to provide income for the Association. Unlike the stores, however, they were conceived as an integral part of the YMCA's programming: a home for young men. This embrace of dormitories meant that the YMCA building no longer operated within the commercial vernacular, but had assumed a new institutional identity.

This conception of the YMCA as a domestic space of sorts was a departure for the organization. When the first New York building opened in 1869 the only living spaces provided in the building were the artists' studios available for rent on the top floors, and Secretary Robert McBurney's own "tower room." Members were intentionally not offered the opportunity to live in the building. Early leaders did not want to *replace* the Christian home entirely. Instead, they made a boardinghouse register available, with lists of respectable establishments and good landladies. This differed significantly from the approach taken by its kindred organization, the Young Women's Christian Association. YWCA buildings conceived and supported by the relatives of YMCA donors were, from their beginnings in the late 1850s, first and foremost residences meant to shelter wage-earning women.

YMCA ideas about the propriety and necessity of an institutional masculine dwelling began to change in 1887, when the Harrisburg, Milwaukee, and Dayton associations first offered dormitory space within their new buildings. The impetus for this change in attitude toward dormitories was, at first, financial. The demand for respectable living arrangements had steadily increased, creating a market among the YMCA membership. In the last quarter of the nineteenth century the demise of the boardinghouse, once the major source of affordable housing in New York City, created a serious shortage of options for the middle class.[22] Small salaries placed most bachelor apartments and apartment hotels beyond the reach of the newcomer, and the flophouses and mission shelters were below his dignity.

Offering dormitories allowed the YMCA to remove the income-producing feature from the street and change its aspect. YMCAs also assured themselves of a steady stream of income, obviating the need for constant fund-raising and the presence of commercial tenants on the ground floor.

This change occurred just as the YMCA was eager to shift its architectural identity from the commercial model it had followed since 1869. As Y leaders soon realized, dorms could be understood as a real service to members and "a legitimate return upon a publicly invested endowment."[23]

Around this time the propriety of all-male living environments was bolstered by changes in residential life at the nation's universities. Before 1880 most students boarded in nearby homes, and fraternities at schools like Dartmouth and Princeton were located off-campus in rented rooms above a store, much like YMCAs.[24] Beginning around 1885, universities began to confront the necessity of providing more housing. Enrollments soared and students had trouble finding living arrangements. University officials realized at this time that dormitory construction would not only serve the students but also provide a steady source of income for school coffers. They developed new buildings modeled on the English residential collegiate models of Oxford and Cambridge. All-male housing became a part of the university experience, not only sanctioned but promoted as an important part of the educational process.

The YMCA, which operated special college branches on most campuses, was surely aware of this development of dormitory life. In fact, rooms at the Y, at least those photographed for advertising and promotional purposes, looked remarkably like college dorm rooms of the day (Figure 4.10). Typically about 7 by 9 feet, a single room contained a bed, dresser, two chairs, and a washbasin. Young men decorated their rooms on a collegiate model, with banners, prints of young women, colorful rugs, and a variety of books. All this was offered for a reasonable price, about half what a comparable hotel room cost at the time.

FIGURE 4.10. Dormitory room, Brooklyn Central YMCA, ca. 1915.

To take advantage of this boon, young men had to relinquish some control over their lives. Many Y leaders strove to view the Association's dormitory space not only as a source of income, but also as an integral part of its character-building program. Secretaries of YMCAs in Cleveland, Pittsburgh, and Columbus, Ohio, urged their colleagues to make the dormitory "proficient with regard to character returns as to actual financial returns."[25] As one fund-raising image suggested, "environment shapes the life" (Figure 4.11). Featuring a young man seated in his dormitory room, it emphasized the importance of and great need for affordable, respectable housing for the nation's young men. The claim to provide a home-like experience for its residents was one of the major challenges of the new buildings. H. M. Shipps, a dormitory official, asserted that "it must not only be a place to eat and sleep, but also a place to study, to make friends, to find diversion that will make the next day easier, happier, and more useful. It must also give him every opportunity to grow and develop into strong Christian manhood."[26]

Unlike hotels run for profit, Association dormitories claimed a particular atmosphere, and required careful management. Unlike an apartment, this alternative domestic arrangement was institutional by nature. Young men were not setting up housekeeping on their own: they dined, bathed, ate, and socialized in group settings. In some dormitories, each resident took part in a governing council that represented the dorm residents to the YMCA administration. This would, it was believed, help young men learn to take *some* responsibility for themselves, although they didn't have to make their beds or clean their rooms. Housekeeping services took place once a week, imposing a modicum of cleanliness and order on their spaces.

This meant that Y employees had to control, or attempt to control, not only the young man's recreation, but his entire social life, in loco parentis. If the Y was to be a place where parents might safely send their boy coming to a strange city, then leaders had to create an environment that would safeguard and stimulate him appropriately. That meant, among other things, a no-smoking policy. This attempt to control private behavior in dorm rooms drove some men away, but most YMCAs, even those that forbade smoking, had a waiting list for their accommodations.[27]

Despite the challenges that dormitories posed, sleeping rooms were so much in demand that they became established features in YMCA buildings. The Milwaukee YMCA, which was one of the first to include dorm rooms in the 1880s, expanded to a new building next door with 161 rooms (Figure

FIGURE 4.11. "A Home Away from Home." Advertisement in *Association Men*, 1908.

FIGURE 4.12. Milwaukee dormitory buildings, Fourth Street and Wisconsin Avenue, constructed in 1887 (*right*) and 1916 (*left*).

4.12). The demand for rooms in Chicago and Buffalo was so great that associations there went so far as to build separate YMCA Hotels in 1913. Most, however, incorporated dormitories into their regular buildings, increasing their size considerably.

Boys' Work

Another feature that added to the bulk of YMCA buildings was the introduction of programs for boys from fourteen through seventeen. Although some YMCA "boys' work," as it was called, dated back to the 1860s, by the 1890s it had been elaborated, and the work of camping begun. Boys' work reflected developments in urban middle-class conceptions of childhood in the late nineteenth century. Fathers who may have been obliged to cut their schooling short at age thirteen to fight their way into the middle class now extended the boyhood and education of their sons long into adolescence.[28] By the 1880s theories and philosophies of education recognized these shifts, moving toward a more age-defined educational experience as reflected in school design, with classrooms divided according to age and level. At this time Y leaders began to assert that their work should be preventative, rather than remedial, and should focus on games, structured play and athletics for boys, especially those in the important developmental years between fourteen and seventeen.

By 1900, when almost 70 percent of city YMCAs operated special programs for boys, the concept began to receive architectural attention.[29] At that point makeshift and temporary appropriations of spaces designed for other purposes no longer seemed adequate. In 1901 boys' work advocates argued for the necessity of separate but equal, or nearly equal facilities.[30] Building manuals suggested that at least half the space of newly planned buildings be allocated to boys' work. Sharing facilities with boisterous youngsters, especially locker rooms and gymnasiums, was unappealing to most older men, and Y officials expressed worries about the "seniors" who *were* interested in youngsters. Some associations purchased additional buildings just for boys in residential neighborhoods, but most continued to carve out space within the main building for the boys, isolated from the adult facilities.[31] In smaller cities like Findlay, Ohio, and Bennington, Vermont, limited funds made such duplication impossible (Figure 4.13). The "compact" $20,000 building

FIGURE 4.13. Findlay YMCA building, 129 East Sandusky Street, Findlay, Ohio, and gymnasium schedule, 1907.

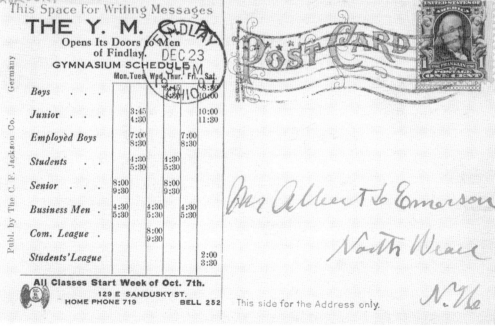

FIGURE 4.14. Twin building design for the Atlanta YMCA, Luckie Street, Atlanta, Georgia, 1914.

in Bennington had just five dormitory rooms, one gym, and one social hall for all to share, boys during the day and men at night.[32]

The addition of boys' work meant further complications in the renovation of older buildings as well as in the planning and arrangement of the modern Y clubhouse. The addition of a duplicate set of facilities, when combined with dormitory floors, doubled the volume of the standard building. One solution, presented in the West Side (New York) YMCA in 1896 and in the Atlanta YMCA in 1904, was the so-called twin-building design: linked side-by-side structures with separate entrances and facilities (Figure 4.14).[33] This visually expressed the spatial distinctions between boys and men, but allowed for an efficient use of common resources on the lower floors where possible.

The more common solution, exemplified in the Brooklyn Big Y, was a single building with two entrances and a zoned area for boys in a separate wing, with its own lobby and reception room, club room, game room, classroom, gymnasium, and locker room, all with appropriately sized furniture (Figure 4.15). In the 1920s a special feature was added to the largest and most sophisticated boys' facilities: the playroom (Figure 4.16). Designed to resemble a log cabin or a ship's cabin, these themed rooms were intended to be more than just novelties. With flagstone floors, hand-hewn log walls, timber roofs, and hickory furniture, the log-cabin rooms were strewn with props of preindustrial masculinity, including imitation muskets, hunting

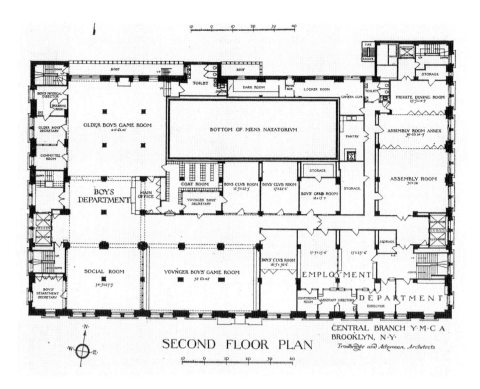

FIGURE 4.15 (*top*). Plan for boys' work, Central Branch, Brooklyn YMCA, 1913.
FIGURE 4.16 (*bottom*). Boys' log-cabin room, Bronx Union YMCA Branch, One Hundred Sixty-first Street and Washington Avenue, New York, 1928.

130 / BEDROOMS, BILLIARDS, AND BASKETBALL

trophies, and a stuffed owl. They were meant to be symbolic reminders to American boys of the vital, character-building experience of frontier life.[34] The playrooms, similar to those used by the Boy Scouts, were also used for club activities, serving as miniature boardrooms where young men could enact community life and leadership.

Parlors and Poolrooms

Although boys' work and dormitories transformed the exterior profile of the Big Y considerably, its most radical change was something only visible to those who entered the building. The tightly organized panoptic arrangement of the nineteenth-century building, with its central reception room and subsidiary parlor, reading rooms, and meeting rooms, changed into a more flexible set of social spaces. A series of individual rooms, formally marked by doorways, passages, and multiple staircases, was exchanged for a more flowing space, including, of all things, a billiards room (Figure 4.17). The game that had once been shunned as too shocking to play at a YMCA became a common architectural feature. The parlor, a standard feature of old, faded into oblivion. In Brooklyn's Big Y the old gendered distinction between the more public masculine reception room, decorated with hunting trophies, and the more removed and private feminine parlor of the 1869 building disappeared into a clubby, welcoming space that embraced masculinity as a respectable scheme throughout.

The disappearance of the parlor was itself a major change, akin to the obsolescence of the revival hall. In the 1850s and 1860s parlors had been important elements of YMCA architecture, a domesticating site of refine-

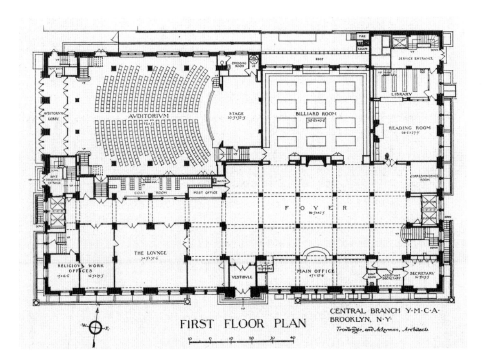

FIGURE 4.17. Plans for the Central Branch Brooklyn YMCA, in *Architecture*, January 1916.

ment and sociability for young members. By 1901 the parlor, which had been included in the modern, up-to-date Chicago skyscraper building just seven years before, was written out of YMCA articles and building manuals. Y officials now dismissed them as "dainty Bohemian boudoirs with pretty draperies and pillows." Most parlors, like the one in the Hyde Park YMCA near Chicago, had been decorated by ladies' auxiliaries in the 1880s with doilies, spindly chairs, and lace curtains.[35] Like the revival halls, they were empty much of the time, no longer used as they had been intended.[36] Parlors now seemed old-fashioned, and despite the YMCA's best attempts to redefine them as male social spaces, they were still associated primarily with women. Following a trend toward "masculinization" in Protestant religious circles, the Y sought new and distinctly male ways to exert religious influence. This meant the definition and design of new kinds of social spaces.[37]

In the Big Y, the architects Trowbridge and Ackerman drew upon the contemporary hotel lobby, organizing the building around a single foyer with a series of public rooms featuring alcoves for specialized activities (Figure 4.18). Divided into a grid by a regular series of massive pillars, it could, when partitioned, host a variety of activities, including socials, sings, shows, talks, and debates. Unlike the reception room of old, this entry space was

FIGURE 4.18. The lobby-foyer of the Brooklyn Central YMCA.

no longer a distributing place, but a multipurpose lounging room decorated with massive oak and leather furniture, overhead beams, and a huge fireplace with blazing logs. Complementing this scheme was a neutral color palette of cherry red, sage green, and Naples ochre, which provided a warm, graceful, and comfortable atmosphere "reminiscent neither of the pretty ladies parlor nor the railway reception room, but the club."[38] Advertisements of the building focus on the fireplace at night, surrounded by young men playing the banjo and roasting chestnuts.

Adjoining the large foyer was another space that significantly changed the atmosphere of the new building: a billiards room. The inclusion of a room specifically dedicated to the game signified a tectonic shift in the YMCA's attitude toward amusements. The question about billiards and other popular games dates all the way back to the New York building of 1869. Schism over the propriety of methods to be used in evangelical work is well illustrated by the awkwardness that followed the donation by Mrs. J. P. Morgan of a billiards table. Conservative religious attitudes toward "commercial entertainments" persisted into the early twentieth century, especially in smaller cities and towns.

In his classic satire of turn-of-the-century Midwestern culture, *The Music Man*, Meredith Willson spoofed the continued fear of the moral influence of billiards, especially the variation known as "pool." In the song "Ya Got Trouble," con man Harold Hill convinces the parents of River City of the moral dangers of the game and other elements of an emerging mass culture: cigarette smoking, dime novels, and ragtime. They fall in with his chant:

> Trouble, oh we got trouble,
> Right here in River City!
> With a capital "T"
> That rhymes with "P"
> And that stands for Pool![39]

Distinguished from billiards by the use of pockets, pool was, as its name suggests, associated with gambling and hustlers, who preyed on the unwary. Billiards, on the other hand, was considered an upper-class game, played in clubs and mansions. The YMCA, hoping to draw men away from poolrooms, began to offer billiards, much in the same way they offered athletics to keep young men away from low-class sporting events. Their billiards experiment was supported by the Brunswick-Balke-Collender Company, which strove to make billiards a respectable middle-class game by donating tables to charitable groups like the YMCA.

Perhaps through the influence of the company, individual YMCAs began to bring billiards into the building itself, where the influences surrounding the game could be controlled. Beginning around 1905, *Association Men* began reporting the appearance of billiards tables in YMCA buildings, first in Salt Lake City, Duluth, Washington, D.C., and Troy, New York. At first, it

FIGURE 4.19. Interior view, with billiards table, of the Geneva YMCA, Castle Street, Geneva, New York.

seems, no one knew quite how to integrate them appropriately into the existing spaces. In Geneva, New York, they were placed somewhat awkwardly in the reception room, under the supervision of the secretaries behind the desk (Figure 4.19). In some cases they were grouped together in the basement with the bowling alleys.

Other YMCAs took a more proactive approach, remodeling their facilities to create an inviting and casual atmosphere reminiscent of popular saloons and poolrooms. The development of special spaces that fused commercial options was necessary to provide the social atmosphere attractive to young men. By 1906 the Brooklyn YMCA introduced "The Inn of Brooklyn Central." This innovative space combined elements of two emerging commercial establishments: the pool hall and the lunch counter. Several billiards tables were placed alongside a long bar, creating a friendly, sporting, but wholesome environment. Instead of liquor bottles, the bar was dominated by large coffee urns, and sandwiches and hot cooked food were available. This introduction of casual food service in Brooklyn and other YMCAs paralleled the rise of lunch counters and cafes in drugstores, including the first Walgreens lunch counter in 1908, and the first automat in 1902 in Philadelphia. Formal restaurants, a feature found in many earlier YMCAs, were increasingly rejected as being ill suited to the needs of young men as well as too expensive to maintain. Instead, YMCAs offered self-serve cafeterias in Chicago, Buffalo, and Omaha.[40]

The Inn at the Brooklyn YMCA was very popular with members, who had obviously frequented pool halls in the past. The general secretary acknowledged that "nearly every man who plays billiards here has played before and is something of an expert in the game." He noted that since the introduction of "The Inn" the social life of the Association had vastly improved and "rough house and nonsense diminished." He cautioned, however, that close supervision was warranted to enforce the distinction between the behavior acceptable in a pool hall and that in a YMCA billiards room.[41] Smoking, rowdy behavior, and fighting were not allowed.

Seven years later, when the original Brooklyn Central YMCA building was replaced with the Big Y, the billiards room was a central feature of the first floor, integrated into a new arrangement of social spaces (see Figure 4.17). As soon as a young man entered the building he could see billiards across the foyer, behind a lounge area anchored by a massive fireplace. Larger than the adjacent library and nearly as big as the auditorium, this twelve-table room gave the game pride of place on the important first floor, while still providing oversight from the main desk directly across the foyer. The design of the rooms was simple and clean, with wood paneling or painted walls, unadorned by the mirrors, risqué posters of women, and liquor bottles that were common in poolrooms. This was intended to communicate the

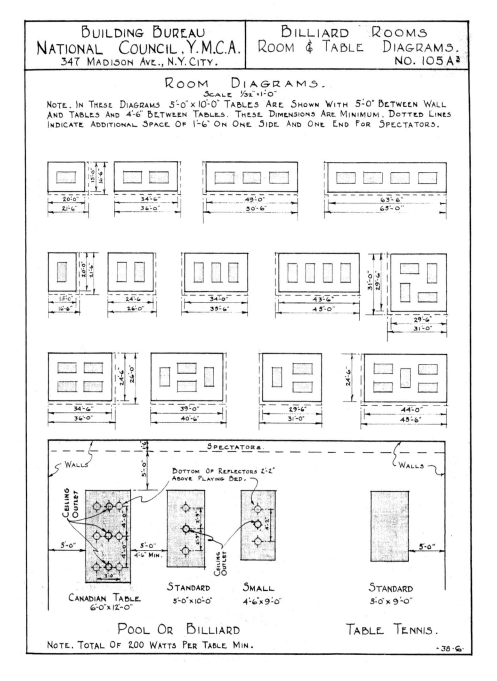

FIGURE 4.20. YMCA Building Bureau, Billiard Room and Table Diagrams.

proper dignity and decorum to players (see Plate 7). The imagery of YMCA billiards rooms emphasizes well-dressed and groomed young men, standing individually with upright posture, engaged in thoughtful play.

In 1869 Mrs. J. P. Morgan's controversial donation of a billiards table to the New York YMCA was a source of embarrassment and misunderstanding: it was relegated to the basement. Forty years later, the Y magazine *Association Men* promoted the inclusion of the game in its model building plans, and provided standardized diagrams for the design of cue racks (Figure 4.20). What had once been shunned as inappropriate was now sanctioned by the YMCA organization, although not without some objections in the provinces. Several donors to the 1908 Greensboro YMCA building campaign refused to fulfill their pledges if a billiards room was in the plans.[42] Still the organization held firm, asserting that there was nothing wrong with billiards itself; only the atmosphere of the poolroom was objectionable. A 1915 article in *Association Men* even argued that, in the proper hands, billiards could be used to win young men to "open discipleship and avowed church membership."[43]

As radical as the inclusion of billiards was, it was not the most symbolic shift in the identity of the YMCA building at the turn of the twentieth century. The ultimate accommodation to the world of mass culture was the acceptance of the electric sign. Just a few years earlier, around 1910, electric signs began to appear in Times Square, shaping the popular image of the Great White Way and the world of mass entertainment.[44] In the world of the big city, with increasingly bright lights, the sedate appearance of the Georgian Revival Big Y was not enough to compete. Soon after the construction of the Big Y, leaders of the Brooklyn Y followed the path pursued by several other cities, purchasing a large red sign with the letters YMCA to serve as a beacon in the night to young men. Soon the signs became a standard feature of the Y building, and electric sign manufacturers were advertising in *Association Men,* noting that all "progressive" associations made use of the stratagem. It was all part of the modern way of doing business.

Conclusion

The transformation of the YMCA building between 1890 and 1915 represented a major change in the organization. Responding to the City Beautiful movement and the rise of mass culture, YMCA architecture evolved from its Victorian origins as a Christian clubhouse, a respectable male space with parlors and gymnasiums, to a more secularized service role, providing leisure, education, and housing to its members. The commercial identity of the YMCA reached its zenith in the design of the Chicago YMCA skyscraper, but decisively moved in another direction after the turn of the century. No longer a building block on Main Street, the model YMCA resembled a club or a hotel and took its place in a civic, public urban landscape.

5
FROM GREENSBORO TO CHINA
YMCA Architecture as International Business

As the story of the Chicago YMCA skyscraper and Brooklyn's Big Y suggests, the model YMCA building was by the early 1900s a complex and quickly evolving mechanism, subject to constant change and inevitable obsolescence, just like the factories to which it was compared. These conditions strained the organization's relationship with the architectural profession. Few commissions were as complicated, and most architects struggled to master the organization of this building type on the strict budget allowed. The acquisition of machinery and the arrangement of the internal features required specialized knowledge and experience.[1] Local building committees, especially outside of major urban areas, lacked the experience to guide the process.

Throughout the first decade of the twentieth century, YMCA leaders attempted to impose order and method on their architectural program. This was a slow process, during which local experience was collected, compared, and codified. With no standard plans distributed by the International Committee, each new building had been an experiment that contributed to the constantly evolving paradigm known as "the modern association building." Building committees learned from the mistakes of their predecessors about how large dormitory rooms should be, or how many toilets were required for a membership of ten thousand. Information about new developments came from a variety of sources: conference reports, journal articles, word of mouth, expert consultants, manufacturers, and specialist architects. This resulted in what one Y official later described as "a modern tower of Babel because of its magnitude and its confusion of tongues and ideas: a tower that was in danger of toppling."[2]

General secretaries and local elites raising money for YMCA buildings were in an increasingly untenable position, risking embarrassment or worse if the structures were nonfunctional, unattractive, or expensive to maintain. As the number of YMCA buildings constructed every year rose, the existing building process became increasingly irksome for YMCA officials, especially their dealings with the architectural profession. Most trained architects, educated in the Beaux-Arts system, were of little help to local YMCAs. Their artistic pretensions were distinctly at odds with the YMCA's business-oriented culture, which valued buildings for their financial and programmatic efficiency.

In their drive for professionalization, American architects intentionally distanced themselves from business interests and the material process of building, emphasizing their cultural superiority and aesthetic values. As Hyungmin Pai has observed, in the American Beaux-Arts system "architecture and its monuments were defined in antithesis to the mundane realities of capitalist society."[3] By contrast, Y officials understood their buildings as equipment whose worth was to be measured graphically in terms of financial value (Figure 5.1).

Although YMCA leaders did attribute some value to aesthetics, in the first decade of the twentieth century the most important aspect of YMCA building design was, to them, the successful interpretation of the program.

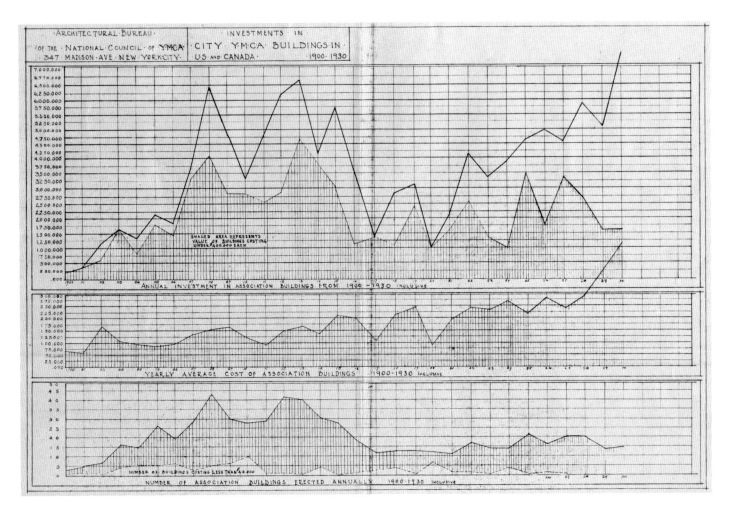

FIGURE 5.1. Investments in City YMCA Buildings in U.S. and Canada, 1900–1930.

Beaux-Arts–trained architects did not share this priority. Instead, they sought to "stage" the client's program in an elegant design.[4] Beaux-Arts–trained architects, Y officials found, focused unduly on the appearance of the exterior and too little on the functionality of the interior. Architects also tended to ignore the increasing standardization and systematization of the building process in favor of an individual aesthetic statement. In an attempt to assert their role as designers rather than builders or contractors, architects eschewed the knowledge of contemporary building technology, mass-produced products, construction supervision, and purchasing that would ensure that a building met the YMCA's standards of success: on time, on budget, and easy to manage and maintain.

A huge spike in construction around 1910 forced the YMCA to reshape the modern building process to meet its own needs. Responding to the complications posed by a national and international construction boom that reached from North Carolina to China and beyond, the International Committee standardized and rationalized their building policies into a bureaucratic system. The systematization of the YMCA's architectural policy took place in two stages: first the collection and codification of past experience, and then the implementation of this code through an official consulting organization, the "Building Bureau." This process, influenced by Frederick Winslow Taylor's principles of scientific management, was a significant and unusual solution to the problems of architecture in the industrial age.

Although the early-twentieth-century YMCA and European architectural modernists Walter Gropius and Le Corbusier shared an interest in standardization, mass production, and the reconciliation of the demands of art and technology in everyday life, the YMCA stood apart from the architectural profession, rejecting the traditionally architect-centered approach to problem solving. It evolved a bureaucratic architectural system that was based upon the manufacturing concept of the division of labor, dividing the responsibility for the process of building into two distinct elements. Technical and planning issues were taken out of the hands of architects and placed in the domain of the accountant, the engineer, and the efficiency specialist.[5] Working in collaboration with these experts, the architect would be responsible for the "artistic" elements. Unlike the slightly later and somewhat similar system evolved by architect Albert Kahn and the Ford Motor Company, the YMCA did not rely upon the leadership of an architect. Instead, it absorbed and subsumed architecture into the world of business.

Expansion

This bureaucratization and modernization of building culture was required by the scale and complexity of the YMCA's twentieth-century architectural agenda. Between 1900 and 1915 the YMCA experienced major expansions both at home and abroad. In the United States the booming economy made construction possible again after the long depression of the 1890s. On all

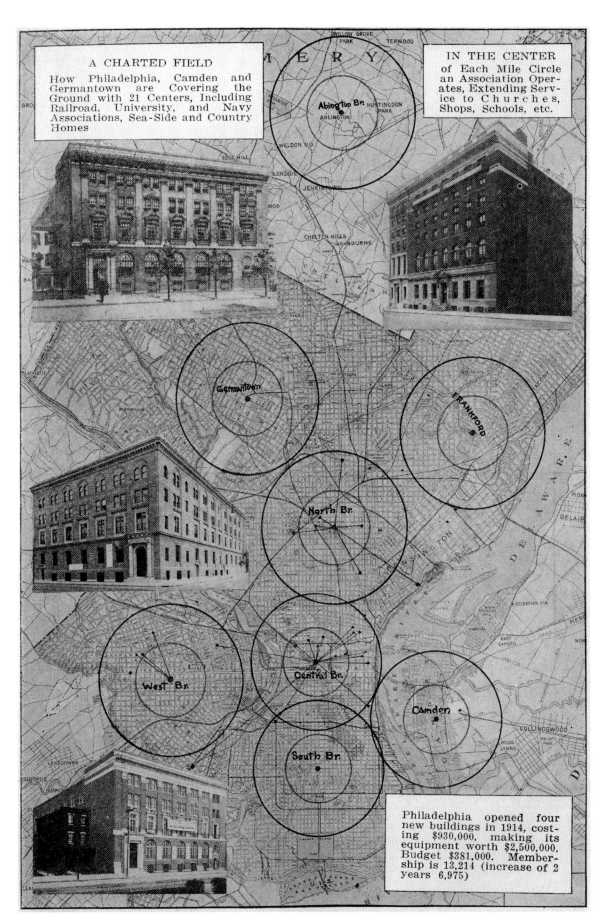

FIGURE 5.2. Map of Philadelphia YMCA expansion plans, 1914.

geographical scales, from the neighborhood to the city, to the state, and around the world, Y buildings appeared by the dozens every year.

The number of urban YMCA buildings increased ten times between 1900 and 1906 and continued on an upward trajectory until World War I halted construction projects. Inspired by the competitive civic rhetoric employed by the International Committee, many smaller cities and towns built their first YMCAs. In addition to the expansion into new territory, YMCA building increased within the larger cities already in possession of an older building from the 1880s or earlier. These "white elephants," with their parlors and halls and old-fashioned appearance, were now obsolete.[6] The paradigm of what the YMCA quite self-consciously described as the "modern" Association building was constantly changing in response to experience and technological improvements, notably the invention of the steel-frame building. Local associations struggled to keep up with the changes. At the same time, large city YMCAs, including those in Brooklyn, Chicago, and Philadelphia, began to plan large expansion campaigns. No longer were leaders content with a single large "central" building; the new "metropolitan" trend was to place the YMCA in every residential neighborhood, within a mile of every young man's residence (Figure 5.2).[7]

In the West, state Y organizations engaged in extensive building promotion, which resulted in a rash of building campaigns within particular regions. Fueled by oil money and an expanding industrial economy, eighteen buildings were constructed in Texas cities just in 1907 alone. In 1908 Nebraskans celebrated nine buildings constructed in the past five years, all located along the Union Pacific Railroad, including Central City, which had grown in population to 1,500 since Robert Weidensall had made his first promotional visit for the YMCA in 1869 (Figure 5.3). Throughout Kansas YMCAs sprouted up all along the railroad lines in Atchison, Topeka, Iola, Salina, Hutchinson, Newton, Winfield, and Pittsburg (Figure 5.4). As a panoramic photograph of the Kansas YMCA State Convention Meeting shows, these clubhouses typically took their place on the edge of Main Street, often across the street from the church and near the residential district (Figure 5.5).

On the national scale, "colored" work took on a new architectural profile. Formerly housed in buildings far inferior to those built for white men, black YMCAs across the United States began to build modern YMCA buildings for themselves. This construction boom was catalyzed by a donation from Julius Rosenwald, executive of Sears, Roebuck and Co. Although Jewish, he admired the work of the YMCA and felt special responsibility for African Americans, who, like the Jews, had suffered so much adversity. In 1910 he promised $25,000 toward the cost of an unlimited number of buildings, if the black community would raise $75,000 on its own.[8] Although this offer institutionalized segregation within the YMCA, thirteen cities responded to the call, including Columbus, Ohio; St. Louis; Kansas City, Missouri; Chicago; Atlanta; Brooklyn; and Philadelphia.

NEBRASKA'S FIVE YEAR BUILDING RECORD

These buildings have been erected in Nebraska within five years and are practically free of debt. The Omaha property is worth $330,000, Lincoln $45,000, Fremont $65,000, Beatrice $45,000, Hastings $37,000, York, $30,000, Columbus $35,000, Chadron (population 2,000) $25,000, Central City (population 1,500) $10,500. South Omaha occupies a temporary building but $10,000 is pledged on a $50,000 building.

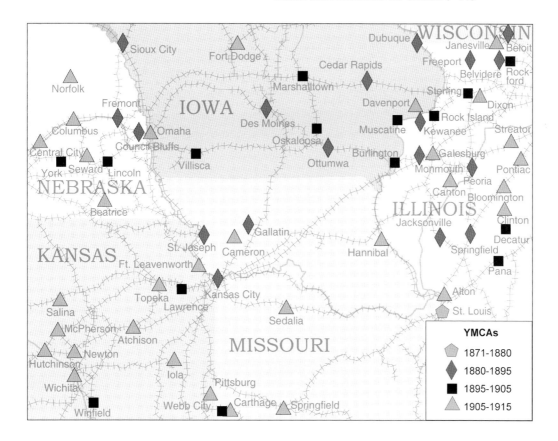

In addition to all of this activity in the United States, the American YMCA initiated an international building campaign during this period. In the wake of the Spanish-American War and in light of an increasing sense of imperial destiny, the International Committee had begun to live up to its name, taking on the responsibility for erecting the most modern YMCA buildings in what might be termed "missionary lands": China, India, Japan, Korea, the Middle East, the Philippines, Portugal, Russia, and the West Indies. At a 1910 conference held at the White House, the YMCA publicized a plan to expand its foreign missionary activity, including fifty new missionary workers and fifty new buildings around the world.[9] According to one Y official: "We are erecting these buildings all over this continent from British Columbia to Maine and from Ontario to the Gulf, also in the Phillipine [sic] Islands, Japan, Korea, and throughout China from Mukden down to Canton."[10]

China, with its rapidly expanding industrial economy, was a special target of this plan, and the site of the most building activity. At the end of the Qin Dynasty and facing a new world under Republican leadership, educated Chinese sought a new cultural and national framework for modernization. Western models, especially in planning and architecture, were tested. City officials, both in the treaty ports and in provincial urban centers like Chengtu and Nantong, initiated planned improvements, including park systems, street paving, and the construction of institutions.[11] The YMCA's focus on buildings for young men was an appealing model since the old system of

FIGURE 5.4. Railroads, urban development, and YMCA buildings: a convergence of railroad lines and the presence of YMCA buildings in Midwest and Plains states at the turn of the twentieth century traces the path of YMCA traveling secretaries, and suggests the influence of this building type on the definition of urban landscape and culture in newly settled regions.

FIGURE 5.3. "Nebraska's Five Year Building Record," in *Association Men*, 1908.

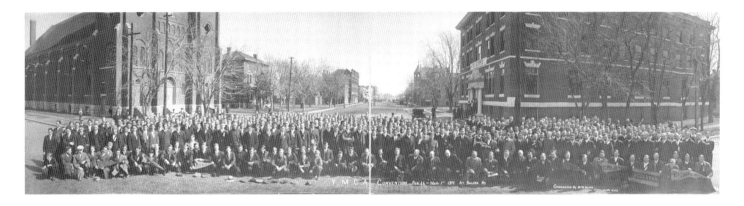

FIGURE 5.5. YMCA State Convention Meeting in front of the new Salina YMCA building, Salina, Kansas, 1914. Gathered across the intersection of Ninth and Iron streets, the local state convention of the YMCA proudly highlights the Salina Association's new $45,000 building, located across the street from the Sacred Heart Parish in a residential and institutional zone just west of the main street, Santa Fe Avenue.

apprenticeship and advancement, the imperial civil service, disappeared in 1905. In its place new educational systems were needed to situate the literati in an unfamiliar capitalist world.

Beginning in 1895 groups of YMCA secretaries traveled not only to the coastal treaty ports of Hong Kong, Amoy, Foochow, Hangchow, Shanghai, and Tientsin, but also to interior cities like Yunnanfu, Chengtu, Changsha, Nanking, Tsinanfu, and Peking to promote the idea, raise money, and train native Chinese in YMCA methods and policies.[12] By 1913 buildings were planned or under construction in more than a dozen locations (Figure 5.6). The success of the YMCA's campaign in China reveals the flexibility of this evangelical model of respectable leisure. The YMCA's emphasis on self-improvement and technical education was particularly appealing to natives, and once they won control of local YMCAs much of the religious origins of the mission to China faded in favor of a nationalist agenda of reform. Just as for people in small-town America, for Chinese a YMCA building provided a tangible model of modernity that they could adapt to their own purposes.[13]

Through its work in China as well as South America and India, the American YMCA became, in a very short time, a major patron of architecture on an international scale, simultaneously planting complex "modern" Association buildings containing the latest in technology in far-flung locations. The management of this process was an overwhelming responsibility, both for the International Committee and for the local associations. The difficulties faced in this building campaign catalyzed a more methodical, systematic architectural policy.

Greensboro and Tientsin

Outside of New York, Chicago, and other major U.S. cities, the challenge of building a modern YMCA building was significant. Whether on Main Street or on the Bohai Sea, local associations had to assimilate an ideal and translate it on the ground within the existing building culture. A YMCA building was a fusion between local, traditional building materials and techniques and imported expertise, technologies, and management. Although the process was slightly more complex abroad, with issues of language, ex-

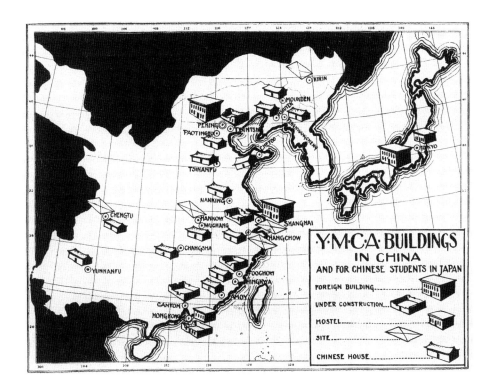

FIGURE 5.6. Map of YMCA buildings in China, 1913.

change rates, and political differences to contend with, the associations at Greensboro, North Carolina, and Tientsin, China, shared the same essential problems. Both were planned by the same architectural firm, Shattuck and Hussey, used similar fund-raising methods, and were constructed within a few years of each other. Despite the distance between them, they looked similar, and their plans were nearly identical. In both cases, the effort exhausted local leaders. The experience of these two communities, and hundreds of others like them, gave rise to a more standardized system of architectural guidance for the YMCA.

Greensboro

In December 1911 the citizens of Greensboro, North Carolina, attended an evening reception to celebrate the long-anticipated opening of their very own YMCA building. Together they had raised $65,000 for a "first-class" building that would help put the city, on the cusp of economic take-off, on the cultural and civic map as well. As one booster put it, "every progressive city in these days believes it is a wise and proper thing to take good physical, intellectual, and moral care of its boys and men."

A square three-story brick building with white stone trim and an overhanging cornice, the refined neo-Georgian clubhouse building offered two entrances: one for men and one for boys (see Figure 3.14). Its gymnasium, bowling alleys, reading room, and billiards room thrilled and surprised the visitors, as did the brilliantly lit decor, furnished with fanciful oriental rugs.[14] At a time when many Greensboro homes still lacked electricity and running water, the building's steam heat, sophisticated plumbing, and "many conveniences" were much remarked upon. The "attractive sleeping rooms," complete with linen, soap, and towels, also received favorable comment.[15] Boy Scouts in uniform were stationed to guide visitors around the unusual new building as though taking them to a strange new land, which in fact it was to many residents. The YMCA was defining a new landscape of leisure and recreation, just around the corner from the landmarks of an emerging mass culture on Elm Street: the new movie theater and the national and regional retailers like the Kress five-and-dime and Meyer's Department Store of Richmond.

The positive reception of the building must have been gratifying to the long-suffering Lewis H. Martin, the general secretary of the Greensboro YMCA. Although the ultimate product was successful, the building process had been torturous. Martin was so frustrated by the building experience that he wrote to the International Committee, relating his experience, or rather lack of experience, and its costly effects. When he and the Greensboro Building Committee began their project they hired a local architect. This turned out to be a fatal mistake. Still rather small and undeveloped in its architectural culture, Greensboro was home to a few practitioners: Frank A. Weston, formerly of Denver; Orlo Epps, a builder-architect; and Frank P. Milburn, who migrated to the area from Washington, D.C. They were responsible for the industrial architecture of the mills, educational architecture at the university, and other small local commissions.

As it turned out, the local architect, unnamed in Martin's account, was unfamiliar with the complexities of the YMCA. He produced an idiosyncratic set of plans at odds with the best practices of Y architecture of the day. Worse yet, his proposal was over budget by $16,000, a cardinal sin against the YMCA's entrenched ethos of efficiency. The useless plans cost the local Y $5,000 in fees and seven months of lost time. Even worse, these mistakes undermined the community's confidence in the Association.[16] The Y leaders, seeking to establish the organization within the city and situate their efforts and the city of Greensboro in a national context, then chose to go outside the state for professional expertise.[17] They felt compelled to toss out the plans and seek guidance from Shattuck and Hussey, the YMCA specialists from Chicago, who could quickly and easily produce an appropriate, if not imaginative, building.

Shattuck and Hussey designed dozens of the nearly two hundred buildings constructed between 1906 and World War I (see Plate 1). Unlike general practice architects, these designers, favored by International Committee officials, became quasi-employees, trusted to produce functional and low-cost buildings. Their understanding of YMCA building principles could be transferred from building to building, reducing risk for local building committees.

The firm had entered into YMCA service through the work of Harry

Hussey, who had begun his career by constructing a few Y buildings in Michigan. Irving K. Pond, a former president of the American Institute of Architects, grumpily noted that "the firm of Shattuck & Hussey specialize in YMCA buildings and have procured a great deal of work through the influence of a relative of Hussey's [Charles Ward], who, as a national secretary engaged in helping out in financial campaigns, sees fit to have the local architect displaced and Shattuck & Hussey appointed in their stead or made to act as advisers." One official later remembered that "Shattuck and Hussey were established and continued in business for many years through his [Ward's] urging them upon Building Committees."[18]

Their experience meant that they carried a certain authority to the building process, especially when planning for the introduction of new technologies to provincial centers: a light plant, elevator, hot and cold water supply, and filtering required for the pool and elaborate bath facilities. Building committees wanted their expertise in calculating the cost of an electricity plant for a building of a particular size, or deciding where they should buy water or drill a well. Questions abounded. Oil or coal? Refiltering for the pool water, or not? How many toilets and shower stalls should be available for a projected membership of one thousand? Should heating system returns be located on the floor or on the wall? General secretaries wanted to ensure the efficiency and ease of building operation so that they could concentrate on helping young men rather than learning mechanical engineering.[19]

Guidance was especially needed when it came time to purchase fixtures and building materials. The specifications for plumbing fixtures, for instance, called for wall hung water closets and lavatories; specially designed urinals; drinking fountains; special cafeteria and kitchen equipment; acid-proof waste lines for chemical laboratories; special cuspidors flushed by the waste of the adjacent drinking fountains in each gym and handball court; special mop sinks that could accommodate mop trucks; liquid soap dispensers; and fire protection systems.[20]

Manufacturers were eager to sell their wares, and many offered free consulting services to YMCA secretaries, both at home and abroad. Nationally circulated Y-published magazines like *Association Men* and *Physical Training* solicited advertisements from materials manufacturers, and encouraged readers to mention the journal when writing for catalogs or more information. As early as the 1880s the Boston Gymnasium Supply Company claimed that its architects had "made special study of the construction of Association Buildings containing gymnasiums" and offered to furnish plans and estimates for proposed buildings. By the 1890s the Narragansett Machine Company was touting its leadership in the field, claiming expertise in developing new machinery and listing by name more than one hundred gyms it had fitted.[21] A 1910 ad for A.G. Spalding and Company openly acknowledged that the "Building Boom is on in the Y.M.C.A." and assured readers of the "quality and quantity of their dumbbells and other equipment."[22]

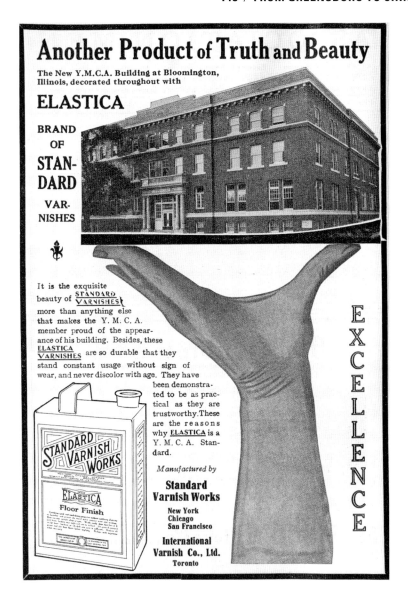

FIGURE 5.7. "Another Product of Truth and Beauty." Advertisement in *Association Men*, 1913.

Everyone from varnish manufacturers to those specializing in china sets for institutional dining rooms sought to demonstrate their practicality and trustworthiness, as well as their appearance (Figure 5.7).[23] Most companies hastened to prove their reliability by listing all of the YMCAs that had successfully used their materials. The National X-Ray Reflector Company of New York and Chicago (Figure 5.8) advertised its "Eye Comfort" lighting system by citing its work on a recent Y project: "There is no glare in Beloit's beautiful new building because the lighting was carefully planned by experts who have made scientific illumination their life work."[24] In its ads Otis Elevator promised availability day or night to render expert service and inspections.[25]

The offers for assistance were real enough, but were advertisers the most reliable sources of information? YMCA officials were quite aware of the competing claims of different manufacturers. One article on gymnasium equipment recommended playing one off the other as a way of gathering information and gauging the accuracy and reliability of the differing brands. Others cautioned against use of manufacturers' agents who had often proved unreliable. Some of the schemes for ventilation, in particular, were deemed "failures" and the YMCAs were stuck with stinky gyms.[26]

Even the decisions of Shattuck and Hussey and other specialists were suspect. They had much power to direct purchasing and seemed to benefit from a very close association with the Medusa Cement Company, whose advertisements pointed out that its products were used in every YMCA building designed by the firm.[27] An article in *Physical Training* urged athletic directors to go to the public library and find out about heating, ventilation, and lighting themselves. "Do not think because you have the best architect, the best contract, and your specifications call for the best, that your work has been done."[28] New gymnasium games, like basketball, required a different kind of artificial lighting than weightlifting, and electricians and architects were not yet familiar with the available fixtures. It was up to the local physical director to decide between arc lights and tungsten and to determine the proper

height and placement of lamps on the ceiling and under and above the running track. Some critics began to call for a department of building supervision, with files on materials and technical information available to help Y leaders master the new and complicated world of modern building.[29]

FIGURE 5.8. "X-Ray Lighting." Advertisement in *Association Men*, 1917.

Tientsin/Tianjin

Across the world, in Tientsin, now known as Tianjin, a very similar-looking building had just opened the year before. Also designed by Shattuck and Hussey, the rectangular four-story building, with a flat roof, stood out amid the lower, hipped-roof buildings of the neighborhood (Figure 5.9). Inside it included all the amenities of an American YMCA, including the signature oval running track around the upper level of the gymnasium, arranged in a plan used, re-used, and slightly adjusted by Shattuck and Hussey at dozens of sites (Figure 5.10). Comparison with the building plan of Galt, Ontario, makes this common heritage clear. In both cases two separate entrances served men and boys, while an efficiently placed reception desk commanded views of both (Figures 5.11 and 5.12). The prime distinction between the two is that in the Tientsin building boys' work was placed on the lower level, rather than on the ground floor as at Galt.

The first modern "Western"-style Y building had been built in the foremost industrial city in Northern China, a treaty port and major trade center.

FIGURE 5.9 (*top*). Tientsin, China, YMCA building.
FIGURE 5.10 (*bottom*). Gymnasium in the Tientsin, China, YMCA building.

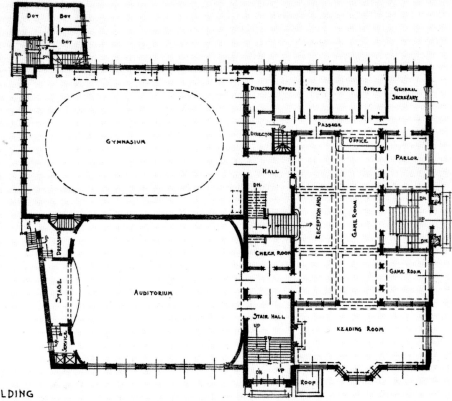

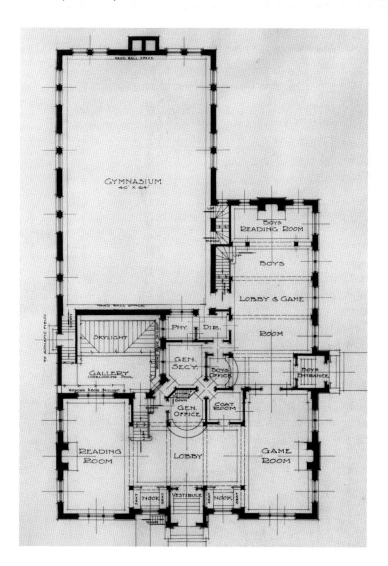

FIGURE 5.11 (*above*). First-floor plan, Tientsin, China, YMCA building, by Shattuck and Hussey, 1910.

FIGURE 5.12 (*left*). First-floor plan, Galt, Ontario, YMCA building, by Shattuck and Hussey, ca. 1905.

Home to just under a million people, Tientsin was connected by railway and telegraph to the rest of the country, and offered residents six government-sponsored schools.[30] Given the city's potential for growth and modern outlook, it is not surprising that the YMCA made its first landfall in China here, in 1895. Unlike Peking (now Beijing), mired in the past, Tientsin looked to the future.

Like many Western institutions, the original Tientsin Y was destroyed in the Boxer Rebellion, but the Association made a quick comeback. The program was in such good standing that in 1909 Sophia Strong Taylor, widow of Cleveland retailing giant John Livingstone Taylor, donated $50,000 for the construction of a new building. As was typical in its missionary work abroad, the YMCA required local Chinese to match the money.[31] It was the YMCA's first attempt to transplant one of its buildings to China, providing an experience that would shape the heavy building campaigns there in the 1910s and 1920s.

The International Committee had hired Shattuck and Hussey to help them build in China.[32] Hussey, something of an adventurer, established himself in Peking, traveled around the country to YMCA sites, and sent sketches back to Shattuck in Chicago. The drawings were then developed into full-fledged plans and returned to American representatives of the International Committee for construction. Unfortunately, concerns about Hussey's ethics and the adaptability of the plans to local conditions soon emerged. His billing practices seemed irregular, and the members of the International Committee were concerned about employing him as an independent contractor to handle the delicate political business of dealing with local and national authorities.[33] Most problematically, Shattuck and Hussey's plans and specifications, manufactured in their Chicago office, had to be extensively revised to suit field conditions, sometimes with the help of Poy Lee, a Chinese-born, American-trained architect who had recently returned to China to assist in YMCA construction (Figure 5.13).

Experience in the United States did not necessarily translate directly to the Chinese city. Shattuck and Hussey did not know, could not know without time and study, how to alter various features of a Y building to suit a different culture. How, for instance, did Chinese negotiate private space, bodily interaction, propriety, and class differences? What should the buildings look like? The Chinese were split over the issue of their own architectural heritage. Some wanted Western-style buildings, which represented progress, while others hoped for some indication of native culture in the building. The YMCA usually solved this dilemma by furnishing the interiors in the Chinese style, but avoiding the expensive and time-consuming timber roofs of historical Chinese architecture. More prosaically and practically, how should the building be heated? As YMCA officials learned over time, the standard air temperature in a gymnasium in the United States was 60 to 70 degrees, a locker room 70 to 75, and the bathroom 75 to 80. Chinese

FIGURE 5.13. Revising Shattuck and Hussey's plans in the Chinese YMCA Building Bureau, Shanghai.

expected bathrooms to be hotter, like their own bathhouses, at least 80 to 85 degrees. Chinese kept their outer clothing on indoors in winter, and therefore their offices only needed to be maintained to 60 degrees, but those for Americans required a minimum of 68 degrees.[34]

Modernizing Building Culture Abroad and at Home

By 1913 YMCA officials in China had rejected the specialist architects and had begun to lobby for a new kind of architectural system to produce foreign buildings. The local building culture, the architects, the contractors, the materials suppliers in China were not prepared to undertake many of the details required in a modern YMCA building. A detailed report and photographic albums compiled by engineer Arthur Q. Adamson reveal the difficulties and humor (often in bad taste) of cultural collaboration in the building process in the late 1910s and 1920s. Hired to superintend YMCA construction from an office in Shanghai, Adamson had ample firsthand knowledge of the difficulties.

At the beginning of the Chinese building boom there was a sharp divergence between local methods and Western building technology. Construction site photographs show that Chinese contractors and workmen used

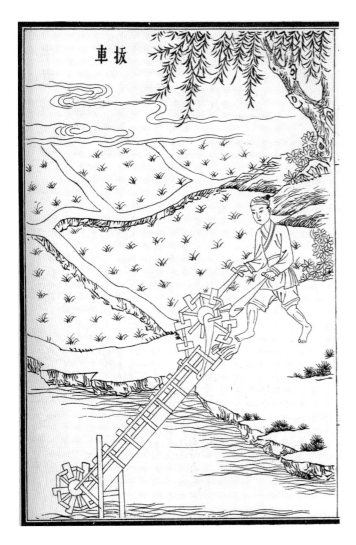

FIGURE 5.14. A manual square-pallet chain pump, illustrated in Joseph Needham, *Science and Civilization in China*, 1954.

old-fashioned frame saws, mallets, and traditional bamboo scaffolding.[35] Chinese workers carried materials in pairs of buckets slung over their shoulders, as they had for thousands of years. Water wheels were constructed to provide energy to lift brick and other materials to the roof, and, when required, filled out with old-fashioned, foot-powered pumps, used for the cultivation of rice. When the YMCA building site at Amoy was flooded in 1927, these irrigation wheels, powered by hand or by animal, were used to remove accumulated water from the foundation (Figure 5.14).[36]

Even if more modern tools and materials were available, the workmen had to be trained to use them. Chinese carpenters were praised by YMCA officials for their skills in mortise-and-tenon joinery, but they had little knowledge of other types of roofing, especially the flat truss roof favored in the American YMCA buildings of the day. In some cases, as in the 1925 Tsinanfu YMCA, reinforced concrete was used alongside Chinese-designed wooden trussed roofs. In more remote areas, Chinese workers took shelter on site in traditional wood-framed temporary sheds enclosed with mats, where they warmed native foods over braziers at lunchtime, for "chow," as YMCA officials called it. Y officials appeared to be simultaneously fascinated by the customs of the Chinese workers and dismissive of their abilities and work ethic.

Standing between the workers and Y officials like Adamson was the Chinese contractor. Photographs from the building scrapbooks show that the contractor was an important figure on the building site, conferring with YMCA officials and directing workers (Figure 5.15). Typically dressed in Western garb with shorn hair and a fedora hat, he occupied two worlds. He served as an intermediary, negotiating traditional relationships in the building trades, while acquiring new knowledge that would enable him to bid competitively for YMCAs and other Western buildings. One observer noted that because workmen had to follow plans they never completely understood, Chinese contracting was a risky business, and high bids were necessary to ensure a profit. Modern equipment, "such as concrete mixers, elevators, hoists, wood- and metal-working machinery, was unfamiliar to them, and they had too little knowledge about how to purchase building materials outside their local area."[37]

Some products, like terra-cotta, porcelain plumbing fixtures, and table-

FIGURE 5.15. Unidentified YMCA official and Chinese contractor at the Tsinanfu YMCA building site, 1924.

ware, were easily available and of good quality in China, but others, like electrical wiring and basic surveying instruments, often had to be imported from the United States. Until the Chinese steel supply increased in the 1920s, beams were provided by the Trussed Concrete Steel Company of the United States. Specialized devices for the gymnasium and pool were imported. One photograph of the filter system imported for the Foochow swimming pool in 1925 was documented quite specifically in the YMCA scrapbook of Chinese building construction (Figure 5.16). Importing raised problems with rates of exchange and with breakage during transit, especially of delicate materials such as plate glass.

Although the building culture was not quite so foreign or difficult in Greensboro, Y construction still required translation. In many smaller communities, the YMCA building challenged the organizational and technical expertise not only of the architects, but also of the local building trades. It was certainly true that Greensboro had both skilled and unskilled workmen, imported for large projects initiated by the textile mills. The city was also home to building material factories that turned the surrounding forests into tiles, shingles, and laths.[38] Nonetheless, the age of the general contractor had yet to arrive in Greensboro, and the YMCA's desire for efficiency, rationalization, and organization exceeded the skills of local builders and technicians. Lewis Martin, the general secretary, pleaded with the International Committee to provide a more concrete system of design assistance

FIGURE 5.16. Filters installed in the Foochow YMCA building, featured in "YMCA Building in China," a scrapbook compiled ca. 1919–24.

that would help local YMCAs negotiate the architectural process from fundraising to furnishing and maintenance.[39] They responded to his letter by printing it in *Association Men* for all to read, and acknowledging that the time had come for change.

The Birth of the Building Bureau

At the 1915 Convention the International Committee assigned responsibility for architectural services to a new department, the Building Bureau.[40] According to a 1917 flowchart of the International Committee's many administrative branches, building became a department, a bureaucratic enterprise on par with record-keeping and publishing (Figure 5.17). A subsidiary Chinese Building Bureau, under the supervision of the "home office," was set up soon afterward. Despite its existence in black and white, the form of the Building Bureau was far from set. Many questions remained about the operation of this new enterprise.[41] What kind of service should it provide and who should pay for it? What would be its relationship to the architectural profession? Although it was clear that specialist architects were not providing the right kind of service, experience showed that leaving the responsibility in the hands of general-practice architects was also unsatisfactory.

Fund-Raising: The Short-Term Building Campaign

It took some time to develop answers to these questions, but there was no doubt that the YMCA building policy was moving toward more complete systematization. The first step, already under way, was a system of fund-raising for building campaigns. This assistance was quite necessary, not only to finance the construction of new buildings, but also to retire crushing debt on many old ones. In the last two decades of the nineteenth century, many associations went into severe debt and even bankruptcy through haphazard fund-raising and overbuilding. Some even lost their buildings. To remedy this situation, a traveling field secretary, Charles Sumner Ward, instituted standard procedures, most notably the "short-term building campaign." Quite familiar today because of the telethons and the appeals of National Public Radio and the United Way, this method of raising funds was unknown at the time—an invention of the YMCA.[42]

Replacing the inefficient and labor-intensive process of individually soliciting wealthy donors, the short-term building campaign was a community-wide appeal dependent on mass psychology, not unlike a political campaign. Local newspapers were called upon to print supportive articles and editorial cartoons. In Denver, one artist reprised the old theme of the Pilgrim's Progress together with the composition of Thomas Cole's *The Cross and the World* in a drawing that paved a young man's path to a temple of "useful manhood" with donation checks to the YMCA (Figure 5.18).

Armed with lists of prospects, a special system of donation slips, and record-keeping equipment, their way prepared by advance publicity in local newspapers, competing teams of young men canvassed a city systematically, attempting to reach the stated goal within a given amount of time, usually a month. A large clock was placed in a prominent downtown location to keep the public abreast of progress toward the YMCA's

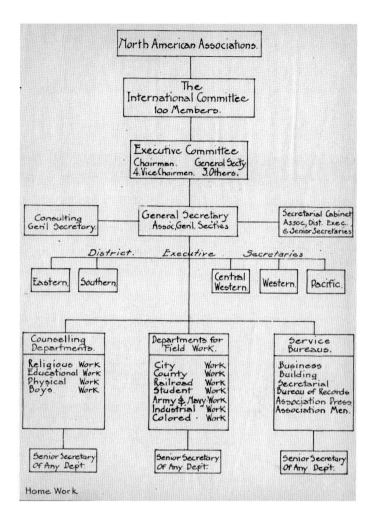

FIGURE 5.17 (*top*). YMCA International Committee organizational chart, 1915. FIGURE 5.18 (*bottom*). "Pave His Way." YMCA fund-raising cartoon, Denver, in *Association Men*, 1906.

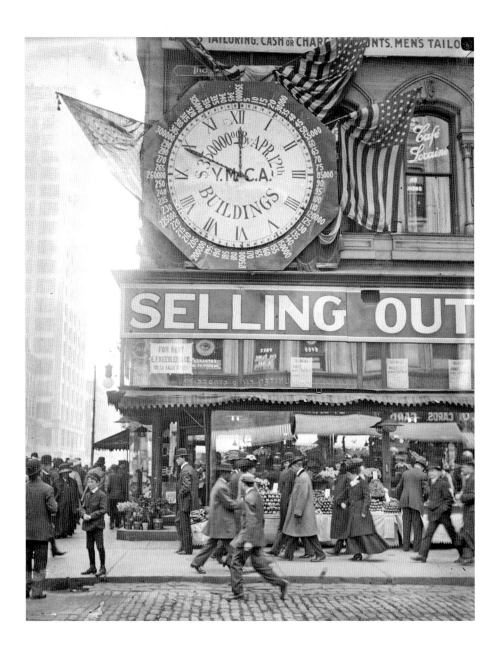

FIGURE 5.19. YMCA campaign clock at the corner of State and Madison, Chicago, 1908.

goal (Figure 5.19). The use of a clock as the marker and symbol emphasized the urgency and competitiveness of the campaign. One fund-raising brochure urged the citizens of Stockton, California, to "Keep Time with Other Cities."

This type of intense, occasional campaign freed Y staff members from the constant and overwhelming need to raise funds and assured the public that should they meet the goal, there would be no further need for them to contribute. Ward improved the existing methods of organization and publicity, establishing a new methodology, and making the short-term campaign a science. He traveled from place to place implementing this method, raising, for example, $800,000 in Toronto in eight days in 1910.[43]

The same techniques were used for fund-raising in Greensboro and China. Joseph Stone, the Greensboro campaign leader, enlisted many of the leading members of the elite into teams, who canvassed citizens in a timed

FIGURE 5.20. Campaign clock in Foochow, China, ca. 1915.

competition marked by a large clock on the courthouse square that tallied the results. Business came to a standstill during the event, where all joined in a celebration of civic spirit. Most residents were impressed by the efficiency of the effort and the persuasive words of the team members, who were well known for their ability to mobilize sentiment behind bond issues and large new projects.[44] In the local effort for a building in Foochow, China, the same idea was adapted, with a clock placed across the major path in and out of the city (Figure 5.20).

Architectural Services

While Ward handled the funds, a new employee, Neil McMillan, was hired to lead a new planning division (Figure 5.21).[45] Trained both as an architect and in the workings of the YMCA, McMillan came well prepared to take on this job. He received his architectural degree from the University of Illinois

FIGURE 5.21. Neil McMillan, director of the YMCA Building Bureau, ca. 1913.

in 1904, and worked for four years as a draftsman and superintendent of construction for the architect of the Chicago Board of Education.[46] Even while he was in architecture school, he showed interest in YMCA work, and after graduation he served the International Committee as secretary of the student and foreign departments. Part of that job included "the purchase in America of materials and equipment for use in the erection of foreign buildings."[47] There seemed to be no man better suited to the job of rationalizing an international building program.

McMillan's first step was to shape the agenda of the planning division. The International Committee had not specified how the Bureau should function, only that it should analyze the building problems confronting associations and adapt its service to assist them.[48] There was the precedent for offering such assistance in architectural planning in the part-time work of Erskine Uhl, who had served in the 1880s and 1890s as a resource through which the accumulated experience in building projects was made available to individual associations. He had collected and distributed plans of well-designed Y buildings and published a series of them in *Association Men,* identifying them as the best plans yet produced for a building of a particular size (Figure 5.22). The articles characterized specific buildings, like the Association building at Lansing, Michigan, as a generalized model that could be adapted for use in any city of a similar size, or by a committee with a particular budget. By 1915 the needs of the associations had grown more complicated, and the standard to which the buildings were constructed had become more demanding.

Buildings needed to be, first and foremost, efficient investments of the community's money in both planning *and* design. Dissatisfied with the ability of general-practice architects in the former and of specialist architects in the latter, McMillan was forced to devise a new system that would incorporate the practice of art in a managerial structure. His system evolved over five years in several intermediary steps that took the Building Bureau from a clearinghouse of technical information to a full-service in-house design firm, responsible for everything from developing the program to hanging the drapes.

The First Phase: Free Advisory Service

In the first six months of his tenure, McMillan collected information and conducted research. There were several different models for a practical or advisory architectural service for the YMCA to emulate. He had firsthand experience in school board design, which in the case of Chicago and other major cities placed responsibility for the construction of all school buildings upon a single salaried architect, who directed his own department.[49] Another model was offered by the British YMCA and the American YWCA,

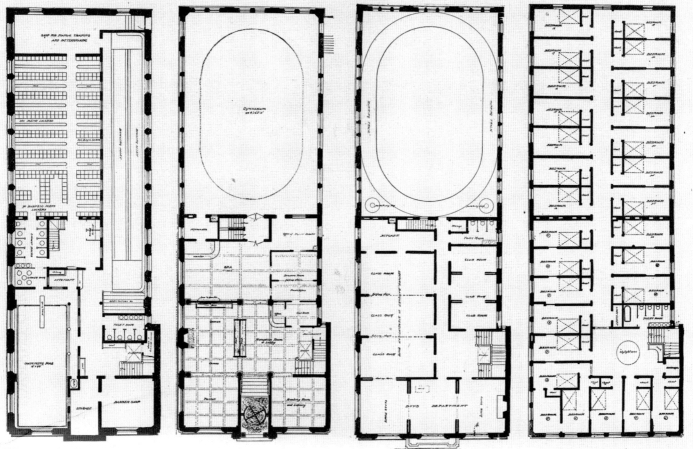

FIGURE 5.22. "The Best Plans Yet Produced for a $50,000 Building, Lansing, Michigan," by White & Hussey, in *Association Men,* 1906.

which retained "an expert [or panel of experts] on the plan, construction, equipment, and furnishing of Association buildings" to review the designs of general-practice architects.[50] Louis Jallade, representing the disgruntled specialist architects, preferred this model and suggested to McMillan that the Bureau "ought to act as a referee, awarding the Associations' architectural work by regions to three specialists."[51] Certain unnamed business leaders lobbied for a complete architectural service that would satisfy all aspects of a building committee's requirements. This vertical integration, a hallmark of modern industrial practice, would give the YMCA coordinated control of all aspects of building.

Faced with all these possibilities, McMillan's first step was modest: a free advisory service that would supplement the work of general-practice architects. Perhaps because of his architectural training, he moved very cautiously into the domain of the architect, assuming only the role of technical advisor. The purview of the Bureau at this stage was limited to counseling local officials on the programmatic and financial aspects of the building process and critically studying the sketches of the architects. This conservative review process represented a firm rejection of a complete design service. Instead, it represented a consolidation of knowledge that had already been gathered.

Early Advice

To begin this advisory experience, McMillan culled through back issues of the International Committee's journal, *Association Men,* which had started in 1899 and served as a regular forum for the discussion of architectural problems. In its pages A. J. Villee of Waycross, Georgia, presented the results of a survey he had conducted on dormitories, with statistics on fees charged, income provided, and comparative information on maintenance and administration.[52] Other contributions addressed a range of planning issues, such as maintenance techniques.[53] On the subject of designing and equipping the building for physical education, the magazine *Physical Training* featured articles on artificial light, equipment, and construction.[54]

McMillan surely also took note of articles published in professional architectural journals, especially *The Brickbuilder.* The first article on YMCA buildings appeared in December 1905, written by Walter M. Wood, then the superintendent of education at the Chicago YMCA.[55] He provided an explanation of the history of the YMCA building and its role in the institution's program, outlined in a general way the different features of the Association building, and defined the most important principles: accessibility, attractiveness, economy, adaptability to both day and night use, possibility of enlargement, composite unity, flexibility of arrangement, minimum internal traffic, ease of control by minimum force, and the arrangement of features to maximize their self-advertising value. Special hints were included on lighting, plumbing, ventilation, gymnasium equipment, and the special needs for storage and toilet facilities. Two architects also contributed articles to *Brickbuilder,* offering readers an architect's viewpoint. Irving K. Pond, responsible along with his brother Allen for the YMCA buildings in Ann Arbor, Michigan, Oak Park, Illinois, and Lake Geneva, Wisconsin, wrote a three-part series in 1906 providing detailed discussion of the issues raised by Wood.[56]

Another source of information was the reports of various conventions and meetings. At the Thirty-seventh Annual Convention in Toronto (1910), A. G. Studer of Detroit presented a paper on "Large Modern Buildings," outlining the increasingly standardized features of a YMCA.[57] At the Fourth Conference of the Metropolitan General Secretaries, Walter Wood presented a paper titled "Types of Buildings Best Suited to Metropolitan Associations."[58] Papers were supplemented by displays, such as the one constructed at the Jubilee Convention in 1901 (see Figure 3.8). In the same year a committee of local secretaries arranged a conference on building matters in Buffalo, an event attended by representatives from forty-seven associations. This conference considered many topics, including the timing and method of a build-

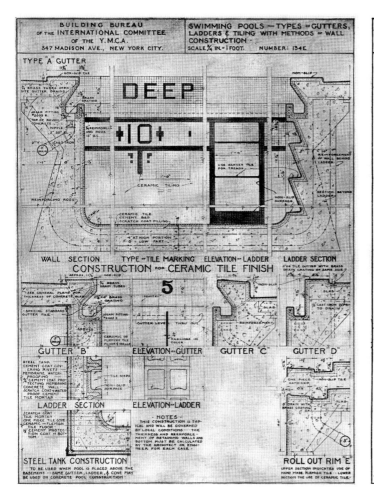 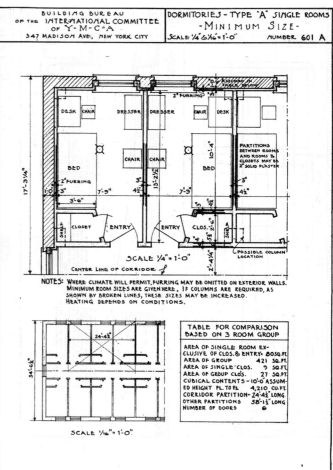

FIGURE 5.23. YMCA Building Bureau standards for swimming pools and dormitory rooms.

ing campaign, how to secure desirable building plans (designated architect, limited competition, or open competition), conducting an architectural competition, supervision of construction, and the evaluation of building plans.

Equipped with this historical information, McMillan and a new employee, R. L. Rayburn, set out to take the current pulse of building activity. During the construction hiatus enforced by wartime restrictions, they traveled to meet building committees and listened to their problems, offered summer training sessions, and held special conferences on YMCA buildings.[59] McMillian analyzed "data" from existing buildings (including photographs, sketches, and specifications) and considered the comparative merits of different sorts of materials and maintenance procedures. After these research trips, he compiled the information, producing drawings for the parts of buildings that could be standardized, including a diagram of pool wall construction with details on gutters, ladders, and tiling. Another Building Bureau plan offered a flexible but ideal layout for minimum-size dormitory rooms, including the placement of the furniture in relation to each other and the windows, and the type of material to be used for partitions (Figure 5.23).

This diagrammatic work seems to have been inspired by collaboration or discussion with Frederick Ackerman, who had designed the Brooklyn Big Y just three years earlier and was busy building war-worker housing for the government. Ackerman later went on to inspire and sponsor the research for *Architectural Graphic Standards* (1932), the first factual reference book for designers. It was in his office that the authors, Charles Ramsay and Harold Sleeper, developed abstract, schematic representations of common architectural problems, everything from the desirable height of doorways to the measurements for an efficient office.[60] This technocratic approach was well suited for McMillan and the Building Bureau's need for an efficient way to design standardized buildings. The Bureau's expertise was not restricted to graphic standards, but was also applied to studies on facility use and the production of checklists for the examination of plans.

The provision of diagrams and checklists, though valuable, was not enough to ensure a successful building. McMillan soon began to recognize the limitations of this free service. The system did not provide enough control or oversight of the process. After eighteen months and much study, McMillan replaced the advisory service with a more efficient, business-like method of producing buildings.

Second Phase: Paid Advisory Service

In late 1917 McMillan's Building Bureau instituted a new system in support of the building projects of seven local associations, offering them a more ambitious service program that ventured further into the architect's territory.[61] Now charging a fee proportional to the size of the building fund, the Bureau not only advised local associations on program and finances and checked the sketches, but actively educated the architect on the special technical aspects of preparing working drawings and specifications for a YMCA. Bureau staff even supervised construction to ensure the quality of the building. Unfortunately, heavy demands on the building material market and high war prices kept construction activity to a minimum and restricted opportunities to test the new system, but a few associations, notably that in Pittsburgh, hired the Bureau to plan a building to be erected after the war.[62]

The work that the Bureau was able to do convinced McMillan to reassess the efficiency of his system again. Although an improvement over the free advisory service, the paid advisory service did not give the YMCA Building Bureau enough control over the building process. Local architects did not fully comprehend the special requirements of a YMCA building and still tended to sacrifice function for effect, despite efforts to educate them. As McMillan later recalled, "As a result it not infrequently happened that the Bureau had to make the sketch plans in order to safeguard the Association's interests."[63] If a specialist architect—with previous YMCA experience—were engaged, the buildings were functional but lacking in stylistic sophistication. Moreover, the specialist architects, many of whom had been building YMCAs for twenty years, understandably resented the advice of the newly formed Bureau.

Third Phase: Complete Service

Faced with these problems, McMillan once more revamped the Building Bureau to provide a more vertically integrated, full-design system. In 1919 the staff was expanded and two additional buildings secretaries, Sherman W. Dean and Albert M. Allen, were added to the payroll. With the assistance of these and other technical specialists in engineering, mechanical systems, building management, and business administration, the Building Bureau was now comparable to an architectural firm and capable of handling all of its functions. In 1920 McMillan unveiled the final stage of the YMCA's building system: a new collaborative arrangement that severely reduced the supervisory role of the outside architect, replacing him with engineers and efficiency experts. In the interwar period the Bureau no longer played an advisory role, but was in control of the building process. It was not only the possessor of information, but the shaper of building policy.[64]

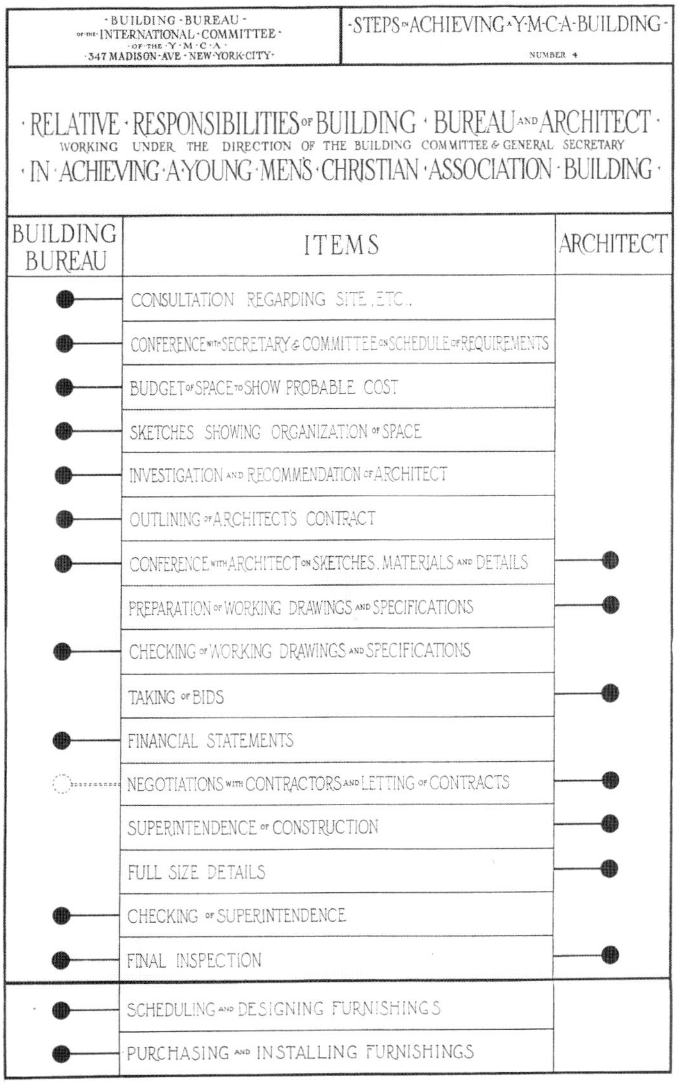

McMillan developed a helpful chart to explain the procedures of the Bureau to clients and architects. It diagrammatically presented the division of responsibility between the Bureau and the local architect. The selection of site, recommendations as to the selection of an architect, and preparation of the architect's contract, the program, budget, specifications, and preliminary plans—even the design of the interiors—were the responsibility of the Bureau (Figure 5.24). The designer was responsible for producing working drawings, handling on-site construction supervision, and clothing the efficient shell in beautiful architectural dress.

FIGURE 5.24. "Steps to Achieving a YMCA Building," YMCA Building Bureau, ca. 1917.

For its work, the Building Bureau took 2 percent of the building's cost, while the architect's standard 6 percent fee, just established by the American Institute of Architects, was reduced to 4 percent. The retention of the independent general-practice architect in the process helped the Bureau adapt its standardized national system to the needs of the local community. It also improved the quality of architectural design and allowed the local YMCA to benefit from the positive publicity of hiring a hometown professional with a knowledge of local weather conditions, materials markets, labor considerations, and costs.[65]

Under this new system, interior decoration was, for the first time, included as a technical service provided by experts at a cousin of the Building Bureau, the Furnishings Service, founded in 1920. This advice was added because noted concerns about the atmosphere in YMCA buildings had been one of the major catalysts for the formation of the Building Bureau. This was not a purely aesthetic concern, but a product of the competitive environment. As one official noted:

> In many cases, the organization was losing out in competition with amusement places, hotels, clubs, and other similar organizations attracting young men because it had failed to provide an environment which appealed to their sense of good taste.[66]

The guiding principle of efficiency had for too long been focused exclusively on the planning process, and the results were clear: buildings that looked and felt too much like factories or tenements.

Even more than the Building Bureau, this new service, under the direction of LaMont A. Warner, former assistant professor of fine arts at the School of Interior Decoration at Columbia University, submitted the artistic arrangement of interiors to the discipline of scientific management.[67] Once the province of volunteer ladies, the decoration of YMCA interiors became a professional and masculine endeavor. This appropriation was possible because the field of interior decoration was less organized than the architectural profession. In 1920 no national body supervised the training or professional practices of decorators, and the design responsibility for interiors varied from commission to commission. Architects and decorators were often brought into conflict. Architects complained that the majority of decorators were not professionals providing a service, but salesmen promoting their own wares at inflated prices.[68] This complicated situation was confusing to building committees, and the potential for inefficiency was great.

FIGURE 5.25. Game table design, YMCA Furnishings Service.

Leaving nothing to chance, the Furnishings Service handled all elements of the process: "the designing of furniture, floor coverings, color schemes and lighting fixtures, and the purchase and installation of the various items, where desired, in such a way as to secure the advantages of quantity buying."[69] Surviving drawings suggest that they designed utilitarian furniture, such as a chess table (Figure 5.25), as well as more elaborate and decorative work such as an "Early English Settee," intended for mass production. For an additional 1.5 percent of the building's cost, the Furnishings Section of the Bureau would provide a trustworthy design and purchase service and ensure coordination with the architect. This would take care of all the difficult decorating decisions, transforming the YMCA from spare simplicity to a comfortable, attractive masculinity—at the right price.[70] The complete design service offered by the Building Bureau in 1920—with its checklists, data tables, and color charts, talented architect and technical specialists—at last put architecture on the same scientific footing as the rest of the Association. Through it this system of architectural practice was rationalized, centralized, and stripped of its unpredictable, individualistic, and potentially inefficient artistic qualities.

The YMCA Building Bureau was a great success, widely used during the building boom of the interwar years by local associations who valued its expertise. Fred Shipp, the general secretary of the Pittsburgh Association, wrote Neil McMillan in March 1919 to praise the new Bureau. Its services justified the expenditure:

> Already we are convinced that the Bureau has saved the Pittsburg [sic] Association many thousands of dollars in construction costs and your layout of floor arrangements and other features are giving us buildings which can be operated at a minimum cost with a maximum of service. We are convinced that not only are we saving the cost of the Bureau's service to us many times over in . . . construction costs, but this service will, in all probability, effect for us an annual saving of operation charges equivalent to the total amount we are paying the Bureau.[71]

Other local associations seemed to agree that buildings supervised by the Building Bureau were more successful, both aesthetically and financially. During the prosperous 1920s, when building funds overflowed, locals overwhelmingly turned to the Building Bureau to handle their new construction. A 1925 Building Bureau report noted that in the previous ten years, seventy-two buildings had been completed under its direction and ninety-three buildings were under way. The work was so successful that within five years nearly 90 percent of the associations initiating building were using the Bureau's services; the staff increased from four to eighteen employees; and a branch office was opened in Chicago.[72]

Aesthetics and the Building Bureau

Because buildings defined how and what services an association could offer to its community, the introduction of the YMCA Building Bureau had a strong impact on both the structure of the organization and its philosophy. By the early 1920s the Building Bureau had become an established element of the YMCA and an important link between local associations and the International Committee. The Bureau helped translate policy changes made in New York into daily practice from Main Street to Shanghai. In addition to acting as a conduit of information, the Bureau also influenced both the local and national conception of the YMCA building. Under its tutelage, the modern YMCA building, long perceived in the organization primarily as a piece of equipment and an apparatus for supervision, became "Architecture," with the power to ennoble the character of young men through exposure to art.

This aestheticizing of the YMCA building was a notable change in institutional culture. Before World War I, the City Beautiful inspired the YMCA to erect buildings they could be proud of—buildings that would give the organization a good name. Yet these structures continued to be viewed as tools rather than works of art. Although "environmental evangelism" continued to motivate the YMCA's building policy, more emphasis was placed on cheap, efficient plans than on aesthetics as a means of suasion. Some even believed that modest furnishings were an important aspect of young men's socialization.

The name-brand architecture and luxurious furnishings that characterized the early, experimental Association buildings by James Renwick Jr. (1869), Addison Hutton (1876), and later, well-equipped big-city clubhouses in Boston (1884), Chicago (1893), and Philadelphia (1911), by Sturgis and Brigham, William Le Baron Jenney, and Horace Trumbauer, respectively, were considered by some to be an inefficient waste of money, something that might communicate the wrong message to young men and the general public. An editorial in *Association Men* in 1911 related the opinion of one architect on the impropriety of providing young men with elaborately furnished buildings:

> [He] declared that the result of furnishing such elegant equipment in dormitory and restaurant at astounding prices "would have the effect of cultivating criminal instincts in young men. It would give men, in the language of George Ade, with a coffee and sinker income a terrapin appetite." While I feel very strongly that the building should be the most attractive in town, it is not our function to equal and excel the equipment of the social clubs of our wealthy men.[73]

This attitude reflects the ongoing debate within the YMCA, dating from the original New York building of 1869, about the propriety of elaborate buildings. Although styles may have changed, the fundamental conception of design remained the same: a medium for construction and communication of identity and class within the hierarchical structure of corporate culture.

With a few exceptions in large cities, the typical YMCA building of the prewar period was a "manhood factory" with a stripped exterior and aseptic interior, designed to grind out young men of character efficiently. Behavior was regulated through the self-monitoring panoptic plan, and, since that method was evidently not sufficient, by posted signs that spelled out pro-

FIGURE 5.26. Sign reads "Self-Respect, Self-Reliance, Self-Control," Lexington, Kentucky, YMCA postcard.

hibitions like "No Profanity," "Please Take Off Your Hat," "Don't Spit on the Floor," and "Have You Written to Mother?"[74] In Lexington, Kentucky, the signage took a more positive tone, reminding men of "self-respect, self-reliance, self-control" (Figure 5.26).

In the 1920s the Building Bureau replaced this mechanical, rather negative, environmental approach with a policy shaped by a belief in the value of art and individualism in the molding of young men. This change was inspired by post–World War I disillusionment in technology, advances in educational psychology, and an increasing interest in aesthetics and interior decoration. Faced with the destruction wrought by technology and efficiency in the Great War, the YMCA reconsidered its mechanical methods of mass-producing young men. At the outbreak of war in Europe one Y leader commented that "In view of the collapse of civilization in some portions of the world which had come to be highly regarded because of their so-called

... efficiency standards, we are compelled to seek a different objective in manhood building."[75] After the war a 1926 editorial in *Association Men* reiterated this idea:

> We become mechanical in our business and our play, in our art, our philosophy, and even in our religion. Many of us get to the point where we regard the smooth and effective doing of things to be more important than what is actually done to the persons involved. Efficiency tends to take precedence over humanity.[76]

The editorial questioned the application of mechanical models to the social sphere of home, school, church, and community and urged the Y to champion the personal against the mechanical view of human life. Greater attention to the individual, it argued, although less easily measured than the results of scientific management, would produce long-term benefits.

With the focus now on the individual, the Building Bureau began to develop the idea that a building could improve men's character less mechanically, through the subtle influence of what it called "cultural atmosphere."[77] R. L. Rayburn, Bureau staff member, rhapsodized that

> Just as with music any of the human impulses and emotions may be created or stimulated, so by use of line, form, and color the Association conceives that it may establish an atmosphere that will tend to stimulate the noblest impulses and emotions and be an impetus to right living, clean thinking, and the highest aspirations in life.[78]

This theory of artistic suasion was strongly influenced by recent developments in educational philosophy. John Dewey, William James, George A. Coe, and others at Teachers College, Columbia University, were proposing that individuals learned through habitual experience, specifically through stimuli within their environment. As Dewey said, "All conduct is interaction between the elements of human nature and the environment, natural and social."[79] This idea was, of course, not new to the YMCA, which had been proceeding upon this principle since 1869. What differed in Dewey's approach was the notion that character could be more easily trained by the positive voluntary responses of individuals to their proper surroundings than by direct attempts to control behavior.

The work of Dewey and others had been studied at the YMCA Training School in Springfield, Massachusetts, since the turn of the century, but this body of literature did not trickle down to the local associations until after World War I, when it was integrated as a dominant educational philosophy into programs for the schoolboys under the YMCA's care.[80] The Building Bureau picked up on this new philosophy, overhauling the Victorian concept of environmental evangelism to reflect the advances of the modern age.[81] Echoing the conclusions of educational psychologists, Dean, an employee of the Building Bureau, noted the change in the YMCA goals: "In the belief that the only type of conduct which will have lasting results is that which is voluntary, the Association is turning from prohibitory mandate to the silent, subtle preachment of atmosphere, surroundings, and example."[82] In a beautifully designed building, the Bureau argued, it would not be necessary to tell young men to take off their hats; they would do so subconsciously, responding to the quality of their surroundings. Here at last, under the professionals at the Building Bureau, the YMCA drew an explicit, direct connection between architecture and behavior, giving "scientific study to the influence of environment and atmosphere on character development."[83]

This design-conscious attitude extended beyond the construction of new buildings. Older associations were urged to redecorate and maintain their buildings in order to provide the right kind of stimulus to members. One article stressed that "an attractive well-cared for building makes the development of Christian character an easier task." Dirt and disorder, it was suggested, provided an unwholesome influence.[84]

A Case Study: The West Side YMCA, New York

The changes instituted by the Building Bureau in the 1920s, both in the procedures for design and construction and in the appearance of YMCA buildings, are exemplified in the story of the construction of the West Side YMCA in New York City of 1930, one of the last buildings constructed before the Depression stunted YMCA building activity. Designed by Dwight James Baum, the West Side Y offers a fairly typical and particularly well-documented instance of the priorities and methods of the Building Bureau in this period.

The decision to erect a new building was easy. The old one, finished in 1896, was no longer adequate to serve the needs of the men of New York. A city-wide survey, taken in 1926, justified this decision statistically, and paved the way for a massive expansion and building program for Manhattan. In October 1926 the Executive Board of the Board of Managers of the YMCA of New York engaged E. L. Mogge of the Financial Services Bureau to run the fund-raising campaign, to take place in December. A new site, on West Sixty-third Street, just off Central Park and Columbus Circle, was purchased.[85] To assist in the fund-raising, the Building Committee contracted with the Building Bureau, recently and significantly renamed the Architectural Bureau, for some preliminary work that would include space budgets and cost estimates. Faced with a huge building campaign that included not only the West Side YMCA but also a new building for Army and Navy men, the board decided, on the basis of the sketches, to engage the Bureau to take care of the whole job, paying them 2.5 percent of the cost of building.

From the moment that the Bureau became involved, the process proceeded according to a strict schedule, with dates assigned to all the steps in their standard checklist.[86] The first stage was drafting a clear program.

This ran over thirty pages, accompanied by sketch plans demonstrating how space would be apportioned.[87] The next step was the selection of the architect. Forty different firms had either requested to be considered or been recommended, representing both the cream of the architectural profession in New York and YMCA specialists. The list included Grosvenor Atterbury, Delano & Aldrich, Arthur Loomis Harmon, Aymar Embury II, Ernest Flagg, Bertram Grosvenor Goodhue Associates, John Russell Pope, George B. Post & Sons, James Gamble Rogers, York and Sawyer, and YMCA specialists Louis Jallade, John F. Jackson, Lucian E. Smith and Harry E. Warren, May and Hillard, and Hohauser and Kuchler.[88]

It was the Architectural Bureau's job to research the experience and reputation of each possibility and select the appropriate architect for the specific job. Neil McMillan laid out the criteria to the Building Committee:

1. Adequate organization to handle the work of a magnitude of either of these buildings.
2. Ability to secure pleasing effects at a reasonable cost.
3. Adaptability to work with others.
4. Facility in design to express the distinctive purpose of the Association under the difficult conditions of an inside city lot.[89]

The list was slowly whittled down, attended by strict confidentiality among the committee members. First dismissed were the old-time YMCA specialists. Some of the Building Committee members, who had worked with the specialist architects before, wondered why they were not being considered. It soon became clear, however, that McMillan was interested in hiring an architect known for his artistic skill rather than an experienced YMCA planner. Surprisingly, Ernest Flagg, whose experience in reform architecture and artistic skill should have made him the perfect choice, was among those dismissed.

The final list of possibilities, all nationally celebrated, was presented to the committee on November 21, 1927: Dwight James Baum; Delano & Aldrich; Arthur Loomis Harmon; Helmle & Corbett; Mayers, Murray & Phillip (Bertram Grosvenor Goodhue's successor firm); John Russell Pope; James Gamble Rogers; and York and Sawyer. Each member of the committee was presented with a packet of information on each candidate, including photographs and plans of earlier works. By December 16, McMillan, representing the Architectural Bureau, had selected Dwight James Baum, who had just designed two YMCA buildings in Florida. Despite this experience, he was a rather strange choice, as neither of these buildings was finished and most of his other work consisted of lavish residences in Riverdale. There was little direct proof that he could handle the complex process of building a skyscraper in New York.

A small delegation of Building Committee members visited his office and some of his residential commissions. They concluded that his work showed originality in design and interior treatment but that this hardly qualified him for the commission. Despite their misgivings, they decided to go with the choice of the Architectural Bureau, placing great faith in its judgment. Walter Wyckoff, real-estate and insurance executive and a member of the committee, concluded that "if the Architectural Bureau is prepared to supplement the work of Mr. Baum where his lack of experience in this class of construction may require assistance and supervision, I should be willing to approve his selection."[90] Having hired the Bureau to superintend the job, the members of the Building Committee committed to a primary relationship and responsibility with it, rather than with the architect. This was, after all, the function of the Bureau, to serve as an advisor, an intermediary between the YMCA and the complex technical and artistic world of the architect. The selection of Baum as the top choice over firms that had experience building skyscrapers and similar buildings was an example of the power of the Bureau to influence local associations. So, despite his inexperience, Baum was appointed on December 23, 1927.

Baum and the Bureau worked in tandem, the Bureau providing the interior sketch plans based on the program, and Baum producing working drawings and the artistic conception of the building. Rather than using the Spanish Colonial style of his YMCA building in Orlando, Florida, for Manhattan, he chose an elegant mixture of twelfth-century North Italian Gothic and Romanesque, a style dubbed "Italianesque" by *New Yorker* architecture critic George S. Chappell (Figure 5.27).[91] Baum's explanation of his choice of style indicated a concern with exterior aesthetics unknown to the YMCA specialist architects.[92] He included details from old palace and cathedral doorways, rendered in pastel terra-cotta–framed entrances (Figure 5.28). In addition to the possibilities in detail and color, the brickwork of this northern Italian style allowed for great variety in pattern and texture. This building's massing was a distinct departure from the earlier efficient box-like YMCA buildings. Setback laws dictated a central service tower surrounded by irregular masses at different levels, which allowed for better-lit bedrooms

FIGURE 5.27. Fundraising brochure, West Side YMCA Building, West Sixty-third Street, by Dwight James Baum, New York, 1927.

FIGURE 5.28. Entrance to the West Side YMCA, by Dwight James Baum, in *Architectural Forum* 53 (August 1930).

in the dormitories, while also masking the size of the building.

In his choice of style and design for the YMCA, Baum was surely influenced by contemporary hotel design in New York City. Like the YMCA, entrepreneurs recognized the need for a sociable, homelike environment for single people and constructed towers for this purpose. The YMCA, which had included Arthur Loomis Harmon, the architect of the extremely influential Shelton Hotel (1924), on its short list, was clearly interested in emulating the design of these structures. The Shelton, an upscale bachelor hotel and a poetic expression of the new setback laws in the "Italianesque" style, had been enthusiastically received by the architectural world. It inspired the design of several other hotels, including Murgatroyd and Ogden's Barbizon Hotel (1927), for women only, and the Beverly Hotel, by Emery Roth and Sylvan Bien (1927).[93] Baum drew upon this tradition for the YMCA. Inside the building Baum also coordinated his design with the recommendations of the Furnishings Service, in a Mediterranean style with tiled floors, stucco walls, leather, brass, and beautifully painted stenciled beamed ceilings, so fashionable in contemporary hotel design (Figure 5.29).[94] With its elaborate facilities, including two restaurants, two tiled swimming pools, and beautifully furnished lounges, the new building was hardly distinguishable from a hotel of the period.

The West Side YMCA was an example of a successful division of technical and artistic activity. The elevations bear Baum's name, the floor plans the insignia of the Architectural Bureau, with its clear division of men's and boys' spaces, accessed by separate entrances and monitored by common offices and counters. It contained all the latest features of YMCA architecture, including a men's spa and refreshment counter, and five themed boys' playrooms, including the log cabin, ship's cabin, and attic room (Figure 5.30). Most notable is the absence of the large open lobby that defined Y buildings like Brooklyn's Big Y fifteen years earlier. The "social room," as it was called, became its own space rather than a distributing point, and the rest of the smaller and highly specialized rooms on the first floor are connected by long narrow hallways that are suited to the site, which stretches between Sixty-third and Sixty-fourth streets. The interior decoration has the unmistakable stamp of the Furnishings Service. The arrangements and furnishings were virtually identical to the interiors it designed at the YMCAs in Harrisburg, Pennsylvania; Little Rock, Arkansas; and San Pedro, California (Figure 5.31).

Reaction from the Architectural Profession

Despite the successful collaboration between Baum and the Bureau, the number of other prominent architects who had indicated their willingness to work with the Bureau on the West Side New York YMCA, and the increased coverage of YMCA commissions in mainstream architectural journals, the

FIGURE 5.29. Lobby of the West Side YMCA.

FIGURE 5.30. Plan for the first floor of the West Side YMCA, 1927.

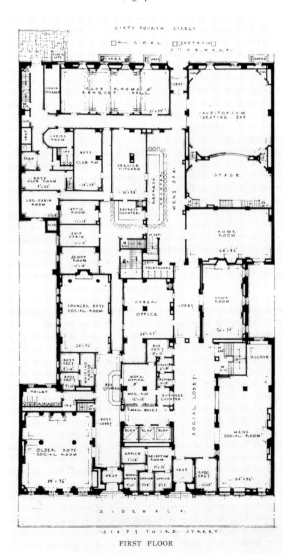

FIGURE 5.31. Lobby of the Little Rock YMCA building, 524 South Broadway, Little Rock, Arkansas, 1928.

response of the architectural profession to the Bureau's service was not uniformly positive. The Bureau had initially anticipated some resistance, and it published a series of defensive articles in March and April 1919 in the *Architectural Record*.[95] This widely circulated trade journal was an appropriate forum to explain the new procedures for YMCA commissions. Anticipating a great increase in construction, the articles appealed to the architectural community to work with the Bureau to create better buildings. "The Bureau . . . places before the architects of this country the opportunity to take part in one of the most important single classes of building in the constructive period that lies ahead."[96]

Realizing that architects might not accept the Bureau's authority, about half of one article was devoted to soothing their fears:

> At the outset it should be made clear that what the Building Bureau is anxious not to do is to usurp the architect's prerogatives or to destroy his initiative. It desires rather to provide a co-operating source of ac-

cumulated and authoritative knowledge, upon which the architect can draw to his own immediate benefit, and ultimately, to that of the organization and its membership.[97]

Another Y official argued that the YMCA Building Bureau was not like other architectural bureaus—for example, those of churches—applying a single formula over and over again, but offered "a method by which a first-class architect could produce a first-class YMCA building in cooperation with the Bureau, even though he had not had previous Association experience."[98] Most important, it was staffed by architectural and engineering professionals.

Despite these soothing explanations, the large number of commissions available to architects, and the fact that several prominent members of the American Institute of Architects (AIA) had indicated a willingness to work with the Building Bureau, by the mid 1920s problems arose with the AIA.[99] Its directors viewed the Bureau as part of a disturbing trend. In addition to the YMCA, local school boards and church denominations, as well as the federal and state governments, were solving their architectural problems without hiring conventional architects. The AIA did not look kindly on these groups, especially the YMCA Building Bureau, which not only insisted on the cooperation of the architect, but took part of his fees as well.[100]

The AIA, which had been founded along the lines of a gentlemen's club in the 1850s, had transformed itself in the twentieth century into a representative of large, business-oriented architectural practices. It published its first Standards of Professional Practice in 1909, which included licensing, a code of conduct, and suggested model contracts.[101] One of its primary goals was to protect the primacy of the architect's role in a time of flux. Although it now seems obvious that the architect should superintend the process of building, at the time organizations like the YMCA Building Bureau, and similar bureaus organized by religious denominations, the Girl Scouts, and other social service groups, posed a threat to this arrangement. The AIA preferred that the YMCA continue to distribute information about its buildings and allow general practitioners to interpret the program on a case-by-case basis.

In 1928 two incidents highlighted the tension between the YMCA and the AIA. The Pittsburgh chapter of the AIA passed a resolution calling on the YMCA to limit the role of the Bureau to the advisory level and place responsibility for design solely in the hands of an architect in general practice. Similarly, the Philadelphia chapter, led by Paul Cret and Edmund Gilchrist, refused to sanction the competition for the Wilmington, Delaware, YMCA because it only called for an elevation, because the architect's fees were curtailed, and because the final responsibility for the success of the building would not rest with the architect.[102]

These disputes were referred to the national leadership of the AIA in

Washington, which considered various resolutions against working for the YMCA under these conditions.[103] Responding to these attacks, a special committee was formed by the National Council of the YMCA in June 1928, and met several times over the following months at the Yale Club in New York. Composed of general YMCA officials, employees of the Building Bureau, and two architects familiar with YMCA projects, it attempted to assess the problem and come up with a solution.[104]

After Neil McMillan exchanged ideas with several AIA officials, including president Louis La Beaume, he identified two basic problems: the YMCA's split fee structure and the restrictions placed upon the architect's role in design. It was immediately apparent that the fees were the real concern. Several AIA members did question the issue of divided responsibility under the YMCA's system, but the solution to that problem seemed to lie in reducing or eliminating the fee paid to the Bureau. After struggling to establish a standard, nationwide architectural fee of 6 percent, AIA members found the Building Bureau's claim to a share of that payment outrageous. They did not accept that any "expert" other than themselves deserved compensation. If the YMCA felt the necessity to charge for its services, it should be in addition to the architect's 6 percent.[105]

The Building Bureau's response to these complaints seems tinged with a genuine lack of understanding of the issues at hand. McMillan, himself an architect, saw the Bureau as supplementary to the architect, technicians in a single design system necessitated by the peculiar requirements of the YMCA building. His report to the special committee pointed out that with their help, the architect saved time and effort—and thus money:

> He does not have to sell himself or his service to his client through extensive cultivation as is the case in most private work. He is saved the cost of a lot of sketches he normally would have to make to aid the client in making up his mind, and is further saved a mass of research because of the data the Bureau supplies.[106]

Accordingly, McMillan felt the Building Bureau had a right to be compensated for its services. He also did not understand why the AIA was not grateful to the Bureau for improving the quality of YMCA architecture and making "it possible to distribute the commissions for designing more than $8 million worth of Association buildings annually among the ablest architects in the localities instead of having it in the hands of a very small group of specialists."[107] Moreover, the Bureau could have provided a full design service, bypassing the architectural profession altogether. What McMillan did not seem to see was that the planning service demoted the architectural profession from leadership to partnership, and, naturally, the AIA also had difficulty accepting the financial demands of this interloper. Faced with a boycott against the Bureau by local chapters of the AIA, McMillan agreed to reduce its own fees to 1.5 percent for the planning service, and half a percent for the furnishing service. This seemed to satisfy the AIA, and there is no further record of dispute in the AIA's files.

Very soon neither architects nor the Bureau had as much to argue about. The Depression changed the focus of the Bureau's building activity from new construction to alterations. Even in this time of crisis, the YMCA building remained central to the organization's mission. This building-centered attitude, born in the 1860s, came to full maturation in the 1920s, when dozens of new buildings were constructed each year.

Perhaps more than any other architectural patron of the modern period, the YMCA responded systematically to the social imperatives and industrial models of the age. Devoted to the use of buildings as tools of persuasion and acculturation, the Y sought to construct them on a mass scale suited to a mass culture using the most modern sophisticated techniques of advertising, fund-raising, and design. In the first years of the twentieth century the American architectural profession had not yet responded to the imperatives of industrialization, forcing the YMCA to devise its own system of construction based on the principles of scientific management.

Unlike European modernists who sought to marry the artistic and the functional, initially the YMCA strictly separated them. The products of this business-like system of architecture were failures, neither wholly efficient nor sufficiently attractive. The Building Bureau was created to respond to that problem, devising a system that encompassed art and business with a strict division of labor, and that ensured artistic quality and efficiency. Assisted by some of the most prominent members of the architectural community, the Bureau made an important contribution to a practical American tradition in which style was not the catalyst, but a side issue in the definition of "modern" architecture.

YOVNG·WOMEN'S·HEBREW·ASSOCIATION

EPILOGUE

Influences Radiate...

Over the course of sixty years, between the Civil War and the Great Depression, the YMCA transformed what had once been a voluntary organization into a highly visible national network of buildings. The environmental evangelism that guided George Williams developed into a permanent physical framework, a standardized building that became a set piece of urban life from New York to San Francisco, from Selma to Shanghai. In a series of 1919 articles on "The Social Center" for *Architectural Record,* historian and critic Fiske Kimball surveyed both philanthropic and for-profit recreational buildings, and noted the leadership of the YMCA:

> In general the Y.M.C.A. may be taken as the type of all.... [I]ts buildings furnish the ideals for others both in their size and provisions. ... [T]he City Y.M.C.A. building ... offers a highly developed type, which has been standardized as the result of immense experience.[1]

The YMCA had the process of building social centers down to a science, with formulae to determine the size, expense, and type of facilities appropriate to communities of different populations, with varying needs and real estate values. They had long ago identified the problems of supervision, of maintenance, and of circulation for each "class" of building (for small, medium, and large cities), and had the benefit of testing many different solutions in its buildings across the country.

Inspired by the YMCA's success, Young Men's Hebrew Associations

(YMHAs) and Protestant churches experimented with a new type of socioreligious building in the first two decades of the twentieth century. Generally, the YMCA was pleased to help other religious organizations follow in its path. A 1912 editorial in *Association Men* suggested that the organization should

> take satisfaction in noting that in Japan its success has stimulated a Young Men's Buddhist Association . . . ; that there has recently opened a handsome building for the Young Men's Hebrew Association in New York City. It has always been the custom of our general secretaries to give every possible aid and encouragement to such organizations where the opportunity has presented.[2]

The Y was evidently proud of its record of producing buildings that did not coerce, attempting instead to shape the behavior of free individuals through persuasion.

The Y was less supportive of a trend toward the public provision of community centers. As concern about the public's leisure time increased in the Progressive era, especially around the issue of Prohibition, the model created by private, religious groups like the Y was adopted by civic authorities in service of a new, secular faith: civil religion. One of the major tenets of this American creed was the productive use of the right kind of leisure. It was in the variations of the community center, including the library, the social center, and the playground, that this right kind of leisure was embodied in architectural form and transmitted to all elements of the urban population: native and immigrant, rich and poor, religious and secular alike.

This appropriation of the YMCA's methods and architecture by civic groups challenged the hegemony of its hierarchical, segregated vision of public culture. There were hundreds of YMCAs for blacks, workingmen, and Native Americans, and YWCAs for women; some YMCAs were devoted specifically to railroad and industrial employees, but these were funded directly by employers and were considered separate enterprises. The grand central YMCA buildings in the nation's cities were aimed primarily at bolstering the hegemony of middle-class Protestant men. Constructed with the financial support of the local community, each elaborate central downtown Y building served not only as a "manhood factory" meant to manufacture young men of worth, but also as a symbol of the city's status and identity. Through the construction of these buildings, the YMCA managed to align its gendered, semireligious vision of modern culture with the public interest.

The impact of the YMCA's buildings on the urban landscape of leisure, both religious and public, can be viewed as both a success and a failure. The Y had undoubtedly shaped amusements into a fully developed cultural system for the modern age. With its buildings for young men, the Y updated the middle-class, evangelical moral geography of separate spheres into a form suited to the corporate organization of society and urban life of the twentieth century. Unfortunately, other groups were eager to copy the idea of a constructive leisure building in service of different priorities and values.

The Institutional Church

The greatest impact of the YMCA's building program was on the Protestant church itself, which developed from the sanctuary-focused structure of the nineteenth century to the elaborate complex of the present day, including recreational, educational, and athletic facilities. The architectural development of the Protestant American church had begun with the inclusion of Sunday school buildings in the early nineteenth century, but it was the YMCA's influence that effected wholesale change in the church's attitude toward leisure and the expansion of the church plant.

From the 1850s through the 1880s the attitude of the Protestant clergy toward the YMCA and its modern methods of evangelism was mixed. A few clergymen accepted the YMCA as the institutional arm of all Protestant denominations. The YMCA always viewed itself as the workday church, the equivalent of a parish house for the entire Protestant community, doing practical things that churches were unwilling or unable to do to bring young men into the Christian fold.[3] More typically, however, the clergy rejected the YMCA when it began to construct elaborate buildings because they feared the YMCA was simply another, suspiciously secular, denomination. The YMCA's straightforward embrace of recreation seemed blasphemous, an accommodation to the forces of evil.

By the end of the 1880s, however, the changing social realities and geography of urban life forced Protestants to reassess the role of recreation in religious life.[4] The introduction of the Social Gospel into Protestant churches in the 1880s required a reconsideration of policies toward the poor and unfortunate. Their condition could no longer be viewed, as it had been in the early nineteenth century, as a result of spiritual failings. The emphasized solution to worldly economic, political, and social problems was shifted from the individual conversion of every inhabitant of the earth to the sponsorship of social welfare programs and the encouragement of activism among church members.[5]

As Social Gospel doctrines began to be preached by Walter Rauschenbusch and others, some church leaders recognized that more could be accomplished in establishing the kingdom of God on earth if the church itself was a center of practical social and educational reform. At the Third Convention of Christian Workers in 1888, the Reverend A. T. Pierson spoke on "Social and Entertainment Accessories in Christian Work." Echoing YMCA rhetoric, he defined the fourfold character of the church: as a place for worship, for work, a school, and a home. He noted that the church was "too much a Sunday institution. . . . Everything therefore, that legitimately draws the people to the place of worship through the week tends to . . . make the church edifice and society associated with the people's employments and enjoyments."[6] He advocated that philanthropic and social reform activities should be channeled through the church, rather than outside it.

This attitude quickly spread across the country. As one observer noted in the *New England Magazine*:

> More and more churches are coming to see that the kingdom of God is not a mere dream of the future or the attainment of personal bliss in heaven, but the building up in America, and throughout the world, of such a national life as will realize the spirit and teachings of Jesus Christ in daily conduct. . . . Slowly a new method of church life and work has come into existence.[7]

Herbert Evans, author of a 1914 handbook on church architecture, also noted the evolving transformation of the church's role:

> There is developing rapidly in our churches a desire to serve the community at the point of need, wherever that may be. Developing the kingdom of God on earth is becoming a dominant motive rather than the preparation of people for life in another world. In the new social world upon which we are just entering, some organization should become the educative influence toward higher civic ideals. Why should not the church accomplish this task for the community?[8]

He acknowledged the existence of the YMCA and did not advocate duplication of its facilities, but in areas unserved by a Y, he saw no reason why the church should not be involved in this work as well. Sounding much like a YMCA booster, he cited the need for a wholesome social environment for urban youth:

> The modern city has multiplied the influences against the highest type of character to such a degree that the church must broaden her efforts to save boys and girls to the higher life. It is not sufficient to plant the Christ ideal . . . it is also necessary to supply as far as possible the wholesome environment in which the Christ ideal may develop to its full normal maturity. . . . Wherever there is a lack in the environment of our youth it is the opportunity and the duty of the agencies of religious education to see that the need is met.[9]

By the turn of the century Protestant evangelical leaders acknowledged the success of the YMCA. Many had viewed leisure activities and sports as suspect thirty years earlier, but they now embraced these as pragmatic and necessary components of their ministry designed to keep the Protestant church relevant within a dynamic and diverse modern urban culture.

This shift to an "institutional church" required architectural adaptation: existing church design was not geared to expanded programs. To assist congregations in adapting to a more "open" or "institutional" plan, publishers produced manuals with practical advice. One example, *Parish Problems: Hints and Helps for the People of the Churches,* was edited by social gospel proponent Washington Gladden in 1888. It contained essays on everything from the collection of dues to the design of buildings and the kind of music the organist should play. Austin Abbott, in an essay titled "Unproductive Property," noted how unfit most church buildings were to this expanded work and offered the YMCA as a model:

> If it is proposed to give more scope to the uses of the church building, we find that as such edifices are usually planned, especially the more expensive ones, they are unfitted for most other uses. . . . The success of the association buildings, which the young men have established in our larger cities, shows that property can be used to advantage every day in the week for the cause of religion. . . . Were it found feasible to enlarge the uses of a part of our church property thus under proper restrictions, and with a view to bring all classes under the influence of the church, and into its place of worship, it cannot be doubted that the moral power exerted by it would be multiplied.[10]

In a 1924 survey of St. Louis churches, Paul Douglass examined the church buildings of the city and found many of them wanting:

> Some of the community-serving churches have buildings designed to meet the conditions of the work as it was understood at the date of their erection, but none has anything like a representative plant for social work if judged by typical enterprises of other cities of the same size. Judged by ordinary Y.M.C.A. standards, the gymnasium and other recreational facilities are nowhere up to par.[11]

The YMCA had become the point of reference for churches engaged in social and community work.

In a manual on *Recreation and the Church,* Herbert Wright Gates, the superintendent of the Brick Church Institute in Rochester, New York, an institutional church, stressed the helpfulness of the YMCA's experience:

> Care should be taken in the choice of an architect to see that someone is secured who has had experience in planning buildings of this type. . . . There are specialists in church architecture as well as in other lines of work, and such should be consulted. Y.M.C.A. secretaries and architects who have designed Association buildings are valuable counselors. It is not to be expected that a pastor or building committee, whose previous experience has had to do only with the ordinary de-

mands of worship and Sunday-school work, should be able to judge of the requirements of institutional and recreational activities; and such should seek competent advice.[12]

Gates singled out the arrangements of the modern YMCA as a model, especially the YMCA's emphasis on economy and efficiency. He cited the panoptic arrangement of the Rochester YMCA, with its cozy lobby, billiards tables, reading rooms, and boys' department in full view of the administrators' offices.[13] Failure to follow this model, he cautioned, might result in an inefficient building, noting that the Brick Church Institute in Rochester, New York, had placed its gymnasium and swimming pool in such a way that control was impossible.[14] Despite this, Evans suggested that the arrangements of the Brick Church Institute were, "as a whole, those of a high-grade city Y.M.C.A. building."[15]

The fact that the Y was the model for institutional churches is not surprising, for many of the leaders of these churches were active supporters of the YMCA. This overlap in membership was especially the case in more wealthy congregations that could afford to build specifically to purpose. Two of the most prominent New York institutional churches were directly connected to the YMCA leadership. The institutional transformation of St. Bartholomew's Episcopal Church was spearheaded by Cornelius Vanderbilt, who had paid for New York's Railroad YMCA Building. The firm of James Renwick, architect of the 1869 building, was responsible for the construction of St. Bartholomew's parish house and other new facilities. St. George's Episcopal, on Sixteenth Street facing Stuyvesant Square, was similarly favored by J. P. Morgan, a member of the Building Committee for the seminal 1869 New York YMCA building. The same situation occurred in other cities, such as Philadelphia, where John Wanamaker, an early leader of the Y locally and nationally, sponsored the institutional efforts of Bethany Church.[16] By the 1920s environmental evangelism and the architectural system of the YMCA, filtered through the experience of inner-city churches, both rich and poor, had begun to affect the design of all churches. Accommodations for social fellowship and athletic activity became generally accepted elements of church architecture, expanding the typical church into a group of buildings. In 1931 Wayne G. Miller, the director of Church Planning, pointed out that "once the church was only a box with a steeple; now it is a highly complex building problem which will tax the best architectural ingenuity."[17] To illustrate his point, he contrasted the plans of an 1875 church by Richard Upjohn to those for the First and Central Presbyterian Church of Wilmington, Delaware, designed by A. G. Lamont in 1931. The first comprised only a sanctuary and chapel, while the second contained eighteen features, including a social hall, club rooms, a carpentry shop, and a gymnasium and bowling alley.[18]

The architectural community was aware of this changing trend in church design as early as the end of 1924. At that time *American Architect* published a series of articles on the design of what they termed "non-ritualistic churches."

Written by Frank G. Dillard, A.I.A., it explicitly linked the YMCA to the new style of church, suggesting that its well-tested panoptic plan for supervision be employed in the reception hall of the educational and social units of a church. He viewed this reception hall, as the YMCA did, as "the heart of the building."[19]

The influence of the YMCA was felt not only in the design of church buildings, but in the actual process of constructing them. Elbert M. Conover, the director of the Bureau of Architecture of the Methodist Episcopal Church, revealed the connections between this organization and the YMCA.[20] Like the YMCA Architectural Bureau, the Methodist church bureau, founded a few years after the Architectural Bureau took its final form in 1918, was intended to facilitate the efficient construction of a large number of churches.[21] In his 1928 guidebook *Building the House of God,* Conover presented a detailed outline of the church building process almost identical to the YMCA's, from the preparation of a survey of the community to the division of responsibility between a bureau or consulting architect.[22] The emphasis on efficiency and the systematic division of the building process into stages clearly identified the source of the church bureau's methods as the YMCA.

The Young Men's Hebrew Association

The Young Men's Hebrew Association, founded in the 1870s, was the clearest beneficiary of the YMCA's architectural experience. Modeled directly upon its Protestant counterpart, the YMHA offered a business-supported network of interdenominational recreation centers, separate from houses of worship and governed by a national supervisory organization. The New York YMHA followed the developments of the YMCA closely, adapting its methods to the specific problems of the Jewish community. The founder remembered later that "it seemed that our Gentile friends had hit upon a way of doing the right thing."[23] The YMHA ignored the evangelical component of the YMCA: because of differences in religious philosophy it did not feel the need to "convert" its members. Its mission was to preserve Jewish identity and, after the arrival of waves of Eastern European Jews in the 1890s, foster an American one as well.

Forced to enlarge its mission to include a large and foreign population, the YMHA envisioned its purpose-built headquarters as a religious-cultural center for a secular age, designed to compete with commercial recreation. Its offerings included not only accounting lessons and athletic activities, but Friday night services and celebrations of Jewish festivals.[24] This fusion of religious, social, educational, and physical activities was reminiscent of the YMCA's fourfold plan. With a specially built recreation building, the YMHA hoped to offer an alternative to the synagogue, a place to forge Jewish identity in an Americanized context. It appropriated the YMCA's concept of a voluntary self-improvement society for middle-class young men that offered lectures and social activities.[25]

FIGURE E.1. The Young Women's Hebrew Association, Central Park North, New York City, by Louis Allen Abramson, 1913.

In 1929 the time came for the design of its building on Ninety-second Street, on the Upper East Side. The YMHA called on the YMCA for help. Its questions about property taxes and the proper way to heat and maintain the swimming pool were typical, not unlike those asked by YMCA building committees in Greensboro and elsewhere. Henry Orne, the associate secretary of the New York YMCA, wrote back quickly, enclosing a cutting of the *Association Notes* editorial and offering practical advice. He pointed out that the International Committee had made studies of Association buildings and offered the help of Erskine Uhl (considered the expert in this field), as well as access to a scrapbook containing views and plans of Association buildings around the country.[26]

The architectural endeavors between the YMCA and YMHA are linked even more firmly through the experience of one architect: Louis Allen Abramson. Abramson, a partner of YMCA specialist Louis Jallade, was responsible for the design of the 1913 building for the Young Women's Hebrew Association in New York (Figure E.1). Members of the Building Committee, which included many of the YMHA's leaders, decided not to hold a competition as had been the case in the Ninety-second Street building, but to hire Abramson based upon his personal connections to the Jewish Y movement as well as his experience constructing buildings of exactly this type for the YMCA.[27]

Abramson had been the author of a series of articles published in *The Brickbuilder* in 1913 titled "The Planning of a Young Men's Christian Association Building" that amply demonstrated his expertise in the by-then-formulaic requirements of a YMCA building.[28] The article was illustrated with extensive drawings detailing issues of circulation, control and management of the members, and the arrangement of the different functions within the building. In association with Jallade he had planned many YMCA buildings and traveled on behalf of the International Committee, collecting data on the special requirements of the building type.[29] A junior partner in a practice devoted entirely to this building type, Abramson claimed to be responsible for the execution of the West Side Young Men's Christian Association on Fifty-seventh Street, the Union Branch YMCA in the Bronx, and other buildings in Pottstown, Pennsylvania; Warren, Pennsylvania; Augusta, Maine; Newport, Rhode Island; and Newport News, Virginia.[30]

The building that he constructed for the Young Women's Hebrew Association in New York was virtually indistinguishable from a contemporary YMCA or YWCA on the exterior, with its dignified red-brick façade trimmed with white stone, quoining, cornice, and classical motifs to relieve the monotony of what was essentially a hotel or apartment house. As Abramson mentioned in his article about YMCAs, the large central entrance, crowned by a classical pediment with cartouche, played an important role. "The main entrances must be accentuated, preferably by exaggerating the scale of the masonry opening in relation to all other fenestration, and so give the entrances an aspect of openness and shelter."[31] Inside, the arrangement and furnishing of the building's reception lobby, auditorium, gymnasium, dining rooms, and dormitories could easily be mistaken for a YWCA, if not a YMCA.

The experience of the Young Men's and Young Women's Hebrew Associations represents two ways that the YMCA model affected other religious groups: through direct assistance of the YMCA, and through the growing expertise of the architectural community already shaped by YMCA work.

Civic and Community Centers

Not only did the established Protestant denominations and Jewish community adapt the innovations of the YMCA, but so did the public-spirited men and women of the Progressive movement. Devoted to political and social reform, this loosely organized effort of the early years of the twentieth century worked to bring order and harmony to the strained fabric of American life. Municipal corruption, immigration, labor unrest, and ethnic tensions, participants in the movement believed, undermined the future of the country, both morally and materially. First in settlement houses, and then with publicly funded playgrounds, parks, libraries, pools, and community centers, Progressives sought to support a new faith for the modern age: what modern scholars call "civil religion."[32]

This new religion, a response to the disestablishment of the Protestant faith in the early nineteenth century, offered to the entire community a set of values free of overt ethnic and religious affiliations. The tenets of this faith were honesty, fair play, trustworthiness, industriousness, voluntarism, good neighborliness, helpfulness, friendliness, equality, universal participation, common purpose, and willingness to work for community betterment.[33] Quite similar to the "practical religion" of the YMCA and embodied in Sinclair Lewis's *Babbitt,* this ideology had its origins in small-town, Main Street Protestantism, but, unlike the YMCA and Babbitt, the civil religionists put civic harmony before material prosperity, although the two were intimately linked. Under this banner of watered-down Protestantism, civil religion adopted athletic, social, and educational activities as the heart of its work, and, with the help of Progressive reformers, housed these functions in temples of its own.

To those committed to civil religion and the architectural means of promoting it, the YMCA was a model, but a limited one. It provided splendid facilities, but limited its membership and imposed fees that further closed it off from certain elements of society. Furthermore, it adopted a patronizing attitude toward its members. This fostered division, rather than healing a disjointed society. According to Progressives, the highest form of community expression had to be public, a civic enterprise, with no element of charity.

The public alternative to the YMCA took many architectural forms, including park facilities and playgrounds, but the closest relative was the "social center" and its successor, the "community center," both dating from approximately 1907 to 1920. One of the originators of the social center, Edward Ward, developed the concept and its building as a result of personal experience in the field of recreation. Ordained as a minister, he was converted to the new civil religion when he experienced the problems of the city firsthand. He then left his church in 1907 to help improve public recreational facilities in his hometown of Rochester, New York, where he became involved in the playground movement, a turn-of-the-century effort to create playgrounds for children in inner-city neighborhoods. Its supporters, encouraged by discoveries in child psychology, believed that the instinct for play could be used to shape the character of children, especially those of immigrant backgrounds.[34] Very quickly, however, Ward began to recognize that the problem of recreation extended beyond the needs of children to embrace the whole community. He sought a competitive alternative to the saloon that would meet the recreational needs of the entire family and promote civic participation and class and racial harmony.[35]

Ward acknowledged the pioneering role of the YMCA, stating that it had been the first institution to provide for young men between school age and maturity. The important innovation of the YMCA, he noted, was the addition of cultural and recreational features to a religious institution. This was done, he contended,

> because the provision of gymnasium, bowling alley, reading room and club opportunities would serve to draw young men into the environment where they might be reached by Protestant church influences . . . and that aside from all special "religious" considerations, young men imperatively need the opportunity for clean, wholesome club association and recreation.[36]

Ward admired the inclusion of athletics but pointed out that the YMCA was a sectarian organization, and the duplication necessary to serve the entire population would be an inefficient use of resources. If there was a YMCA for Protestant men, this required a YWCA for Protestant women, a YMHA and YWHA for Jews, and similar Catholic organizations, to say nothing of those not strongly religiously affiliated. "There are differences between the sacred books used in these several organizations, but there is no difference between the basket-ball rule books they use in their several gymnasiums."[37] The YMCA may have codified the architectural principles, but that did not mean that religion had to be the basis of recreation. Ward even claimed to have the support of the church. In an address to the National Education Association in 1912, he cited the experience of one "leading" clergyman as proof of the inefficiency of separate religious structures:

> Some time ago, when I began to recognize the need of a recreation place, especially for the young people, I thought of building a parish house in connection with my church. I then thought that it would be more economical to unite forces with others in the building of a Y.M.C.A. Today I see that the money a Y.M.C.A. plant would cost would go very much farther and benefit a hundred fold more people if it were devoted to the equipment, supervision, and opening of schoolhouses for physical training, club work, and entertainment.[38]

Not only was the YMCA an inefficient agent for providing the public with facilities, it also divided the population. Ward condemned the separate construction of playgrounds, libraries, and other municipal facilities.[39] Instead, he offered the school as a model center of democratic community life.

Envisioning a renewal of neighborhood life based on mutual interest and good citizenship, Ward and a nationwide group of Progressive supporters proposed in the years before World War I to replace religious, ethnic, and commercial recreational centers like the saloon, the dance hall, and the nickelodeon with recreational centers that already stood on common ground: the public schools.

In 1916, leaders of the group, which included reformers Clarence Perry and John Collier, formed the National Community Center Association (NCCA). Its members publicized the social center idea through pamphlets, articles in the *American School Board Journal, The American City,* and the *American Journal of Sociology,* and sponsored discussions at conferences of the National Education Association. Starting in 1917 they published their own newspaper, the *Community Center,* to share methods and policies among the 554 cities that had created social centers.

Ward, Perry, and other Social Center leaders soon realized that their vision would require more than a few rooms in an existing school if they were to attract adults away from the saloon. One official proclaimed that

> brilliant light, polished floors, and comfortable seats are the inducements that enable commerce to fatten on the petty savings of wage-earners.... [W]e must learn from our commercial competitors in readjusting old buildings and erecting new ones for community use.[40]

They joined school officials in promoting the construction of modern school buildings with electric lighting, an adequate gymnasium, an elevated stage for the auditorium, baths, storage space, handball courts in the school yard, and bowling alleys in the cellar.[41] The influence of the Social Center movement on the improvement and diversification of the architecture of the American public school cannot be isolated, but it was definitely a factor in changing school architecture.

The social center idea not only helped to transform school architecture but also inspired the development of stand-alone community centers. After World War I many communities, seeking an appropriate memorial to fallen soldiers, built community or "liberty" buildings. Envisioned as a separate structure from the school, the community building combined the civic qualities of the social center and the program and architectural model of the YMCA. Its features included a meeting hall, gymnasium, swimming pool, bowling alleys, social lounges, reading rooms, and club rooms to house meetings of community agencies like the Rotary Club, Boy Scouts, and war veterans' associations.[42] These new buildings were not extensions of the social center concept, but replacements—the result of identical needs but changing priorities of the American people.

First proposed in 1918 by Harold S. Buttenheim, the editor of *The American City* (a journal devoted to municipal development), the concept quickly spread across the country.[43] By August 1919 the newly established Federal Bureau of Memorial Buildings of the War Camp Community Service reported that 265 cities and towns had committed themselves to a building, and more than a thousand others were considering the idea.[44] Constructed in the years after the Great War with voluntary public donations, these buildings were viewed by their proponents and a large majority of the public as the most fitting memorials for the soldiers who had fought and died to preserve the American way of life.

A dedicated memorial community building seemed an appropriate symbol of healing, of practical idealism. As Buttenheim suggested in his initial call for these buildings, "if, when the war shall end, we of America can turn to constructive works of peace our new spirit and energy of public service, we shall have achieved Liberty and Democracy indeed."[45] The influence of the YMCA was present in most of these buildings.[46] Martha Candler noted influences from several sources, recognizing the interrelatedness of the development of buildings for the use of the community:

> Except that its appeal is essentially to the whole community rather than to a special class or to the people of a particular district, it might vary little in design and equipment from the better type of modern settlement houses. Except that it appeals to men and women, old and young, alike, it might vary little from big central Y.M.C.A. buildings recently erected in a number of larger cities.[47]

There is evidence that the technical planning experience of the YMCA was particularly valued in the design of memorial community buildings. Jallade, one of the YMCA specialists displaced by the Building Bureau, was called in to display his expertise in this new field. Another article by Candler, this time specifically on community buildings for industrial towns, features Jallade's plans (Figure E.2).[48] His designs display evidence of the lessons learned from his YMCA experience, especially the central placement of the secretary and physical director's offices. The plan is almost indistinguishable from that of the YMCA at Galt, Ontario, designed by Shattuck and Hussey (see Figure 5.12). Jallade was given the opportunity to construct a community house at Dalton, Massachusetts, in 1923, and, as the *Community Center* noted, its arrangements for easy supervision were perfect:

> An attendant at the desk off the main lobby has command of the bowling alleys, the billiard room, social room, check room, gymnasium, and entrance to the locker rooms on the lower floor. Many community center buildings have been designed on the assumption that they were to be free from the stigma of supervision. It has not taken social workers who have used that type of building long to decide, however, that this idea, while attractive, was scarcely practical.[49]

Whether public or private, religious or civic, the community buildings that followed in the footsteps of the YMCA benefited from its experience. Although they tried to improve its program or mission, there was little they could fault in its buildings.

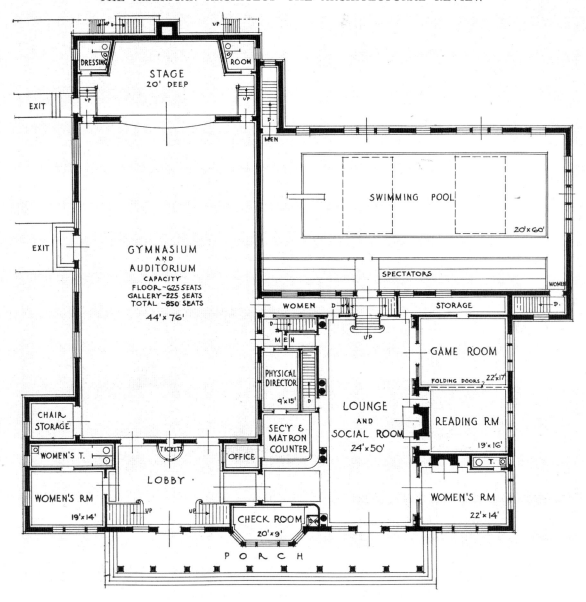

FIGURE E.2. First-floor plan for "Community Building—Scheme B," by Jallade, Lindsay & Warren, 1919. Based on his earlier work for the YMCA, Jallade produced this standardized community center plan intended for use in industrial towns.

Response by the YMCA

By the end of the Great War, the YMCA's competition included institutional churches, YMHAs, Catholic parish halls, the Salvation Army, and the facilities of nonreligious social welfare agencies, including municipal facilities, Boys' Clubs, and settlement houses. To some, the YMCA's place in this emerging world of recreation was that of a pioneer, important but outdated. John Daniels, a settlement-house worker from Boston, dismissed the YMCA as unconcerned with the interests of immigrants:

> But, great as its services are in instruction and enjoyment, the Y.M.C.A. has established remarkably few organic relations with immigrant groups and has enlisted comparatively little co-operation on the part of such groups. . . . The chief reason for lack of neighborhood

relations, however, is that the Y.M.C.A. has developed more along institutional lines than in the direction of identifying itself with neighborhood interests outside its own walls.[50]

This criticism was echoed by municipal officials. A question posed in 1910 to the editors of *The American City* gave voice to a common criticism of the YMCA. The city of Augusta, Maine, considering the construction of a building with a gymnasium, asked whether they should invite the YMCA to build it. The editor's answer, which reflected the general attitude of those involved in civic management, was that this sort of work belonged to the city, rather than some private organization. The YMCA, it was implied, only catered to a small segment of the population, and was thus not as efficient an investment as its leaders contended.[51]

The Reverend Raymond Calkins, a temperance advocate who investigated the problem posed by the saloon, concurred with the municipal experts, but for another reason. In 1901 he published *Substitutes for the Saloon,* in which he contended that the YMCA did not qualify as an adequate substitute for the "workingman's club" because of its religious focus. As he noted, "here stand expensive and splendidly equipped buildings by no means filled to their utmost capacity, which thousands of men will never think of entering so long as they remain centers for religious or evangelistic work." By this he refers not only to nonreligious middle-class young men, but the working-class men who regularly frequented the saloons. This critique was seconded by *The Christian Century* in 1925, which called on the YMCA to extend its mission beyond white-collar workers and embrace the industrial worker.

In addition to the YMCA's policies on class, gender, and age, the apparent hypocrisy of the YMCA was also the target of criticism. As the Reverend Calkins pointed out, the YMCA still purported to be a Christian organization, but in reality, some suggested, it argued for a much larger role.[52] A 1909 editorial in a Chicago-based journal, *The Interior* (which was quoted in *Association Men*), asked the rhetorical question, "Can an institution dependent on large public benevolence maintain itself permanently unaffected by the character of the sources from which it solicits support?" The answer was, of course, no, and the financial demands of any building program required the organization to approach donors outside the evangelical community, raising a sticky issue:

> In order to get money from such men—Romanists, Jews, ethical culturists, infidels and indifferent—the Association has been obliged to put forward its social usefulness as its plea and hold back the original ultimate purpose of these social activities—the persuasion of men to individual trust in a saving Christ.[53]

Although the editors of *Association Men* vehemently denied this charge, there was much truth in the accusation. Starting with the New York building of

1869, the YMCA was in a constant state of adaptation and growth, building on its successes by taking on more responsibility until it was an unwieldy international organization, called upon by the U.S. government to coordinate recreational activities for all U.S. soldiers during World War I (see Plate 11). By the end of the war, with increasing competition, the YMCA had to acknowledge that it could not be all things to all people, and made a decision about its intended role.

Opinion concerning the future direction of the YMCA took two basic forms. Some leaders believed that the way to justify the YMCA's large building program was to identify its unique identity as a Protestant moral force, while others, emphasizing the YMCA's years of expertise, suggested that the YMCA continue in its tradition of adaptation and expand and redefine its work, incorporating the methods of its competitors. At a 1916 meeting on the problems facing the urban YMCA, Wilbur Messer, general secretary of the Chicago Association, explained the problem and suggested a variety of solutions:

> The Association of today is facing a complicated, and in some places a dangerous situation, as to the leadership and permanency of the Association in community life. The growing consciousness of state and municipal responsibility for conserving and safeguarding the youth has led to increasing investments in playgrounds, parks, and social centers, etc.[54]

He also acknowledged some of the YMCA's weaknesses: "Superficiality lies at the bottom of many of our failures and produces waste. Matured, well-planned, and adapted measures, thoroughly worked out, count most in the long run."[55] Fearing that the public perceived the results of the expensive building program to be meager, he suggested that more be done for "the unfavored class," and that personal contact and influence, rather than surveillance, might be a more successful means of affecting character. Most important, he contended, the Y must emphasize its distinctly Christian contribution:

> While commercial organizations are making the city prosperous, and while civic improvement organizations are making it beautiful, the Association must help make it a place of moral health—a place where it is easy and natural for boys to grow up in the likeness of the Master; a place where the finer things of Christian civilization may come to their fullest development.[56]

In response to, and in competition with, the institutional church and the social center, Messer urged the YMCA to continue with its civilizing Christian mission, extending its work for middle-class young men to a broader audience.

The impact and influence of this call for an expansion of the YMCA's mission is embodied in the introduction of smaller, more flexible "community"-type buildings. Branch buildings had existed before, as had buildings of different sizes for cities of different populations, but this was the first time that the model for design was not the large, complex "city" building. The new community Y building was designed by the Building Bureau and presented to the public as a central element of its post–World War I construction program. Smaller and more domestic in appearance than the typical YMCA building, it was well suited to residential neighborhoods in the outlying areas between city and suburb. Usually only one or two stories tall, the new community-type YMCAs contained a combination gymnasium/auditorium, a billiards room, a small classroom, a social room, and, in a major departure, a ladies' room.[57]

Those in favor of these smaller buildings acknowledged the pressing concern of community work advocates about the needless duplication of facilities in urban and suburban neighborhoods, but justified continued construction by asserting that, more than any other group, the YMCA should be entrusted with responsibility for the community's leisure. Messer explained why the YMCA should do more than serve as social coordinators, as its community workers suggested:

> Because of its trained leadership, the public confidence it enjoys, its long record of successful achievement; its long experience in the administrative and financial tasks incident to such enterprises, the Association ought to be able to do this work better than these new untried movements.[58]

With finite resources, the YMCA avoided neighborhoods already well served by other institutions, instead choosing to build in areas most in need of help. Whether or not the Y would have constructed redundant buildings had they had unlimited funds is unclear. The continued construction of YMCA buildings throughout the 1920s does indicate, however, that the YMCA was unwilling to relinquish its architectural identity in the face of competition.

Conclusion

The YMCA's remarkable ability to adapt to changing circumstances, including war, immigration, and the rise of a mass culture, ensured its continued relevance throughout the vicissitudes of late nineteenth- and early twentieth-century American life. Only one challenge proved impossible to overcome—the Great Depression. This brought an end to the YMCA's massive and ambitious building program, and, when money became available again after World War II, the city was no longer the primary object of YMCA attention. As the middle class migrated to the suburbs, the YMCA followed. With this, what had once been a religious and commercial organization intrinsically connected to city growth and city life completed its metamorphosis, emerging from its chrysalis as a secularized recreational building: a place to learn to swim or go to day camp.

The only survivors of the early years of the YMCA are the buildings of the central city, altered, sold, in disrepair. These stand as monuments to the status the YMCA once enjoyed within the city, as one of its most prominent institutions, invested in the problems of the industrializing city and devoted to their solution by architectural means. Although they are now often overshadowed by taller buildings, YMCA buildings played an important role in the community of their day. At a time when many new building types were changing the appearance of American cities, the YMCA was a particularly bold invention, a sign of modernity and civic pride.

Although there is evidence that the initial function of the YMCA building, to mold young Christian men, was not fulfilled in reality, other aspects of the building's reception suggest that the YMCA had a significant effect in carrying out one of its larger missions: defining the nature of leisure activity in an emerging mass culture. One indication of the YMCA building's success in this regard is the imitative behavior of other religious and civic groups. The explosion of Y-inspired recreational buildings at the turn of the century offers proof of widespread confidence in the YMCA solution to the social problems of modern urban culture. With the invention, development, and distribution of its Christian clubhouses in the last quarter of the nineteenth century, the YMCA blazed a path for those committed to the perpetuation of traditional values in a mass-culture society. Faced with the well-coordinated and well-funded attempts by advertisers and merchants to socialize the American public into a culture of consumption, individualism, and self-gratification, the YMCA acknowledged the necessity of competition rather than retreat with its building program. By the turn of the century other groups, aware of the YMCA's seeming monopoly on "respectable" recreation, copied the well-tested techniques branded as radical and even blasphemous only thirty years earlier.

Whether or not the YMCA can be credited with the saving of souls will probably never be established, but its centrality in the lives of millions of Americans is clear. This national organization's influential building program helped to define the concept of productive and respectable leisure, easing the transition of American culture from theocracy to the mass market.

NOTES

Introduction

1. See Bogrette, "The Abington YMCA." One exception is the study of an architecturally distinguished YMCA building by Gitler, "The Architecture of the Jerusalem YMCA."

2. One notable exception is Groth's *Living Downtown,* which focuses primarily on the YMCA's dormitory spaces.

3. William McKinley and Theodore Roosevelt, "The Association: A National Defense"; and "For More 'Manhood Factories,'" *Association Men* 34 (February 1909): 234–36. The first buildings appeared in the bonanza economy of the late 1860s. The Panic of 1873 put plans for a national program of YMCA construction on hold until the 1880s, when financial recovery made it possible for local communities to support building enterprises. Hundreds of YMCAs were constructed in this period across the country, especially in the urbanized Northeast and Midwest, and in the New South cities. Financial depression in the early 1890s meant another halt in new YMCA projects. Recovery began in 1896 and a boom period of YMCA building construction lasted until World War I, with dozens of buildings constructed each year, filling in the western and southern sections of the country. In the flush 1920s the trajectory of YMCA building continued upwards, with significant expansion abroad, especially in China, until the Great Depression put a stop to the phenomenon.

4. Hale, *Making Whiteness,* 6.

5. The general literature on this subject is voluminous. Seminal works include: Douglas, *The Feminization of American Culture*; Cott, *The Bonds of Womanhood*; Ryan, *Cradle of the Middle Class*; Halttunen, *Confidence Men and Painted Women*; and Kerber, "Separate Spheres, Female Worlds, Women's Place."

6. Van Slyck, *Free to All*; Isenberg, *Downtown America*; and Spain, *How Women Saved the City*.

7. Van Slyck, *Free to All*; Isenberg, *Downtown America*; Spain, *How Women Saved the City*; Stansell, *City of Women*; Wilson, *The Sphinx in the City*; and Domosh and Seager, *Putting Women in Place*.

8. For a general introduction see Mjagkij and Spratt, *Men and Women Adrift*. Developed monographic studies include Winter, *Making Men, Making Class*; Mjagkij, *Light in the Darkness*; Chauncey, *Gay New York*; Chudacoff, *The Age of the Bachelor*; and Gustav-Wrathall, *Take the Young Stranger by the Hand*.

9. Gustav-Wrathall, *Take the Young Stranger by the Hand*; Chauncey, *Gay New York*; and Winter, *Making Men, Making Class*.

10. Gendered space has been explored in recent work on the Young Women's Christian Association. Julia Morgan, one of the best-known women architects in the United States, designed clubhouses for the YWCA on the West Coast. Those seeking to find female designers in the historic register and the historical record have studied these buildings as part of Morgan's architectural biography, and, to some degree, as the creation of female space. See Boutelle, *Julia Morgan, Architect*; and Dubrow and Goodman, *Restoring Women's History through Historic Preservation*.

11. Moore, *Masonic Temples*.

12. Bederman, *Manliness and Civilization*, 7.

13. Kimmel, *Manhood in America*; Rotundo, *American Manhood*; Kwolek-Folland, *Engendering Business*; Chandler, *The Essential Alfred Chandler*; Zunz, *Making America Corporate*; and Hilkey, *Character Is Capital*.

14. Bederman, "'The Women Have Had Charge of the Church Work Long Enough,'" 432–35.

15. Nelson, *National Manhood*, 3.

16. Trachtenberg, *The Incorporation of America*, 3–7.

17. For an application of Joseph Schumpeter's economic theories to the built environment, see Page, *The Creative Destruction of Manhattan,* and Cronon, *Nature's Metropolis*.

18. Trachtenberg, *The Incorporation of America*, 213.

19. Ibid., chapter 7.

20. The Chicago YMCA's image of its buildings assembled into a single site was modeled on the tradition of the Turner Construction Company, which marked its annual progress with a similar assemblage of its completed projects. The company continues with this tradition today. Turner City Collection, National Building Museum, Washington, D.C.

21. Key books redefining modern through a consideration of the process of making include Terry Smith, *Making the Modern,* chapter 2; Willis, *Form Follows Finance*; Solomonson, *The Chicago Tribune Tower Competition*; and Isenberg, *Downtown America*.

1. Reconciling Morality and Mammon

1. Letters, Henry Baldwin to Robert McBurney, February 13, 1864, and March 24, 1864. Robert McBurney Correspondence, Y.CNY.9, box 17, Kautz Family YMCA Archives, University of Minnesota Libraries, Minneapolis.

2. Fisher, *Public Affairs and the Y.M.C.A.,* 17.

3. Donoghue, *An Event on Mercer Street,* 15.

4. For an account of "colored" YMCAs, see Mjagkij, *Light in the Darkness*.

5. Binfield, *George Williams and the Y.M.C.A.,* 18–19.

6. Noll, *A History of Christianity in the United States and Canada,* 176.

7. Fishman, *Bourgeois Utopias.* The concept of women's sphere and their unquestioned role as children's role model has been questioned in recent scholarship. On the role of men in the home, see Marsh, "Suburban Men and Masculine Domesticity." For a discussion of men as consumers, see Breward, *The Hidden Consumer,* introduction. On the presence of working-class women in the public sphere, see Stansell, *City of Women,* and Benson, *Counter Cultures.* For a discussion of middle-class women, see Spain, *How Women Saved the City.*

8. Baldwin, *Domesticating the Street,* 14–15. Bushnell himself followed the logic of his arguments in *Christian Nurture* with a treatise on city planning in 1854 and a proposal for a large urban park for Hartford, Connecticut, where he preached.

9. Ryan, *Cradle of the Middle Class,* 129.

10. Gunn, *The Physiology of New York Boarding-Houses,* 32.

11. V. Morse, *An Analytical Sketch,* 54.

12. Peel, "On the Margins," 813–15.

13. Gorn, *The Manly Art*; Gilfoyle, *City of Eros,* 92–104; Chudacoff, *The Age of the Bachelor*; and Sante, *Low Life,* 92.

14. Foster, *New York by Gas-Light,* 84–85.

15. Abell, *The Urban Impact on American Protestantism,* 6; Kilde, *When Church Became Theatre,* 56–83.

16. Browne, *The Great Metropolis,* 169.

17. Abell, *The Urban Impact on American Protestantism,* 12–14.

18. Stansell, *City of Women,* 68.

19. New York Young Men's Christian Association, *Ninth Annual Report,* 1861.

20. New York Young Men's Christian Association, *Eleventh Annual Report,* 1863, 12.

21. Dedmon, *Great Enterprises,* 53–56.

22. Hopkins, *History of the YMCA in North America,* 16–17; R. C. Morse, *History of the North American Young Men's Christian Associations,* 20.

23. "Nason Collins," New York, vol. 341, p. 200qq, R. G. Dun & Co. Collection, Baker Library Historical Collections, Harvard Business School.

24. Schwantes, *Vision and Enterprise,* 31.

25. "Jacob Wyckoff," New York, vol. 195, pp. 837, 900, R. G. Dun & Co. Collection, Baker Library Historical Collections, Harvard Business School.

26. Zunz, *Making America Corporate,* 2.

27. See Cronon, *Nature's Metropolis.*

28. George Templeton Strong, quoted in P. B. Dodge, *Tales of the Phelps-Dodge Family,* 231.

29. Satterlee, *J. Pierpont Morgan,* 110–17.

30. Gregory, *Families of Fortune,* 96.

31. Satterlee, *J. Pierpont Morgan,* 148.

32. New York Young Men's Christian Association, *Sixteenth Annual Report,* 1868, 17.

33. Clyde and Sally Griffen have shown in their study of Boston that between 1870 and 1900 there was a dramatic drop in the number of proprietorships and an increase in the number of dead-end clerkships. Demand for new clerical workers increased from four to eighteen thousand between 1870 and 1900. Griffen and Griffen, *Natives and Newcomers.*

34. Zunz, *Making America Corporate,* 2.

35. Attie, "Warwork and the Crisis of Domesticity in the North."

36. New York Young Men's Christian Association, *Sixteenth Annual Report*, 1868, 17.

37. Bederman, "'The Women Have Had Charge of the Church Work Long Enough,'" 437.

38. For some other reasons why businessmen became involved in the YMCA and other evangelical philanthropic organizations, see Abell, *The Urban Impact on American Protestantism*, 3–18; Bremner, *The Public Good*, 181–85, 208–211; and Trachtenberg, *The Incorporation of America*.

39. Srole, "'A Position That God Has Not Particularly Assigned to Men,'" 119; Griffen and Griffen, *Natives and Newcomers*, 60.

40. Abell, *The Urban Impact on American Protestantism*, 9–10.

41. Dodge was paraphrasing Ralph Waldo Emerson; quoted in *Federal Council Bulletin: A Journal of Religious Co-operation* 16 (April 1932): 356.

42. Bederman, "'The Women Have Had Charge of the Church Work Long Enough,'" 434.

43. V. Morse, *The Work of the Young Men's Christian Association: What It Is and How to Do It*, essay read before the New York Young Men's Christian Association, September 26, 1864, 6, box 339, Records of the YMCA of the City of New York, YMCA of Greater New York, Y.GNY.0020, Kautz Family YMCA Archives, University of Minnesota Libraries, Minneapolis.

44. *A Memorandum Respecting New York as a Field for Moral and Christian Effort Among Young Men* (New York: by the Association, 1866), 14, Pamphlet Files, SHP p.v.5 no. 9, New York Public Library.

45. New York Young Men's Christian Association, *Sixteenth Annual Report*, 1868, 12.

46. Doggett, *Life of Robert R. McBurney*, 69.

47. New York Young Men's Christian Association, *Thirteenth Annual Report*, 1865, 17.

48. Putney, *Muscular Christianity*.

49. Librarians also employed similar tactics, offering novels to get people in the door. Van Slyck, "Managing Pleasure," 222.

50. Nolte, *The Sokol in the Czech Lands*, 9.

51. *Historical Journal*, n.p.

52. Conzen, "Ethnicity as Festive Culture"; and Gerber, "The Germans Take Care of Our Celebrations," 39–60. The turnverein was directly mentioned in an earlier version of the *Memorandum*, published in 1863. This report chronicles the existence of more than twelve ethnic German organizations, including the turnverein. The fear, and perhaps envy, of the successful cultural program of these organizations inspired the founding of a German branch of the YMCA in 1865. Frank Ballard, "New York City: A Mission Field" (1863), box 339, Records of the YMCA of the City of New York, YMCA of Greater New York, Y.GNY.0020, Kautz Family YMCA Archives, University of Minnesota Libraries, Minneapolis; *A Memorandum Respecting New York* (cited in note 44), 11.

53. Women were involved in many of these activities but were not full members even as late as 1950. They did not take part in gymnastics at this early date in the organization's history, but gained admission to the gym floor in the 1890s.

54. New York Young Men's Christian Association, *Thirteenth Annual Report*, 1865, 8, 19.

55. *Journal of the Proceedings of the Annual Conventions of the Y.M.C.A.s of the United States and British Provinces* (hereafter cited as *Journal of the Proceedings*), Chicago,

June 4–7, 1863, 14. The issue of baseball was a timely one to discuss at this convention. During the Civil War thousands of soldiers were introduced to the game and brought the sport back home with them, laying the foundation for the national pastime.

56. Board of Directors Minutes, Young Men's Christian Association of New York, vol. 3 (May 13, 1865, to May 18, 1868): 87, box 386, Young Men's Christian Association of New York, Y.GNY.0020, Kautz Family YMCA Archives, University of Minnesota Libraries, Minneapolis.

57. Stephen Tyng, in New York Young Men's Christian Association, *Fourteenth Annual Report,* 1866, 78.

58. Verranus Morse, *Amusements: An Essay* (New York: James L. Hastie, 1868), 8, 19, box 339, Young Men's Christian Association of New York, Y.GNY.0020, Kautz Family YMCA Archives, University of Minnesota Libraries, Minneapolis.

59. Ibid.

60. Donoghue, *An Event on Mercer Street,* 47.

61. New York Young Men's Christian Association, *First Annual Report,* 1852, 7.

62. New York Young Men's Christian Association, *Twelfth Annual Report,* 1864, 10.

63. One of J. P. Morgan's first acts as treasurer of the organization was to find a new set of rooms. Sinclair, *Corsair,* 26; Bayless, *The YMCA at 150,* 10.

64. See letters by Jacob Wyckoff (February 17, 1864), Verranus Morse (February 18, 1864), Hugh Stebbins (February 16, 1864), and Henry Matthews (February 18, 1864) to Robert McBurney, box 337, Robert McBurney Correspondence, Y.GNY.0020, Kautz Family YMCA Archives, University of Minnesota Libraries, Minneapolis.

65. Snyder, *The Voice of the City,* 5.

66. McCabe Jr., *Lights and Shadows of New York Life,* 133.

67. Quoted in McNamara, *The New York Concert Saloon,* 18.

68. Sinclair, *Corsair,* 26.

69. Stern, Mellins, and Fishman, *New York 1880,* 35.

70. M. C. Boyer, *Manhattan Manners*; Gilfoyle, *City of Eros.*

71. Fairfield, *The Clubs of New York,* 111.

72. Most early clubs did not provide accommodation. Members lived with their families or in hotels and elite boardinghouses.

73. J. P. Morgan, the Dodges, the Browns, and the Colgates settled in the East 30s on both sides of 5th Avenue. A few adventurous souls, such as railroad financier J. S. Kennedy, ventured even farther north, to the southern edge of Central Park. Building new brownstones and houses of worship, these wealthy and influential neighbors created a new kind of domestic landscape.

74. An invaluable source on the Ladies' Mile and an important source for my maps is M. C. Boyer, *Manhattan Manners.*

75. Complaints about the cost can be found in a report of the Committee on Library and Rooms to Samuel Stebbins, President, in early 1864, box 337, Records of the YMCA of the City of New York, YMCA of Greater New York, Y.GNY.0020, Kautz Family YMCA Archives, University of Minnesota Libraries, Minneapolis.

76. Donoghue, *An Event on Mercer Street,* 44.

77. New York Young Men's Christian Association, *Thirteenth Annual Report,* 1865, 23.

78. *A Memorandum Respecting New York* (cited in note 44).

79. Bulmer, Bales, and Sklar, *The Social Survey in Historical Perspective,* 27–43.

80. *A Memorandum Respecting New York* (cited in note 44), 4–10.

81. "The Young Men's Christian Association," *The Nation,* March 15, 1866, 327.

82. Rev. William Adams, "The Duty of Christian People to Those in Their Employ" (New York: Robert Carter and Brothers, 1866), box 339, Records of the YMCA of the City of New York, YMCA of Greater New York, Y.GNY.0020, Kautz Family YMCA Archives, University of Minnesota Libraries, Minneapolis.

83. New York Young Men's Christian Association, *Twelfth Annual Report,* 1864, 11.

84. M. C. Boyer, *Manhattan Manners,* 83.

85. For a partial list of donors, see New York Young Men's Christian Association, *Fifteenth Annual Report,* 1867; and "Dedication of the New Building of the Young Men's Christian Association of the City of New York" (New York: by the Association, 1869), box 8, McBurney Branch YMCA Records, 1858–1992, Y.GNY.013, Kautz Family YMCA Archives, University of Minnesota Libraries, Minneapolis.

2. Inventing the YMCA Building

1. *The New York Young Men's Christian Association Building: Resume of the Edifice* (New York: YMCA, 1869), 2. Robert McBurney Correspondence, Records of the YMCA of the City of New York, YMCA of Greater New York, Y.GNY.0020, Kautz Family YMCA Archives, University of Minnesota Libraries, Minneapolis.

2. "Historical Sketch of the Building of the Association," New York Young Men's Christian Association, *Eighteenth Annual Report,* 1870, 56.

3. Joseph Thompson, "The Association in Architecture," *Association Monthly* 1 (January 1870): 3–4. The editor of *Association Monthly,* Richard Morse, notes in his memoirs that, though not published in the article, Thompson extended his list of modern Christian buildings to include the Sunday school room and the press rooms of the Bible and Tract Societies. See R. C. Morse, *My Life with Young Men,* 63.

4. Moore, *Selling God*; see also Oberdeck, *The Evangelist and the Impresario.*

5. John Wanamaker, instrumental in the similar transformation of the YMCA in Philadelphia, is an excellent example of this reconciliation. See Leach, *Land of Desire,* chapter 7.

6. The choice of an architect at all, let alone one with a prominent name, distinguishes this project from most earlier philanthropic or evangelical endeavors, like missions, Sunday schools, or houses of refuge, which were executed by contractors or builders. The building committee clearly sought an artistic identity for their building, a certain status within the community. Board of Directors Minutes, Young Men's Christian Association of New York, vol. 3, September 16, 1867 (cited in chapter 1, note 56).

7. Culter, "The First and Latest Architect for the Smithsonian."

8. Amsden, "Historians and the Spatial Imagination."

9. Doggett, *Life of Robert R. McBurney,* 74.

10. Ibid.

11. Ibid.

12. New York Young Men's Christian Association, *Seventeenth Annual Report,* 1869, 16.

13. Frank Ballard to Robert McBurney, February 15, 1864, box 337, Robert McBurney Correspondence, Records of the YMCA of the City of New York, YMCA of Greater New York, Y.GNY.0020, Kautz Family YMCA Archives, University of Minnesota Libraries, Minneapolis.

14. *Proceedings of the Sixteenth Anniversary of the Young Men's Christian Association of Philadelphia* (Philadelphia: by the Association, 1871), 24, YMCA of Philadelphia, 1854–1967, 22, Urban Archives, Temple University, Philadelphia.

15. Landau, *P. B. Wight,* 24–25.

16. Building Committee Minutes, Young Men's Christian Association of New York, January 23, 1868, vol. 1, Y.GNY.0020, Kautz Family YMCA Archives, University of Minnesota Libraries, Minneapolis.

17. Kwolek-Folland, *Engendering Business;* Bluestone, *Constructing Chicago.*

18. Stern, Mellins, and Fishman, *New York 1880,* 390–91.

19. Scobey, *Empire City,* 173–74; Kwolek-Folland, *Engendering Business,* 103.

20. Board of Directors Minutes, Young Men's Christian Association of New York, vol. 3, February 5, 1868 (cited in chapter 1, note 56).

21. *Resume of the Edifice* (cited in note 1), 3; Rattner, "James Renwick," 546.

22. "Cooper Union," *Harper's Weekly* 5 (March 30, 1861): 200.

23. Stern, Mellins, and Fishman, *New York 1880,* 203–4; Irwin, May, and Hotchkiss, *A History of the Union League Club of New York City,* 68–69.

24. My discussion of the YMCA's studio space is heavily indebted to Oaklander, "Studios at the YMCA."

25. Irwin, May, and Hotchkiss, *A History of the Union League Club of New York City,* 85–94.

26. Hunt had already challenged such hierarchies in his unsuccessful proposal for the National Academy of Design (1861), which incorporated stores on the ground level. The jury found Peter Bonnett Wight's Venetian Gothic palace, without stores, a more appropriate and dignified architectural interpretation of the organization's identity. See Stern, Mellins, and Fishman, *New York 1880,* 170–71.

27. Institutional histories credit Dodge Jr. and McBurney with significant responsibility for "designing" the building, claiming that "it was really an evolution—the work of the secretary [McBurney], the committee, the board, and the architects." Doggett, *Life of Robert R. McBurney,* 74.

28. *A Memorandum Respecting New York* (cited in chapter 1, note 44), 14.

29. Board of Directors Minutes, Young Men's Christian Association of New York, vol. 4, April 2, 1866 (cited in chapter 1, note 56).

30. Oaklander, "Studios at the YMCA," 20.

31. Harris, *The Artist in American Society,* 263.

32. Strong, *The Diary of George Templeton Strong,* February 13, 1869, 4:241.

33. *Resume of the Edifice* (cited in note 1), 4–6. This attention to detail in the auditorium was partly owing to the fact that it was intended to provide additional income for the association through rentals. As was the case with artists' studios, fine assembly space was in short supply, and the YMCA's leaders sought to take advantage of the demand by providing an elegant space.

34. Boyer, *Manhattan Manners,* 84.

35. "New York Y.M.C.A. Building," *Watchman* 2 (October 1876): 1; quotation from *Resume of the Edifice* (cited in note 1), 5.

36. Johnson, *The History of YMCA Physical Education,* 34–43.

37. Kwolek-Folland, *Engendering Business,* 101; Grier, *Culture and Comfort,* 62–63; Berger, "A House Divided"; Blumin, *The Emergence of the Middle Class,* 185–88.

38. Brucken, "In the Public Eye."

39. Boettger, "Eastman Johnson's 'Blodgett Family.'"

40. The New York Mercantile Library, an important precedent and model for the

New York YMCA, had closed stacks. Members had to request books, which were retrieved by an attendant. Augst, *The Clerk's Tale,* 159.

41. On alcoves and surveillance, see Van Slyck, "Managing Pleasure."

42. Fairfield, *The Clubs of New York,* 113.

43. "The Cross and the World," published by the Association, n.d., McBurney Branch YMCA Records, 1858–1992, Y.GNY.13, Kautz Family YMCA Archives, University of Minnesota Libraries, Minneapolis. An article in the New York YMCA's newspaper suggested that art's function is to convey ideas: "Conversational Intelligence," *Association Notes* 4 (February 1889): 6, McBurney Branch YMCA Records, 1858–1992, Y.GNY.13, Kautz Family YMCA Archives, University of Minnesota Libraries, Minneapolis.

44. Richard C. Morse, *The Young Men of Our Cities, and of What Use the Young Men's Christian Association Has Been and Can Be to Them* (privately published by the author, 1885), 3, in uncatalogued box marked "City Association Materials," Kautz Family YMCA Archives, University of Minnesota Libraries, Minneapolis.

45. On the applications of the Panopticon, see R. Evans, "Bentham's Panopticon," and Vidler, "Architecture, Management, and Morals."

46. Foucault, *Discipline and Punish,* 202–3.

47. On the Akron Plan, see Lawrence, *Housing the Sunday School,* 83–92; and H. F. Evans, *The Sunday-School Building and Its Equipment,* 5–13.

48. Verranus Morse, "Improvement of the Social Condition of Young Men," *Journal of the Proceedings,* Albany, N.Y., June 1–5, 1866, 57.

49. The building-as-machine metaphor was common in the building literature. Two examples: Nelson F. Evans, "The Work of the Young Men's Christian Association," *Journal of the Proceedings,* San Francisco, May 11–15, 1887, 90; and E. S. Turner, "What Advantages Have Accrued to Work for Young Men as a Result of Securing Association Buildings?" In *Journal of the Proceedings,* Milwaukee, Wis., May 16–20, 1883, 121–31, 1885, 1, box 1, Buildings and Furnishings Service Materials, Administrative Records, Kautz Family YMCA Archives, University of Minnesota Libraries, Minneapolis.

50. *Resume of the Edifice* (cited in note 1), 2.

51. "The Young Men's Christian Association," *Harper's New Monthly Magazine* 41 (October 1870): 644.

52. New York Young Men's Christian Association, *Thirty-Second Annual Report,* 1884, 24–29. Annual Reports of the Young Men's Christian Associations of Greater New York, Kautz Family YMCA Archives, University of Minnesota Libraries, Minneapolis.

53. Ibid.

54. Boyer, *Manhattan Manners,* 84; Cantor, "The Public Architecture of James Renwick, Jr.," 154–58; McKenna, "James Renwick, Jr. and the Second Empire Style."

3. Accepting the Call to Build

1. Scobey, *Empire City,* 23.
2. Ibid., 110.
3. Ibid., 21–24.
4. Ibid., 27.
5. "Booth's New Theatre, Twenty-third Street and Sixth Avenue, New York,"

Harper's Weekly (January 9, 1869): 29; "The New Post-Office and Sub-Treasury Building, Boston, Massachusetts," *Harper's Weekly* 13 (May 1, 1869): 89; "Our Common Schools," *Harper's Weekly* 14 (February 26, 1870): 141.

6. Scobey, *Empire City,* 25.

7. "The New Building of the Y.M.C.A.," *Harper's Weekly* 12 (November 21, 1868): 740–41; "The Young Men's Christian Association's New Building," *Harper's Weekly* 13 (October 23, 1869): 685–86; and "The New York Young Men's Christian Association," *Harper's Weekly* 13 (December 11, 1869): 785–86.

8. Moore, *Selling God,* 34.

9. Ibid.

10. Hopkins, *History of the YMCA in North America,* 109.

11. Dedmon, *Great Enterprises,* 63–68.

12. Gustav-Wrathall, *Take the Young Stranger by the Hand,* 125.

13. Ibid., 117–18.

14. "Design for the Y.M.C.A. Building, Philadelphia, Pa.," 397; "The Philadelphia Young Men's Christian Association," *Watchman* 5 (June 15, 1879): 133–34.

15. Decker, *Fortunes and Failures,* 11, 19, 48.

16. Richardson, *Garnered Sheaves*; published posthumously by his wife, this title includes a series of letters, "Through to the Pacific," written for the *New York Tribune* in May–June 1869.

17. Hopkins, *History of the YMCA in North America,* 111–14, 116–18.

18. Ibid., 119.

19. R. Morse, *My Life with Young Men,* 65.

20. Hopkins, *History of the YMCA in North America,* 137.

21. "Ecclesiastes 3:1: A Time to Build," *Association Monthly* 1 (June 1870): 132.

22. Hopkins, *History of the YMCA in North America,* 131, 141.

23. "Why Should We Have a New Association Building?" *Watchman* 8 (June 15, 1882): 181.

24. Robert A. Orr, "The First Year's Experience in a New Association Building" (New York: International Committee, [1885]), box 1, Buildings and Furnishings Service Materials, Administrative Records, Kautz Family YMCA Archives, University of Minnesota Libraries, Minneapolis; and Turner, "What Advantages Have Accrued?" (cited in chapter 2, note 49).

25. Darling, *Advantages of a Permanent Home,* 4.

26. Ibid., 9; Ruskin, *The Seven Lamps of Architecture,* 16–19. Ruskin was a popular figure with the YMCA, often quoted and lionized.

27. "Views of Association Buildings," *Watchman* 6 (May 1, 1880): 103; "Buildings," *Watchman* 12 (June 1, 1886): 126.

28. "Building Pamphlet," *Watchman* 12 (April 1, 1886): 78.

29. Atherton, *Main Street on the Middle Border,* 40, 58, 135–42, 149.

30. Longstreth, *The Buildings of Main Street,* 24–29; Blackmar, "Rewalking the Walking City."

31. "Is It Expedient to Open the Rooms of Our Associations on the Sabbath?" *Journal of the Proceedings*, Portland, Maine, July 14–18, 1869, 33–34.

32. Van Slyck, "The Lady and the Library Loafer."

33. Darling, *Advantages of a Permanent Home,* 11.

34. "The Function of the Association: Is It a Permanent One?" *Association Monthly* 1 (February 1870): 35.

35. R. C. Morse, *The Young Men of Our Cities* (cited in chapter 2, note 44), 10–11.

36. Darling, *Advantages of a Permanent Home*, 5.

37. Longstreth, *The Buildings of Main Street*, 14; Rifkind, *Main Street*.

38. As Van Slyck notes, even within communities there might be disagreement between men and women about how to site such buildings: within the domestic and religious sphere, or in the civic/commercial area. Van Slyck, *Free to All*, 137–43.

39. A good example of the local resistance and transformation and accommodation of mass culture is Waller, *Main Street Amusements*.

40. Vidler, "A Note on the Idea of Type in Architecture," xix. Vidler suggests that it was not until the 1880s that the idea that a building's form should be related to its specific function, which dates back to the Enlightenment, took hold in the United States with the publication of Leopold Eidlitz's *The Nature and Function of Art, More Especially of Architecture* in 1881.

41. Doyle, *New Men, New Cities, New South*, 36.

42. "Recent Architecture in Atlanta," *Harper's Weekly* 33 (August 3, 1889): 623–24.

43. Currey, "The Virtuous Soldier," 134.

44. "Negro Not Admitted to Y.M.C.A.," *Cleveland Gazette,* March 12, 1887, 94.

45. Mjagkij, *Light in the Darkness*, 67–85.

46. Hale, *Making Whiteness,* 6; J. Allen, *Without Sanctuary*, 165–203.

47. For a discussion of the development of the booster ethos in the early-nineteenth-century Midwest as a masculine, regional phenomenon, see Tim Mahoney, *Provincial Lives*.

48. See "Dedication and Openings," box 4, A–T folders, Buildings and Furnishings Service Materials, Administrative Records, Kautz Family YMCA Archives, University of Minnesota Libraries, Minneapolis.

49. "Trinity of Constructive Forces," *Association Men* 33 (November 1908): 55.

50. *Founders and Builders of Greensboro*; I. J. Issacs, *Progressive Greensboro*.

51. M. A. Brown, *Greensboro,* 28; Kipp, "Old Notables and Newcomers," 385.

52. See background on Greensboro in Bishir and Southern, *A Guide to the Historic Architecture of Piedmont, North Carolina*, 322–38.

53. "The Handsome New Building of the Young Men's Christian Association," *Greensboro Daily Record,* October 15, 1911, Clippings Files, Greensboro Public Library, Greensboro, North Carolina.

54. Isenberg, *Downtown America,* 42–43.

55. Ames, "Words to Live By," chapter 3 in *Death in the Dining Room,* 97–149.

56. Good general histories of the picture postcard can be found in Jakle, *Postcards of the Night,* 20–21; Dotterrer and Cranz, "The Picture Postcard," 46; and Meikle, "A Paper Atlantis," 271.

57. Jakle, *Postcards of the Night,* 20–21; Dotterrer and Cranz, "The Picture Postcard," 46.

58. Trachtenberg, *Reading American Photographs*; Hales, *Silver Cities*; Earle, ed., *Points of View*.

59. Dotterrer and Cranz, "The Picture Postcard," 44.

60. Baggett, "Birmingham and the Picture Postcard."

61. All postcards discussed in the text can be found in the Cliff Smith YMCA Postcard Collection, Archives and Special Collections, Babson Library, Springfield College, available at http://ymcapostcards.spfldcol.edu/, accessed July 15, 2008.

62. Spears, *100 Years on the Road,* 149–52.

4. Bedrooms, Billiards, and Basketball

1. "From the Editor's Viewpoint," *Association Men* 36 (December 1910): 116.

2. I. E. Brown, "Brief History of the Building Movement in America," in *Book of Young Men's Christian Association Buildings*, n.p.

3. R. W. Cooke, "Some Significant Gleanings from the History of the Young Men's Christian Association of Chicago," 1940, 7–8, box 7, folder 6, Young Men's Christian Association of Metropolitan Chicago Collection, Archives and Manuscripts, Chicago Historical Society, Chicago.

4. Bluestone, *Constructing Chicago*, 105–150; Donald Hoffman, "The Setback Skyscraper City of 1891."

5. Undated clipping, YMCA Scrapbook, box 89, folder 14, Young Men's Christian Association of Metropolitan Chicago Collection, Archives and Manuscripts, Chicago Historical Society, Chicago.

6. W. L. Jenney to C. S. McCormick, box 88, folder 8, Young Men's Christian Association of Metropolitan Chicago Collection, Archives and Manuscripts, Chicago Historical Society, Chicago.

7. Gibbs, *Business Architectural Imagery in America,* 78.

8. Halsey Hammond, "Fully Use the Auditorium," *Association Men* 39 (May 1913): 413.

9. "Experience Teaches," *Association Men* 38 (February 1912): 241.

10. Putney, "Character Building in the YMCA." Roosevelt, who had grown up in New York on Madison Square in a social circle that included the Dodges and other YMCA families, was an ardent supporter of the organization and was responsible for coining the term "manhood factories" to describe its buildings.

11. For a discussion of the shift in the perception of swimming from bathing to athletics, see Van Slyck, *A Manufactured Wilderness,* chapter 5.

12. Johnson, *The History of YMCA Physical Education,* 41. Collegiate athletic facilities, especially Harvard's Hemenway Gymnasium (1888), were also influential.

13. Turkish baths appeared in Scranton in 1901, in Washington, D.C., in 1905, in Detroit in 1908, and in St. Paul in 1911.

14. H. I. Allen, "Special Equipment for Business Men."

15. Johnson, *The History of YMCA Physical Education*, 41.

16. It is ironic, or perhaps inevitable, that locker rooms designed to control, classify, and organize male bodies became the site of resistance to control, the scene of surreptitious or even overt cruising by gay men. See Gustav-Wrathall, *Take the Young Stranger by the Hand,* and Chauncey, *Gay New York*.

17. Cited in Dedmon, *Great Enterprises,* 129.

18. Nelson F. Evans, "The Work of the Young Men's Christian Association" (cited in chapter 2, note 49), 90.

19. Ibid.

20. Gordon, "Association Architecture: Part I."

21. Wharton, *Building the Cold War,* chapter 6.

22. Groth, *Living Downtown,* 57.

23. Barr, "Y.M.C.A. Dormitories," 6–7, box 5, Buildings and Furnishings Service Materials, Administrative Records, Kautz Family YMCA Archives, University of Minnesota Libraries, Minneapolis. The Chicago (1913) and Buffalo (1910) associations also erected separate YMCA hotels to serve their patrons, but most associations incorporated living space into their buildings.

24. Willard, "The Development of College Architecture in America"; Heald, "Fraternity Life at Dartmouth."

25. Barr, "Y.M.C.A. Dormitories" (cited in note 23), 8.

26. H. M. Shipps, "The Y.M.C.A. Dormitories," quoted in Barr, "Y.M.C.A. Dormitories" (cited in note 23), 21, box 5, Buildings and Furnishings Service Materials, Administrative Records, Kautz Family YMCA Archives, University of Minnesota Libraries, Minneapolis.

27. "From the Editor's Viewpoint" (cited in note 1), 116–17.

28. Macleod, *Building Character in the American Boy,* 7–8.

29. Ibid., 74–78.

30. The Report of an Informal Conference on Young Men's Christian Association Buildings, July 25 and 26, 1901 (Buffalo: 1901), box 1, Buildings and Furnishings Service Materials, Administrative Records, Kautz Family YMCA Archives, University of Minnesota Libraries, Minneapolis.

31. H. S. Ninde, J. T. Bowne, and Erskine Uhl, eds., *A Handbook of the History, Organization, and Methods of Work of Young Men's Christian Associations* (New York: International Committee of the Young Men's Christian Associations, 1892), 166, box 1, Buildings and Furnishings Service Materials, Administrative Records, Kautz Family YMCA Archives, University of Minnesota Libraries, Minneapolis.

32. C. S. Ward, "The Short-Term Building Campaign," *Association Men* 32 (October 1906): 19–21, esp. 20; "Bennington, Vermont," *Association Men* 32 (October 1906): 20.

33. Robinson, "Provision for Boys' Work in Association Buildings."

34. Van Slyck, *A Manufactured Wilderness.*

35. "Furnish the Building," *Association Men* 39 (April 1913): 342.

36. This change echoed a general shift away from the parlor in American homes during the Progressive period. Wright, *Building the Dream,* 172.

37. Bederman, "'The Women Have Had Charge of the Church Work Long Enough,'" 432–35.

38. "A Building in Which the Decorations, Furnishings and Color Scheme and Effects Have Been Happily Used to Enhance Its Effectiveness," *Association Men* 31 (November 1904): 76–77; "Barren Reading Rooms," *Association Men* 39 (October 1913): 22; Louis E. Jallade, "Suggestions for Association Furnishings," *Association Men* 37 (October 1911): 15; and "Passing Things in Association Architecture," *Association Men* 31 (May 1905): 378.

39. Willson, *The Music Man,* act 1, scene 2.

40. "Keeping the Building Up," *Association Men* 35 (May 1909): 381.

41. "The Social Room and the 'Inn' of Brooklyn Central," *Association Men* 33 (August 1906): 475.

42. "Centennial of Y Movement Being Observed This Month: Local Organization Keeps Step with International Progress," *Greensboro Daily Record,* ca. 1944, Clippings Files, Greensboro Public Library, Greensboro, North Carolina.

43. Christian F. Reisner, "Christians and Pool," *Association Men* 41 (August 1915): 573.

44. "New Electric Signs Offending the Eye," *New York Times,* September 7, 1910, 4.

5. From Greensboro to China

1. I. K. Pond, "Buildings of the Young Men's Christian Association," 28.

2. Sherman Dean, "Putting Character into Buildings," *Association Men* 53 (January 1928): 215.

3. Pai, *The Portfolio and the Diagram,* 21.

4. Ibid., 62.

5. "The Business of Developing Men and Boys to Higher Efficiency," *Association Men* 34 (January 1909): 155; C. M. Wonacott, "Scientific Association Management," *Association Men* 37 (May 1912): 398–99; "Are the Associations Efficient?" *Association Men* 37 (November 1912): 79; Charles R. Towson, "Engineers of Environment: A New Evangelism in the Industrial World," *Association Men* 34 (September 1909): 580–81.

6. On obsolescence, see "Passing Things in Association Architecture" (cited in chapter 4, note 38); and Hammond, "Fully Use the Auditorium" (cited in chapter 4, note 8).

7. This trend was echoed in school and library construction as well. See Van Slyck, *Free to All*, 101–120.

8. Hopkins, *History of the YMCA in North America,* 458.

9. "Conference on the World-Wide Expansion of the Young Men's Christian Association Held at the White House, October 20, 1910," box 62, Building Records, Records of YMCA International Work in China, Y.USA.9-2-4, Kautz Family YMCA Archives, University of Minnesota Libraries, Minneapolis.

10. "Heating of the Young Men's Christian Association Buildings," *Radiation* 2 (May 1913): 10–14, Buildings and Furnishings Service Materials, Administrative Records, Kautz Family YMCA Archives, University of Minnesota Libraries, Minneapolis.

11. Shao, *Culturing Modernity*; Stapleton, *Civilizing Chengdu*.

12. To maintain clarity I use the Wade-Giles, historical spelling of Chinese cities employed by the YMCA in its records.

13. Risedorph, "Reformers, Athletes, and Students," 17–21.

14. "Brilliant Reception Marks the Opening of the YMCA Building," *Greensboro Daily Record*, December 9, 1911, 3, Clippings Files, Greensboro Public Library, Greensboro, North Carolina.

15. Ibid.

16. Letter from Lewis H. Martin to John Glover, May 1, 1911, box 1, Buildings and Furnishings Service Materials, Administrative Records, Kautz Family YMCA Archives, University of Minnesota Libraries, Minneapolis.

17. Bishir, *North Carolina Architecture,* 363.

18. Neil McMillan to Fred B. Shipp, July 18, 1932, Buildings and Furnishings Service/Property Management Historical Records, YMCA of the USA Headquarters, Chicago; Irving K. Pond to William Stanley Parker, secretary of the American Institute of Architects, April 8, 1919, Biographical File: Walter F. Shattuck, box 231, folder 39, Membership Files, Record Group 803, The American Institute of Architects Archives, Washington, D.C. Pond noted that the AIA had received many complaints about Shattuck and Hussey during his tenure as president.

19. "Heating of the Young Men's Christian Association Buildings" (cited in note 10), 13.

20. Hansen, "YMCA Swimming Pool Equipment."

21. Narragansett Machine Company advertisement, *The Triangle* 3 (April 1891); "A Century of Y.M.C.A. Gymnasiums," *Association Men* 26 (January 1901).

22. "The Building Boom Is On in the YMCA."

23. "Another Product of Truth and Beauty," *Association Men* 38 (March 1913): 24.

24. National X-Ray Reflector Company advertisement, *Association Men* 40 (November 1915): 105.

25. Otis Elevator advertisement, *Association Men* 40 (January 1915): 229.

26. Foss, "Equipment and Construction of the Physical Department," *Physical Training* 7 (May 1910): 3–7.

27. "Shattuck and Layer and Medusa," *Association Men* 50 (July 1925): n.p.

28. Foss, "Equipment and Construction of the Physical Department," *Physical Training* 7 (May 1910): 5.

29. "Clinton Wire Cloth Company," *Association Men* 41 (April 1916): 123.

30. Risedorph, "Reformers, Athletes, and Students," 137.

31. The International Committee wanted to build a native organization, rather than an outpost of the American YMCA. Thus they offered seed money and expertise, but did not fully fund building projects.

32. Shattuck and Hussey went on to construct buildings in Shanghai, Hankow (now Wuhan), Foochow (now Fuzhou), Canton (now Guangzhou), Hong Kong, and Manila. Cody, *Building in China,* 78.

33. A letter from C. W. Harvey to Fletcher Brockman dated March 6, 1914, seems to suggest that the International Committee entered into a contractual agreement with Shattuck and Hussey, one they soon regretted; box 27, 1913–1924, Building Records, Records of YMCA International Work in China, Y.USA.9-2-4, Kautz Family YMCA Archives, University of Minnesota Libraries, Minneapolis.

34. Roy Creighton, "Annual Report: Building in Central China," 1920, n.p., box 67, Building Records, Records of YMCA International Work in China, Y.USA.9-2-4, Kautz Family YMCA Archives, University of Minnesota Libraries, Minneapolis.

35. Needham, *Science and Civilisation in China,* Vol. 4, Part 2, *Mechanical Engineering,* 97.

36. Hommel, *China at Work,* 49–55.

37. Cody, *Building in China,* 78.

38. Bishir, *North Carolina Architecture,* 313.

39. L. H. Martin, "Everybody's Editorials," *Association Men* 37 (December 1911): 123.

40. Executive Committee of the International Committee of the YMCA Minutes, Report of the Commission Appointed at the Atlantic City Conference to Further Consider and Propose Desirable Re-Adjustments in the Work of the International Committee, December 12, 1912, 50, Administrative Records, Board/Council Minutes, Kautz Family YMCA Archives, University of Minnesota Libraries, Minneapolis.

41. "The Builders' Bureau," *Cleveland's Young Men* (May 2, 1912), clipping, box 1, Buildings and Furnishings Service Materials, Administrative Records, Kautz Family YMCA Archives, University of Minnesota Libraries, Minneapolis.

42. Cutlip, *Fund Raising in the United States,* 41.

43. Hopkins, *History of the YMCA in North America,* 599.

44. "Centennial of Y Movement Being Observed This Month" (cited in chapter 4, note 42), 6.

45. "An International Building Bureau," *Association Men* 41 (December 1915): 149.

46. It is not clear exactly when McMillan worked for the Chicago Board of Education, but it seems likely to have been at least partially under the directorship of Dwight Heald Perkins, architect of settlement houses and park systems, who held the post between 1905 and 1910, the years just after McMillan's graduation from architecture school. See Davis and Indeck, *Dwight Heald Perkins,* 10–12.

47. "Neil McMillan," 29; "An International Building Bureau" (cited in note 45), 149.

48. The resolution in its report to the Cincinnati Convention stated that "the International Committee establish and maintain in its headquarters in New York an association building bureau through which special services could be rendered to Associations in connection with their building enterprises." *Report of the International Committee to the Thirty-Eighth International Convention of YMCAs* (New York: International Committee, 1913), 38, Administrative Records, General Assemblies, Kautz Family YMCA Archives, University of Minnesota Libraries, Minneapolis.

49. This was similar to the federal and state practice at the time. See Hamlin, "The State Architect." On federal architectural practices, see Wodehouse, "Ammi Burnham Young," "Alfred B. Mullett," and "W. A. Potter"; on school district arrangements, see D. R. Nelson, "School Architecture in Chicago during the Progressive Era."

50. L. H. Martin, "A National Building Expert Needed," *Association Men* 36 (June 1911): 376.

51. Neil McMillan to Fred B. Shipp, July 18, 1932, Buildings and Furnishings Service/Property Management Historical Records, YMCA of the USA Headquarters, Chicago.

52. *The Dormitory Problem in the Young Men's Christian Association*, Commission of the Association of General Secretaries, May 19–23, 1915, Residences/Dormitories File, Buildings and Furnishings Service Materials, Administrative Records, Kautz Family YMCA Archives, University of Minnesota Libraries, Minneapolis.

53. Halsey Hammond, "To Keep the Building Up," *Association Men* 35 (March 1909): 294; "Keeping the Building Up" (cited in chapter 4, note 40).

54. Allen, "Artificial Light for Gymnasiums"; Foss, "Equipment and Construction of the Physical Department"; see also J. H. McCurdy, "Notes on Gymnasiums and Athletic Grounds for the Young Men's Christian Associations," Springfield, Mass., 1899, box 1, Physical Education Programs, 1887–1997, Y.USA.5, Kautz Family YMCA Archives, University of Minnesota Libraries, Minneapolis.

55. Wood, "Buildings of the Young Men's Christian Association," 264–69.

56. Abramson, "The Planning of a Young Men's Christian Association Building"; and Pond, "Buildings of the Young Men's Christian Association."

57. A. G. Studer, "Large Modern Buildings," *Journal of the Proceedings,* Toronto, Canada, October 28–31, 1910, 78–80.

58. Walter Wood, "Types of Buildings Best Suited to Metropolitan Associations," *Proceedings of the Fourth Conference of Metropolitan General Secretaries*, December 3–7, 1914, 12–19, Buildings and Furnishings Service Materials, Administrative Records, Kautz Family YMCA Archives, University of Minnesota Libraries, Minneapolis.

59. *Yearbook of the Young Men's Christian Associations of North America,* 1916–17, 26.

60. Emmons, "Diagrammatic Practices," 8.

61. Statement for Consideration of Special Committee on Architectural Bureau's Policy and Charges, September 10, 1928, 9, Buildings and Furnishings Service/Property Management Historical Records, YMCA of the USA Headquarters, Chicago.

62. "Building Bureau," *Yearbook of the Young Men's Christian Associations of North America*, 1918, 26.

63. Statement for Consideration of Special Committee on Architectural Bureau's Policy and Charges, September 10, 1928, 8, Buildings and Furnishings Service/Property Management Historical Records, YMCA of the USA Headquarters, Chicago.

64. Minutes of the Executive Committee of the International Committee of the Young Men's Christian Association of North America, September 11, 1919, 376, Administrative Records, Board/Council Minutes, Kautz Family YMCA Archives, University of Minnesota Libraries, Minneapolis; and Neil McMillan, "Building Bureau Service," in *The Building Enterprise of a City Young Men's Christian Association* (New York: International Committee, 1919), 11–13, box 1, Buildings and Furnishings Service Materials, Administrative Records, Kautz Family YMCA Archives, University of Minnesota Libraries, Minneapolis.

65. C.C. May, "A Post-War Construction Program," 223, 328; R.L. Rayburn, letter dated August 23, 1940, Buildings and Furnishings Service/Property Management Historical Records, YMCA of the USA Headquarters, Chicago.

66. "Some Gains to the Association Movement from the Service of the Architectural Bureau," statement prepared for Mr. Urice for Home Division Summary, September 8, 1927, 2, box 1, Buildings and Furnishings Service Materials, Administrative Records, Kautz Family YMCA Archives, University of Minnesota Libraries, Minneapolis.

67. Minutes, Executive Committee of the International Committee, September 11, 1919, 376, Administrative Records, Board/Council Minutes, Kautz Family YMCA Archives, University of Minnesota Libraries, Minneapolis; "Building Bureau," *Yearbook of the Young Men's Christian Association of North America,* 1920, 33–34; "Outline of the Furnishings Service," The Building Bureau of the International Committee of the Young Men's Christian Associations, April 15, 1922, 1, box 1, Building and Furnishings Service Materials, Administrative Records, Kautz Family YMCA Archives, University of Minnesota Libraries, Minneapolis.

68. See Price, "Architect and Decorator"; "The Interdependence of Architecture and Interior Decoration"; Moran, "Interior Decoration"; and "Interior Architecture: Cooperation between Architect and Decorator."

69. "Building Bureau," *Yearbook of the Young Men's Christian Associations of North America*, 1921, 32; Obsolete Furniture Designs, box 6, Buildings and Furnishings Service Materials, Administrative Records, Kautz Family YMCA Archives, University of Minnesota Libraries, Minneapolis.

70. "Building Bureau," 1924 Report of the International Committee of the Young Men's Christian Association to the National Council, 94, box 1, Buildings and Furnishings Service Materials, Administrative Records, Kautz Family YMCA Archives, University of Minnesota Libraries, Minneapolis.

71. Fred B. Shipp to Neil McMillan Jr., March 7, 1919, Buildings and Furnishings Service/Property Management Historical Records, YMCA of the USA Headquarters, Chicago.

72. The 10 percent not utilizing the Bureau either had feelings against the International Committee, or had strong personal connections to the specialist architects. See "Statement for Consideration of the Special Committee on the Architectural Bureau's Policy and Charges," September 10, 1928, Buildings and Furnishings Ser-

vice/Property Management Historical Records, YMCA of the USA Headquarters, Chicago; and Report of the Architectural Bureau to the National Council of YMCAs for the period from December 1, 1924, to October 5, 1925, 2–4, box 1, Buildings and Furnishings Service Materials, Administrative Records, Kautz Family YMCA Archives, University of Minnesota Libraries, Minneapolis.

73. Paul C. Foster, "Opinions, Plans, and Policies," *Association Men* 37 (December 1911): 123.

74. Rayburn, "The Purpose of the New Type of 'Y.'"

75. George B. Hodge, "Efficiency at Too High a Price," *Association Men* 41 (July 1916): 560–61.

76. "The Watchtower," *Association Men* 51 (August 1926): 567, 595.

77. Neil McMillan Jr., "Are We Getting Better Buildings?" *Association Men* 51 (January 1926): 228.

78. Rayburn, "The Purpose of the New Type of 'Y,'" 151.

79. Dewey, *Human Nature and Conduct,* 10. See also Pence, *The Y.M.C.A. and Social Need*, 244, 276–77; and Hopkins, *History of the YMCA in North America*, 550–51. Some of the other important primary sources cited by the YMCA are Coe, *Social Theory of Religious Education*, and Kilpatrick, *Foundations of Method*.

80. Hopkins, *History of the YMCA in North America,* 550.

81. Rayburn, "The Purpose of the New Type of 'Y.'"

82. Sherman Dean, "The Advancing Wave of Color," *Association Men* 54 (January 1929): 216.

83. Report of the Special Committee Appointed to Review General Policies and Budget Problems of the Architectural Bureau, 1928, 2, box 1, Buildings and Furnishings Service Materials, Administrative Records, Kautz Family YMCA Archives, University of Minnesota Libraries, Minneapolis. There is an indication that the Bureau intended to do a comprehensive research study on this subject, but the study, if it was carried out, is now lost. See also "Outline for Study of the Character of Association Buildings," February 1, 1923, Buildings and Furnishings Service/Property Management Historical Records, YMCA of the USA Headquarters, Chicago; and Super, *Formative Ideas in the YMCA,* 113–14.

84. S. O. Houser, "Polish the Handle of the Big Front Door," *Association Men* 50 (January 1925): 210, 226.

85. In papers preserved at the Kautz Family YMCA Archives, the Building Committee left a record of the process of selecting and working with an architect and the Building Bureau. West Side YMCA Records, 1896–1980s, Y.GNY.14, Kautz Family YMCA Archives, University of Minnesota Libraries, Minneapolis.

86. New York YMCA Building Committee Minutes, November 21, 1927, Document B27-11, Board of Directors/Committees box, Building Committee Minutes, 1926–1929, New York YMCA, Y.GNY Records, Kautz Family YMCA Archives, University of Minnesota Libraries, Minneapolis.

87. "West Side Y.M.C.A. Statement of Program," Building Committee Minutes, Document B28-1A, Board of Directors/Committees box, Building Committee Minutes, 1926–1929, New York YMCA, Y.GNY Records, Kautz Family YMCA Archives, University of Minnesota Libraries, Minneapolis.

88. "Architects Who Have Been Suggested in Connection with the Building Program of the New York Association," Document B-27-7, September 14, 1927, Board of Directors/Committees box, Building Committee Minutes, 1926–1929, New York

YMCA, Y.GNY Records, Kautz Family YMCA Archives, University of Minnesota Libraries, Minneapolis.

89. Building Committee Minutes, December 5, 1927, 3, Board of Directors/Committees box, Building Committee Minutes, 1926–1929, New York YMCA, Y.GNY Records, Kautz Family YMCA Archives, University of Minnesota Libraries, Minneapolis.

90. Frank Totten to F. Louis Slade, December 22, 1927, Document B-27-13; Walter Wyckoff to F. Louis Slade, December 22, 1927, Document B-27-12. Board of Directors/Committees box, Building Committee Minutes, 1926–1929, New York YMCA, Y.GNY Records, Kautz Family YMCA Archives, University of Minnesota Libraries, Minneapolis.

91. Stern, Gilmartin, and Mellins, *New York 1930,* 203.

92. "West Side Y.M.C.A., New York, Dwight James Baum, Architect."

93. Stern, Gilmartin, and Mellins, *New York 1930,* 203, 208–213.

94. "Interior Architecture: The Spirit of the Old Spanish in Modern Decoration."

95. C. C. May, "A Post-War Construction Program."

96. Ibid., 343.

97. Ibid., 223.

98. Jay Urice, "Some Gains to the Association from the Service of the Architectural Bureau," September 8, 1927, Buildings and Furnishings Service/Property Management Historical Records, YMCA of the USA Headquarters, Chicago.

99. La Beaume & Klein and Helmle & Corbett, two firms with AIA presidents among their members, had either worked for the YMCA or expressed their desire to do so. Letter from Neil McMillan to Jay Urice, February 10, 1927, box 1, Buildings and Furnishings Service Materials, Administrative Records, Kautz Family YMCA Archives, University of Minnesota Libraries, Minneapolis.

100. The YMCA's fee structure and cooperative arrangements were copied by similar bureaus in charge of the planning of churches and hospitals. "1924 Report of the International Committee to the National Council," 94–95, box 1, Buildings and Furnishings Service Materials, Administrative Records, Kautz Family YMCA Archives, University of Minnesota Libraries, Minneapolis.

101. Saint, *The Image of the Architect,* 158.

102. "Wilmington YMCA Competition, Minutes of Combined Meeting of Competitors, Committee on Competitions, AIA, Building Committee, Chairman, and Architectural Bureau Director, February 29, 1928," Buildings and Furnishings Service/Property Management Historical Records, YMCA of the USA Headquarters, Chicago.

103. "Minutes of the Regular Meeting Held at the Fort Pitt Hotel," Tuesday, September 18, 1928, *The Charrette*, appended to "Notes of Interview with A. W. Rice, Chairman, AIA Committee on Competitions," September 24, 1928, Buildings and Furnishings Service/Property Management Historical Records, YMCA of the USA Headquarters, Chicago.

104. "Statement for Consideration of the Special Committee on the Architectural Bureau's Policy and Charges, September 10, 1928"; "Statement for Second Meeting of Special Committee on Policy and Charges of the Architectural Bureau at Edgewater Beach Hotel, Chicago, October 21, 1928"; "Minutes of the Third Meeting of Special Committee on Architectural Bureau Policy and Charges, April 10, 1929," Buildings and Furnishings Service/Property Management Historical Records, YMCA of the USA Headquarters, Chicago.

105. "Wilmington YMCA Competition" (cited in note 102), 2; "Minutes of the Third Meeting" (cited in note 104), 1.

106. "Minutes of the Third Meeting" (cited in note 104), 3.

107. Letter from Neil McMillan to Louis La Beaume, Director, American Institute of Architects, April 16, 1929, Buildings and Furnishings Service/Property Management Historical Records, YMCA of the USA Headquarters, Chicago.

Epilogue

1. Kimball, "The Social Center: Part I," 433.
2. Editorial, *Association Men* 38 (February 1912): 284.
3. "Denver's Institutional Church," *Association Men* 29 (October 1903): 12.
4. Gates, *Recreation and the Church,* 146.
5. Bennett, "What Is the Social Gospel?"
6. *Proceedings of the Third Convention of Christian Workers*, November 1888, 70, Records of the YMCA of the City of New York, 1852–1980s, Y.GNY.20, Kautz Family YMCA Archives, University of Minnesota Libraries, Minneapolis.
7. Cook, "The Institutional Church," 645–46, 647.
8. H. F. Evans, *The Sunday-School Building and Its Equipment,* 42.
9. Ibid., 86–87.
10. Austin Abbott, "Unproductive Property," in Gladden, ed., *Parish Problems,* 126–28.
11. Douglass, *The St. Louis Church Survey*, 114.
12. Gates, *Recreation and the Church*, 149–50.
13. Ibid., 1–2.
14. Ibid., 154.
15. H. F. Evans, *The Sunday-School Building and Its Equipment,* 92.
16. Gibbons, *John Wanamaker,* 328.
17. Miller, "Churches Are Not What They Used to Be . . ."
18. Ibid.
19. Dillard, "Regarding Design of Non-Ritualistic Church Buildings," 164.
20. Conover, "Building a Seven-Day-a-Week Church."
21. The founding of church bureaus is obliquely referred to in Betts, "Protestant Churches Work to Improve Public Taste in Architecture."
22. Conover, *Building the House of God,* 84–93.
23. S. Newton Leo, "The Beginnings of the YMHA," [New York] *YMHA Bulletin* (March 1924): 16.
24. Nadel, "The Y.M.H.A. and the Jewish Center."
25. In an anonymous typescript preserved at the Ninety-second Street Y in New York titled "Talk to YMCA," February 25, 1930, the speaker notes that "In a general way the purposes of the Young Men's Hebrew Association are similar to those of the Y.M.C.A. In fact, the early history of my organization indicates clearly that, in its inception, our association was patterned after yours." YMCA-YMHA Materials, Ninety-second Street YM-YWHA Archives, New York City.
26. Henry M. Orne to Perceval Menken, January 13, 1899, Building Committee files, 1899, Ninety-second Street YM-YWHA Archives, New York City.
27. Minutes of the YWHA Building Committee, February 27, 1913, YWCA Files, Ninety-second Street YM-YWHA Archives, New York City.
28. Abramson, "The Planning of a Young Men's Christian Association Building."

29. Letter from Louis Allen Abramson to Henry M. Toch, June 28, 1927, Architects File, 1929 Building Materials, Ninety-second Street YM-YWHA Archives, New York City.

30. Letter from Louis Allen Abramson to Sidney B. Crystal, July 6, 1927, Architects File, 1929 Building Materials, Ninety-second Street YM-YWHA Archives, New York City. His claim to the West Side Building is confusing since the building's architects were Parish & Schroeder, with no reference to either Jallade or Abramson.

31. Abramson, "The Planning of a Young Men's Christian Association Building: Part I," 51.

32. Expertise in the design of YMCAs led to commissions to build settlement houses and public facilities, and vice versa. Irving Pond and his brother Allen were the architects of Hull House, the nation's best-known settlement house, in the 1890s, along with several YMCAs at the turn of the century and, in the 1910s and 1920s, student unions.

33. Hughey, *Civil Religion and Moral Order,* 87–89.

34. P. Boyer, *Urban Masses and Moral Order in America,* 242–43.

35. Calkins, *Substitutes for the Saloon*, and Freeman, *If Not the Saloon—What?*

36. E. J. Ward, *The Social Center,* 129.

37. Ibid., 130.

38. E. J. Ward, "The Schoolhouse as the Civic and Social Center of the Community," 445.

39. Ward is referring primarily to the 10 million dollars expended on the Chicago South Park System by 1910, money that could have been expended on the improvement of public schools. For a discussion of the South Parks, see G. R. Taylor, "Recreation Developments in Chicago Parks," 88.

40. Quoted in Perry and Williams, *New York School Centers and Their Community Policy,* 39.

41. Stitt, "Evening Recreation Centers," 48–50.

42. "Liberty Buildings as Victory Monuments."

43. Bard, "Community Houses as War Memorials," 129.

44. Otis, "The Financing of Memorial Buildings," 103.

45. "Liberty Buildings as Soldiers' Memorials," *American City* 19 (September 1918): 173.

46. For a discussion of the Y as architectural model, see Kimball, "The Social Center," and Candler, "The Community House as a War Memorial," 199.

47. Candler, "The Community House as a War Memorial," 199.

48. Candler, "Community Buildings for Industrial Towns," 313.

49. "Dalton Erects Splendid Community House," *The Community Center* 5 (January–April 1923): 4.

50. Daniels, *America via the Neighborhood*, 300.

51. "The Question Box."

52. Review of *Substitutes for the Saloon, Association Men* 27 (April 1902): 304; reference to *The Christian Century* cited in "The Watch Tower," *Association Men* 50 (November 1925): 115.

53. "The Dilemma of the Y.M.C.A.," *Association Men* 34 (August 1909): 532–33.

54. Quoted in John W. Cook, "The Problems of the City Association Field and Relationships," paper presented at the Garden City conference, March 3, 1916, 3, uncatalogued materials, box marked City Department Counseling Commission, Build-

ings and Furnishings Service/Property Management Historical Records, YMCA of the USA Headquarters, Chicago.

55. Ibid., 4.

56. Young Men's Christian Association of Chicago, Prospectus, 1921, 21, Chicago Historical Society Archives and Manuscripts, box 10, folder 6, Young Men's Christian Association of Metropolitan Chicago Collection, Archives and Manuscripts, Chicago Historical Society, Chicago.

57. C. C. May, "A Post-War Construction Program," 220–30.

58. Young Men's Christian Association of Chicago, Prospectus (cited in note 56).

BIBLIOGRAPHY

This first scholarly study of the YMCA building's architectural and social significance in the American city has been drawn from a variety of sources. Unfortunately the YMCA, typically a highly organized and bureaucratic organization, did not preserve most of its building records. Though thousands of YMCAs were constructed according to a systematic procedure, little manuscript material is extant. There is no complete institutional record of these buildings or the building process.

In order to create such a record, I have used material from contemporary architectural periodicals and the monthly building columns in the YMCA journal *Association Men* to supplement the pamphlets, photographs, plan-books, scrapbooks, and administrative records available to me.

The development of the YMCA building occurred on both national and local levels. Through the International Committee and later the Building Bureau, the concept of a YMCA building was promoted and information pertaining to buildings was collected and distributed. The Kautz Family YMCA Archives at the University of Minnesota in Minneapolis, the Buildings and Furnishings Service at YMCA of the USA headquarters in Chicago, and the Archives of the American Institute of Architects are essential sources for piecing together the YMCA's national building policy.

Equally important to any study of YMCA architecture are the records of the local associations, which interpreted and helped to shape the national architectural policy. The associations in Chicago and New York were leaders in the architectural development of the Y. The YMCA collection at the Chicago Historical Society contains building committee minutes, plans, scrapbooks, correspondence, and other important records pertaining to its building activities.

Archival Sources

Administrative Records, Kautz Family YMCA Archives, University of Minnesota Libraries, Minneapolis.

Annual Reports of Local Associations in China, 1901–1945, Records of YMCA International Work in China, Y.USA.9-2-4, Kautz Family YMCA Archives, University of Minnesota Libraries, Minneapolis.

Annual Reports of the YMCAs of China, Korea, and Hong Kong, 1902–1904, Records of YMCA International Work in China, Y.USA.9-2-4, Kautz Family YMCA Archives, University of Minnesota Libraries, Minneapolis.

Annual Reports of the Young Men's Christian Associations of Greater New York, Kautz Family YMCA Archives, University of Minnesota Libraries, Minneapolis.

Board of Directors Minutes, Young Men's Christian Association of New York, Y.GNY.0020, Kautz Family YMCA Archives, University of Minnesota Libraries, Minneapolis.

Building Committee files, Ninety-second Street YM-YWHA Archives, New York City.

Building Committee Minutes, New York YMCA, Y.GNY Records, Kautz Family YMCA Archives, University of Minnesota Libraries, Minneapolis.

Building Records, Records of YMCA International Work in China, Y.USA.9-2-4, Kautz Family YMCA Archives, University of Minnesota Libraries, Minneapolis.

Buildings and Furnishings Service Materials, Administrative Records, Kautz Family YMCA Archives, University of Minnesota Libraries, Minneapolis.

Buildings and Furnishings Service/Property Management Historical Records, YMCA of the USA Headquarters, Chicago.

Clippings Files, Greensboro Public Library, Greensboro, North Carolina.

Committees, Competitions, Correspondence, and Reports, 1917–1954, Record Group 801, AIA Office Files, Series 2.1, The American Institute of Architects Archives, Washington, D.C.

Executive Committee Minutes, Record Group 509, AIA Board of Directors, Series 2, The American Institute of Architects Archives, Washington, D.C.

McBurney, Robert, Correspondence, 1866–1885, 1890s, Records of the YMCA of the City of New York, Y.GNY.0020, Kautz Family YMCA Archives, University of Minnesota Libraries, Minneapolis.

McBurney Branch YMCA Records, 1858–1992, Y.GNY.13, Kautz Family YMCA Archives, University of Minnesota Libraries, Minneapolis.

Membership Files, Record Group 803, The American Institute of Architects Archives, Washington, D.C.

Pamphlet Files, New York Public Library, New York City.

Physical Education Programs, 1887–1997, Y.USA.5, Kautz Family YMCA Archives, University of Minnesota Libraries, Minneapolis.

Records of the YMCA of the City of New York, YMCA of Greater New York, Y.GNY.0020, Kautz Family YMCA Archives, University of Minnesota Libraries, Minneapolis.

R. G. Dun & Co. Collection, Baker Library Historical Collections, Harvard Business School, Cambridge, Massachusetts.

Smith, Cliff, YMCA Postcard Collection, Archives and Special Collections, Babson Library, Springfield College, Springfield, Massachusetts.

YMCA Biographical Files, Kautz Family YMCA Archives, University of Minnesota Libraries, Minneapolis.
YMCA of Philadelphia, 1854–1967, 22, Urban Archives, Temple University, Philadelphia.
YMCA-YMHA Materials, Ninety-second Street YM-YWHA Archives, New York City.
Young Men's Christian Association of Metropolitan Chicago Collection, Archives and Manuscripts, Chicago Historical Society, Chicago.
YWCA Files, Ninety-second Street YM-YWHA Archives, New York City.

Periodicals

Association Men, New York. Monthly, 1899–1930.
Association Monthly, New York: New York Young Men's Christian Association. Monthly, 1870–1873.
The Community Center, New York. Bimonthly, 1917–1924.
Journal of the Proceedings of the Annual Conventions of the Y.M.C.A.s of the United States and British Provinces. Annually, 1854–1877; Biennially, 1878–1901; Triennially, since 1902.
The Watchman, Chicago: Chicago Young Men's Christian Association. Weekly, 1873–1889.
Yearbook of the Young Men's Christian Associations of North America. Annually, since 1875.

Articles and Books

Abell, Aaron Ignatius. *The Urban Impact on American Protestantism, 1865–1900.* Hamden, Conn.: Archon, 1962.
Abramson, Louis Allen. "The Planning of a Young Men's Christian Association Building." *The Brickbuilder* 22 (March 1913): 49–54, 77–80, 127–31.
"Accepted Design for the Y.M.C.A. Building, Richmond, Va." *American Architect and Building News* 18 (November 14, 1885): 234.
Adelman, Melvin. *A Sporting Time: New York City and the Rise of Modern Athletics, 1820–70.* Urbana: University of Illinois Press, 1986.
Adler, Jeffrey S. *Yankee Merchants and the Making of the Urban West: The Rise and Fall of Antebellum St. Louis.* Cambridge, Eng.: Cambridge University Press, 1991.
Agnew, Jean-Christophe. *Worlds Apart: The Market and the Theatre in Anglo-American Thought, 1550–1750.* New York: Cambridge University Press, 1986.
Alexander, B. G., G. S. Bilheimer, and G. D. McDill. *How to Establish a City Young Men's Christian Association with Modern Building and Equipment.* New York: Association Press, 1916.
Allen, Harvey I. "Artificial Light for Gymnasiums." *Physical Training* 7 (May 1911): 20–23.
———. "Special Equipment for Business Men." *Physical Training* 10 (March 1913): 140.
Allen, James. *Without Sanctuary: Lynching Photography in America.* Santa Fe, N.Mex.: Twin Palms Publishers, 2000.
Ames, Kenneth. *Death in the Dining Room and Other Tales of Victorian Culture.* Philadelphia: Temple University Press, 1992.

Amsden, Jon. "Historians and the Spatial Imagination." *Radical History Review* 21 (Fall 1979): 12.
"The Association Building in San Francisco." *Watchman* 5 (November 15, 1879): 253–54.
Atherton, Lewis. *Main Street on the Middle Border.* Bloomington: Indiana University Press, 1984.
Attie, Jeanie. "Warwork and the Crisis of Domesticity in the North." In *Divided Houses: Gender and the Civil War*, edited by Catherine Clinton and Nina Silber, 247–59. New York: Oxford University Press, 1992.
Augst, Thomas. *The Clerk's Tale: Young Men and Moral Life in Nineteenth-Century America.* Chicago and London: University of Chicago Press, 2003.
Baggett, James L. "Birmingham and the Picture Postcard." *Alabama Heritage* (Spring 1999): 22–27.
Bailey, Peter. *Leisure and Class in Victorian England: Rational Recreation and the Contest for Control, 1830–1885.* London: Routledge & Kegan Paul, 1978.
Baldwin, Peter C. *Domesticating the Street: The Reform of Public Space in Hartford, 1850–1930.* Columbus: Ohio State University Press, 1999.
Banner, Lois. "Religious Benevolence as Social Control: A Critique of an Interpretation." *Journal of American History* 60 (June 1973): 23–41.
Bard, Albert S. "Community Houses as War Memorials." *National Municipal Review* 8 (March 1919): 129.
Barr, Chester D. "Y.M.C.A. Dormitories: Theory and Practice." Master's thesis, Ohio State University, 1927.
Barth, Gunther. *City People: The Rise of Modern City Culture in Nineteenth-Century America.* New York: Oxford University Press, 1980.
Bayless, Pamela. *The YMCA at 150: A History of the YMCA of Greater New York.* New York: YMCA of Greater New York, 2002.
Bederman, Gail. *Manliness and Civilization: A Cultural History of Gender and Race in the United States, 1880–1917.* Chicago: University of Chicago Press, 1995.
———. "'The Women Have Had Charge of the Church Work Long Enough': The Men and Religion Forward Movement of 1911–1912 and the Masculinization of Middle Class Protestantism." *American Quarterly* 41 (September 1989): 432–65.
Bennett, John C. "What Is the Social Gospel?" In *The Social Gospel: Religion and Reform in Changing America,* edited by Ronald C. White, Jr., and C. Howard Hopkins, xi–xix. Philadelphia: Temple University Press, 1976.
Benson, Susan Porter. *Counter Cultures: Saleswomen, Managers, and Customers in American Department Stores, 1890–1940.* Urbana: University of Illinois Press, 1986.
———. "Palace of Consumption and Machine for Selling: The American Department Store, 1880–1940." *Radical History Review* 21 (Fall 1979): 199–221.
Berger, Molly W. "A House Divided: The Culture of the American Luxury Hotel, 1825–1860." In *His and Hers: Gender, Consumption, and Technology*, edited by Roger Horowitz and Arwen Mohun, 39–66. Charlottesville and London: University Press of Virginia, 1998.
"The Best Plans Yet Produced for a $50,000 Building, Lansing Michigan, White & Hussey, Architects." *Association Men* 31 (June 1906): 393.
Betts, Benjamin. "Protestant Churches Work to Improve Public Taste in Architecture." *American Architect* 137 (February 1930): 63.
Binfield, Clyde. *George Williams and the Y.M.C.A.: A Study in Victorian Social Attitudes.* London: Heinemann, 1973.

Bishir, Catherine. *North Carolina Architecture.* Chapel Hill and London: University of North Carolina Press, 1990.

Bishir, Catherine, and Charlotte V. Brown. *Architects and Builders in North Carolina: A History of the Practice of Building.* Chapel Hill and London: University of North Carolina Press, 1990.

Bishir, Catherine, and Michael T. Southern. *A Guide to the Historic Architecture of Piedmont, North Carolina.* Chapel Hill and London: University of North Carolina Press, 2003.

Blackmar, Elizabeth. "Rewalking the Walking City: Housing and Property Relations in New York City, 1780–1840." *Radical History Review* 21 (Fall 1979): 131–48.

Bluestone, Daniel. *Constructing Chicago.* New Haven, Conn.: Yale University Press, 1991.

Blumin, Stuart. *The Emergence of the Middle Class: Social Experience in the American City, 1760–1900.* New York: Cambridge University Press, 1989.

Boettger, Susan. "Eastman Johnson's 'Blodgett Family' and Domestic Values during the Civil War Era." *American Art* 6 (Autumn 1992): 50–67.

Bogrette, Christine Durham. "The Abington YMCA: A Case Study of an American Institutional Building Type." Master's thesis, University of Pennsylvania, 1993.

Boutelle, Sara Holmes. *Julia Morgan, Architect.* New York: Abbeville Press, 1995.

Bowron, James. "Gymnasiums and Bath Rooms—Their Place and Usefulness." *Watchman* 14 (February 1, 1888): 30.

Boyer, M. Christine. *Dreaming the Rational City.* Cambridge, Mass.: MIT Press, 1983.

———. *Manhattan Manners: Architecture and Style, 1850–1900.* New York: Rizzoli, 1985.

Boyer, Paul. *Urban Masses and Moral Order in America, 1820–1920.* Cambridge, Mass.: Harvard University Press, 1978.

Boylan, Anne. *Sunday School: The Formation of an American Institution, 1790–1880.* New Haven, Conn.: Yale University Press, 1988.

Bremner, Robert Hamlett. *The Public Good: Philanthropy and Welfare in the Civil War Era.* New York: Knopf, 1980.

Breward, Christopher. *The Hidden Consumer: Masculinities, Fashion, and City Life, 1860–1914.* Manchester, Eng.: Manchester University Press, 1999.

Brown, I. E. *Book of Young Men's Christian Association Buildings.* Chicago: Young Men's Era, 1895.

———. *Young Men's Christian Association Buildings.* 1st ed. Chicago: W. W. Vanarsdale, 1885.

———. *Young Men's Christian Association Buildings.* 2nd ed. Chicago: W. W. Vanarsdale, 1886.

———. *Young Men's Christian Association Buildings.* 3rd ed. Chicago: W. W. Vanarsdale, 1887.

Brown, Marvin A. *Greensboro: An Architectural Record.* Greensboro, N.C.: Preservation Greensboro, 1995.

Browne, Junius Henri. *The Great Metropolis: A Mirror of New York.* 1869. Reprint, New York: Arno Press, 1974.

Brucken, Carolyn. "In the Public Eye: Women and the American Luxury Hotel." *Winterthur Portfolio* 31 (December 1996): 203–220.

"The Building Boom Is On in the YMCA." *Physical Training* 10 (March 1910): 38.

Bulmer, Martin, Kevin Bales, and Kathryn Kish Sklar. *The Social Survey in Historical Perspective, 1880–1940.* Cambridge, Eng.: Cambridge University Press, 1991.

Burns, Sarah. "The Country Boy Goes to the City: Thomas Hovenden's *Breaking Home Ties* in American Popular Culture." *American Art Journal* 20 (1988): 59–73.

Butsch, Richard, ed. *For Fun and Profit: The Transformation of Leisure into Consumption.* Philadelphia: Temple University Press, 1990.

Calkins, Raymond. *Substitutes for the Saloon.* 1901. 2nd ed. Boston: Houghton Mifflin, 1919.

Candler, Martha. "Community Buildings for Industrial Towns." *American Architect* 121 (April 12, 1922): 311–16.

———. "The Community House as a War Memorial." *American Architect* 116 (August 13, 1919): 195–211.

Cantor, Jay E. "The Public Architecture of James Renwick, Jr.: An Investigation of the Concept of an American National Style of Architecture during the Nineteenth Century." Master's thesis, Winterthur Program in American Material Culture, University of Delaware, 1967.

Carnes, Mark, and Clyde Griffen, eds. *Meanings for Manhood: Constructions of Masculinity in Victorian America.* Chicago: University of Chicago Press, 1990.

Cavallo, Dominick. *Muscles and Morals: Organized Playgrounds and Urban Reform, 1880–1920.* Philadelphia: University of Pennsylvania Press, 1981.

Cawelti, John G. *Apostles of the Self-Made Man: Changing Concepts of Success in America.* Chicago: University of Chicago Press, 1965.

"Central Branch Y.M.C.A., Brooklyn, N.Y., Trowbridge & Ackerman, Architects." *Architectural Record* 45 (May 1917): 434–35.

Chandler, Alfred D., Jr. *The Essential Alfred Chandler: Essays toward a Historical Theory of Big Business.* Cambridge, Mass.: Harvard University Business School Press, 1991.

———. *The Visible Hand: The Managerial Revolution in American Business.* Cambridge, Mass.: Belknap Press of Harvard University Press, 1990.

Chauncey, George. *Gay New York: Gender, Urban Culture, and the Making of the Gay Male World, 1890–1940.* New York: Basic Books, 1994.

"Chicago Young Men's Christian Association Gymnasium." *Watchman* 12 (February 14, 1886): 44.

Christensen, Ellen. "A Vision of Urban Social Reform." *Chicago History* 22 (March 1993): 50–61.

Chudacoff, Howard P. *The Age of the Bachelor: Creating an American Subculture.* Princeton, N.J.: Princeton University Press, 1999.

Cieplik, Raymond. "Physical Work and Amusements as Concerns of the Young Men's Christian Association, 1851–1884." Ph.D. diss., University of Massachusetts, 1969.

Cody, Jeffrey W. *Building in China: Henry K. Murphy's "Adaptive Architecture," 1914–1935.* Seattle: University of Washington Press, 2001.

———. *Exporting American Architecture, 1870–1920.* London: Routledge, 2003.

Coe, George A. *Social Theory of Religious Education.* Chicago: University of Chicago Press, 1917.

Conover, Elbert M. "Building a Seven-Day-a-Week Church." *American Architect* 126 (August 27, 1924): 179–80.

———. *Building the House of God.* New York: Methodist Book Concern, 1928.

Conzen, Kathleen Neils. "Ethnicity as Festive Culture: Nineteenth-Century German America on Parade." In *The Invention of Ethnicity,* edited by Werner Sollors, 44–76. New York: Oxford University Press, 1989.

Cook, George Willis. "The Institutional Church." *New England Magazine* 14 (August 1896): 645–60.

"Cornerstone, Young Men's Christian Association New Building." *New York Times,* November 1, 1868, 2.

Corrigan, John. *Business of the Heart: Religion and Emotion in the Nineteenth Century.* Berkeley: University of California Press, 2002.

Cott, Nancy F. *The Bonds of Womanhood: "Woman's Sphere" in New England, 1780–1835.* New Haven, Conn.: Yale University Press, 1977.

"The Country Boy Leaving Home." *Association Men* 39 (March 1914): 282–83.

Cronon, William. *Nature's Metropolis: Chicago and the Great West.* New York: W.W. Norton, 1992.

Cross, Whitney. *The Burned-Over District: The Social and Intellectual History of Enthusiastic Religion in Western New York, 1800–1850.* Ithaca, N.Y.: Cornell University Press, 1950.

Culter, Carol. "The First and Latest Architect for the Smithsonian." *Smithsonian* 2 (February 1972): 62–63.

Currey, David. "The Virtuous Soldier: Constructing a Usable Confederate Past in Franklin, Tennessee." In *Monuments to the Lost Cause: Women, Art, and the Landscapes of Southern Memory,* edited by Cynthia Mills and Pamela H. Simpson, 133–48. Knoxville: University of Tennessee Press, 2003.

Cushing, Charles Phelps. "In Quest of Homeyness." *Association Men* 49 (January 1924): 199–200.

Cutlip, Scott M. *Fund Raising in the United States: Its Role in American Philanthropy.* New Brunswick, N.J.: Rutgers University Press, 1965.

Cuyler, Theodore L. "Popular Amusements." *Watchman* 7 (October 1, 1881): 246.

Daniels, John. *America via the Neighborhood.* New York: Harper & Brothers, 1920.

Darling, T. G. *Advantages of a Permanent Home for a Young Men's Christian Association with Suggestions Concerning How It Can Be Secured.* New York: International Committee, 1881.

———. *Why Should We Have a Young Men's Christian Association in Our Town?* New York: International Committee, 1888.

Davis, Eric Emmett, and Karen Indeck. *Dwight Heald Perkins: Social Consciousness and Prairie School Architecture.* Chicago: Gallery 400 at the University of Illinois at Chicago, 1989.

Davis, John. "Children in the Parlor: Eastman Johnson's 'Brown Family' and the Post–Civil War Luxury Interior." *American Art* 10 (Summer 1996): 73.

Decker, Peter R. *Fortunes and Failures: White-Collar Mobility in Nineteenth-Century San Francisco.* Cambridge, Mass.: Harvard University Press, 1978.

Dedmon, Emmett. *Great Enterprises: 100 Years of the YMCA of Metropolitan Chicago.* New York: Rand McNally, 1957.

"Design for the Y.M.C.A. Building, Philadelphia, Pa." *American Architect and Building News* 1 (December 9, 1876): 397.

Dewey, John. *Human Nature and Conduct.* New York: Henry Holt, 1922.

Dillard, Frank G. "Regarding Design of Non-Ritualistic Church Buildings." *American Architect* 127 (February 25, 1925): 159–66.

Dodge, Cleveland E. *"YMCA": A Century at New York (1852–1952).* New York: Newcomen Society in North America, 1953.

Dodge, Phyllis B. *Tales of the Phelps-Dodge Family: A Chronicle of Five Generations.* New York: New York Historical Society, 1987.

Dodge, William. "How to Secure a Building." *Watchman* 5 (May 1, 1879): 99.

Doggett, L. L. *Life of Robert R. McBurney.* Cleveland, Ohio: F. M. Barton, 1902.

Domosh, Mona, and Joni Seager. *Putting Women in Place: Feminist Geographers Make Sense of the World.* New York and London: Guilford Press, 2001.

Donoghue, Terry. *An Event on Mercer Street: A Brief History of the YMCA of the City of New York.* New York: privately printed, 1951.

Dotterrer, Steven, and Galen Cranz. "The Picture Postcard: Its Development and Role in American Urbanization." *Journal of American Culture* 5 (Spring 1982): 44–50.

Douglas, Ann. *The Feminization of American Culture.* New York: Knopf, 1977.

Douglass, H. Paul. *The Church in the Changing City: Case Studies Illustrating Adaptation.* New York: George H. Doran, 1927.

———. *The St. Louis Church Survey: A Religious Investigation with a Social Background.* New York: George H. Doran, 1924.

Doyle, Don H. *New Men, New Cities, New South: Atlanta, Nashville, Charleston, Mobile, 1860–1910.* Chapel Hill: University of North Carolina Press, 1990.

Drury, Clifford M. *The San Francisco YMCA: One Hundred Years by the Golden Gate.* Glendale, Calif.: Arthur H. Clark, 1963.

Dubrow, Gail Lee, and Jennifer Goodman. *Restoring Women's History through Historic Preservation.* Baltimore, Md.: Johns Hopkins University Press, 2003.

Duis, Perry. *The Saloon: Public Drinking in Chicago and Boston, 1880–1920.* Urbana: University of Illinois Press, 1983.

Earle, Edward W., ed. *Points of View: The Stereograph in America—A Cultural History.* Rochester, N.Y.: Visual Studies Workshop, 1979.

Eddy, George Sherwood. *A Century with Youth: A History of the Y.M.C.A. from 1844 to 1944.* New York: Association Press, 1944.

Emmons, Paul. "Diagrammatic Practices: The Office of Frederick Ackerman and Architectural Graphic Standards." *Journal of the Society of Architectural Historians* 64 (March 2005): 4–21.

"An Episcopal Convention through Its Bishop Advocating an Association Building." *Watchman* 12 (August 1, 1886): 173.

Erenberg, Lewis A. *Steppin' Out: New York and the Transformation of American Culture, 1890–1930.* Chicago: University of Chicago Press, 1981.

Evans, Herbert Francis. *The Sunday-School Building and Its Equipment.* Chicago: University of Chicago Press, 1914.

Evans, Robin. "Bentham's Panopticon: An Incident in the Social History of Architecture." *Architectural Association Quarterly* 3 (Spring 1971): 21–37.

Fairfield, Francis Gerry. *The Clubs of New York.* New York: Harry Hinton, 1874.

Farmer, Silas. "Build." *Association Monthly* 1 (October 1870): 261.

Fisher, Galen Merriam. *Public Affairs and the Y.M.C.A., 1844–1944.* New York: Association Press, 1948.

Fishman, Robert. *Bourgeois Utopias: The Rise and Fall of Suburbia.* New York: Basic Books, 1987.

"For More 'Manhood Factories.'" *Association Men* 34 (February 1909): 234–36.

Foss, M. I. "Equipment and Construction of the Physical Department." *Physical Training* 7 (May, September, October, November 1910): 3–7, 19–24, 18–20, 15–25, respectively.

Foster, George G. *New York by Gas-Light and Other Urban Sketches.* 1850. Edited and with an introduction by Stuart Blumin. Berkeley: University of California Press, 1990.

Foucault, Michel. *Discipline and Punish: The Birth of the Prison.* New York: Vintage Books, 1979.

Founders and Builders of Greensboro, 1808–1908. Greensboro, N.C.: Joseph J. Stone, 1908.

Freeman, James E. *If Not the Saloon—What?* New York: Baker & Taylor, 1903.

Gates, Herbert Wright. *Recreation and the Church.* Chicago: University of Chicago Press, 1917.

Gerber, David A. "The Germans Take Care of Our Celebrations: Middle-Class Americans Appropriate German Ethnic Culture in Buffalo in the 1850s." In *Hard at Play: Leisure in America, 1840–1940,* edited by Kathryn Grover, 39–60. Amherst, Mass., and Rochester, N.Y.: University of Massachusetts Press and the Strong Museum, 1992.

Gibbons, Herbert Adams. *John Wanamaker.* New York: Harper & Brothers, 1926.

Gibbs, Kenneth Turney. *Business Architectural Imagery in America, 1870–1930.* Ann Arbor, Mich.: UMI Research Press, 1984.

Gilbert, James. *Perfect Cities: Chicago's Utopias of 1893.* Chicago: University of Chicago Press, 1991.

Gilfoyle, Timothy. *City of Eros: New York City, Prostitution, and the Commercialization of Sex, 1790–1920.* New York: W. W. Norton, 1994.

Gitler, Inbal Ben-Asher. "The Architecture of the Jerusalem YMCA, 1919–1933: Constructing Multiculturalism." Ph.D. diss., Tel Aviv University, 2006.

Gladden, Washington, ed. *Parish Problems: Hints and Helps for the People of the Churches.* New York: Century, 1888.

Gordon, H. B. "Association Architecture: External Appearance and Interior Arrangement of Buildings, Part I." *Young Men's Era* 16 (April 17, 1890): 241.

———. "Association Architecture: External Appearance and Interior Arrangement of Buildings, Part II." *Young Men's Era* 16 (April 24, 1890): 257.

Gorn, Eliot. *The Manly Art: Bare-Knuckle Prize Fighting in America.* Ithaca, N.Y.: Cornell University Press, 1999.

Gray, Lee Edward. "The Office Building in New York City, 1850–1880." Ph.D. diss., Cornell University, 1993.

Greenberg, Dolores. *Financiers and Railroads, 1869–1889: A Study of Morton, Bliss, and Co.* Newark: University of Delaware Press, 1980.

Gregory, Alexis. *Families of Fortune: Life in the Gilded Age.* New York: Vendome Press, 1993.

Grier, Katherine C. *Culture and Comfort: Parlor Making and Middle-Class Identity, 1850–1930.* Washington, D.C.: Smithsonian Institution Press, 1988.

Griffen, Clyde, and Sally Griffen. *Natives and Newcomers: The Ordering of Opportunity in Mid-Nineteenth-Century Poughkeepsie.* Cambridge, Mass., and London: Harvard University Press, 1978.

Griffin, Clifford S. "Religious Benevolence as Social Control, 1815–1860." *Mississippi Valley Historical Review* 44 (December 1957): 423–44.

———. *Their Brothers' Keepers: Moral Stewardship in the United States, 1800–1865.* New Brunswick, N.J.: Rutgers University Press, 1960.

Groth, Paul. *Living Downtown: The History of Residential Hotels in the United States.* Berkeley: University of California Press, 1994.

"The Growth of Clubs in New York City." *Real Estate Record and Guide* 45 (March 8, 1890): 1–13.

Gunn, Thomas Butler. *The Physiology of New York Boarding-Houses.* New York: Mason Brothers, 1857.

Gustav-Wrathall, John Donald. *Take the Young Stranger by the Hand: Same-Sex Relations and the YMCA.* Chicago: University of Chicago Press, 1998.

Haber, Samuel. *Efficiency and Uplift: Scientific Management in the Progressive Era, 1890–1920.* Chicago: University of Chicago Press, 1964.

Hale, Grace Elizabeth. *Making Whiteness: The Culture of Segregation in the South, 1890–1940.* New York: Pantheon Books, 1998.

Hales, Peter B. *Silver Cities: The Photography of American Urbanization, 1839–1915.* Philadelphia: Temple University Press, 1984.

Halttunen, Karen. *Confidence Men and Painted Women: A Study of Middle-Class Culture in America, 1830–1870.* New Haven, Conn.: Yale University Press, 1982.

Hamlin, A. D. F. "The State Architect." *Architectural Record* 53, 54 (1923): 26–43, 265–76, respectively.

Hansen, A. E. "YMCA Swimming Pool Equipment." *Architectural Forum* 56 (August 1930): 240.

Harris, Neil. *The Artist in American Society: The Formative Years, 1790–1860.* New York: G. Braziller, 1966.

Heald, Franklin E. "Fraternity Life at Dartmouth." *American University Magazine* 3 (November 1895): 60.

Henry, Anne W. D. *The Building of a Club: Social Institution and Architectural Type.* Princeton, N.J.: Princeton University, School of Architecture and Planning, 1976.

Hilkey, Judy. *Character Is Capital: Success Manuals and Manhood in Gilded Age America.* Chapel Hill: University of North Carolina Press, 1994.

Hinding, Andrea. *Proud Heritage: A History in Pictures of the YMCA in the United States.* Norfolk, Va.: Donning, 1988.

Hints about the Construction of Association Buildings. New York: Association Press, 1909.

Historical Journal: A Souvenir of the Centennial Celebration of the New York Turn Verein, January 1st to November 11, 1950. New York: New York Turnverein, 1950.

Hoffman, Donald. "The Setback Skyscraper City of 1891: An Unknown Essay by Louis H. Sullivan." *Journal of the Society of Architectural Historians* 29 (May 1970): 184–85.

Hommel, Rudolf P. *China at Work: An Illustrated Record of the Primitive Industries of China's Masses, Whose Life Is Toil, and Thus an Account of Chinese Civilization.* Doylestown, Pa., and New York: Bucks County Historical Society and the John Day Company, 1937.

Hopkins, C. Howard. *History of the YMCA in North America.* New York: Association Press, 1951.

Horlick, Allan Stanley. *Country Boys and Merchant Princes: The Social Control of Young Men in New York.* Lewisburg, Pa.: Bucknell University Press, 1975.

Horowitz, Helen Lefkowitz. "Hull House as Women's Space." *Chicago History* 12 (Winter 1983–84): 40–55.

———. *Rereading Sex: Battles over Sexual Knowledge and Suppression in Nineteenth-Century America.* New York: Knopf, 2002.

Hughey, Michael W. *Civil Religion and Moral Order: Theoretical and Historical Dimensions.* Westport, Conn.: Greenwood Press, 1983.

Hume, Leland. *Successful and Safe Methods for Securing Money for Current Expenses or Buildings.* New York: International Committee, 1888.

"The Interdependence of Architecture and Interior Decoration." *Good Furniture* 10 (January 1918): 33–42.

"Interior Architecture: Cooperation between Architect and Decorator." *American Architect* 126 (July 2, 1924): 17–23.

"Interior Architecture: The Spirit of the Old Spanish in Modern Decoration." *American Architect* 126 (December 17, 1924): 573–80.

Irwin, Will, Earl Chapin May, and Joseph Hotchkiss. *A History of the Union League Club of New York City.* New York: Dodd Mead, 1952.

Isaacs, I. J. *Progressive Greensboro, the Gate City of North Carolina.* Greensboro, N.C.: Joseph J. Stone, 1903.

Isenberg, Alison. *Downtown America: A History of the Place and the People Who Made It.* Chicago: University of Chicago Press, 2004.

Jackson, John F. "Constructive Criticism on Association Building." *Association Men* 36 (March, April, June, July 1911): 263, 303, 410, 455, respectively.

Jakle, John. *Postcards of the Night: Views of American Cities.* Santa Fe: Museum of New Mexico Press, 2003.

Jallade, Louis E. *The Association Building 1. Supervision and Circulation.* With an Introduction entitled, The Evolution of the Modern Association Building by Thornton B. Penfield. New York: Association Press, 1913.

Johnson, Elmer. *The History of YMCA Physical Education.* Chicago: Association Press, 1979.

Johnson, Paul. *A Shopkeeper's Millennium: Society and Revivals in Rochester, New York, 1815–1837.* New York: Hill and Wang, 1978.

Johnson, Ronald M. "Forgotten Reformer: Edward J. Ward and the Community Center Movement." *Mid-America* 74 (January 1992): 17–35.

Kasson, John. *Amusing the Million: Coney Island at the Turn of the Century.* New York: Hill and Wang, 1978.

Kaufman, David. *Shul with a Pool: The "Synagogue-Center" in American Jewish History.* Hanover, N.H.: University Press of New England, 1999.

Kerber, Linda. "Separate Spheres, Female Worlds, Women's Place: The Rhetoric of Women's History." *Journal of American History* 75 (1988): 9–39.

Kilde, Jeanne Halgren. *When Church Became Theatre: The Transformation of Evangelical Architecture and Worship in Nineteenth-Century America.* New York: Oxford University Press, 2002.

Kilham, Walter H. "Community and Social Halls." *Architecture* 59 (May 1929): 267–76.

Kilpatrick, William H. *Foundations of Method.* New York: McMillan, 1925.

Kimball, Fiske. "The Social Center." *Architectural Record* 45, 46 (May and July 1919): 417–40, 526–43, 29–46, respectively.

Kimmel, Michael. *Manhood in America: A Cultural History.* New York: Free Press, 1996.

Kingsdale, John. "The Poor Man's Club: Social Functions of the Urban Working-Class Saloon." *American Quarterly* 25 (October 1972): 472.

Kipp, Samuel M., III. "Old Notables and Newcomers: The Economic and Political

Elite of Greensboro, North Carolina, 1880–1920." *Journal of Southern History* 43 (August 1977): 373–94.

Klauder, Charles Z., and Herbert C. Wise. *College Architecture in America and Its Part in the Development of the Campus.* New York and London: Charles Scribner's Sons, 1929.

Kwolek-Folland, Angel. *Engendering Business: Men and Women in the Corporate Office, 1870–1930.* Baltimore and London: Johns Hopkins University Press, 1994.

Landau, Sarah Bradford. *P. B. Wight: Architect, Contractor, and Critic, 1838–1925.* Chicago: Art Institute of Chicago, 1981.

Landau, Sarah Bradford, and Carl W. Condit. *Rise of the New York Skyscraper, 1865–1913.* New Haven, Conn.: Yale University Press, 2006.

Lawrence, Marion. *Housing the Sunday School.* Philadelphia: Westminster Press, 1921.

Leach, William. *Land of Desire: Merchants, Power, and the Rise of a New American Culture.* New York: Pantheon, 1993.

Lectures on the Operation and Maintenance of Association Buildings. Floor Layout or Arrangement of Space. Lake Geneva, Summer School of City Association Administration 1915: The Young Men's Christian Association College, Chicago, 1915. Box 1, Buildings and Furnishings Service/Property Management Historical Records, YMCA of the USA Headquarters, Chicago.

Lefebvre, Henri. *The Production of Space.* Translated by Donald Nicholson-Smith. Cambridge, Mass.: Basil Blackwell, 1984.

Lewis, Sinclair. *Babbitt.* New York: P. F. Collier & Son, 1922.

"Liberty Buildings as Soldiers' Memorials." *American City* 19 (September 1918): 173.

"Liberty Buildings as Victory Monuments." *American City* 19 (December 1918): 471.

Longstreth, Richard. *The Buildings of Main Street: A Guide to American Commercial Architecture.* Washington, D.C.: Preservation Press, 1987.

Lupkin, Paula. "'Manhood Factories': Architecture, Business, and the Evolving Role of the YMCA, 1869–1915." In *Men and Woman Adrift: The YMCA and the YWCA in the City,* edited by Nina Mjagkij and Margaret Spratt, 40–64. New York: New York University Press, 1997.

———. "A Temple of Practical Christianity." *Chicago History* 24 (Fall 1995): 22–41.

———. "YMCA Architecture: Building Character in the American City, 1869–1929." Ph.D. diss., University of Pennsylvania, 1997.

Macleod, David I. *Building Character in the American Boy: The Boy Scouts, YMCA, and Their Forerunners, 1870–1920.* Madison: University of Wisconsin Press, 1983.

Mahoney, Tim. *Provincial Lives: Middle-Class Experience in the Antebellum Middle West.* Cambridge, Eng., and New York: Cambridge University Press, 1999.

Mahy, Geo. G. "The Modern Association Building." *Association Men* 29 (December 1903): 97–103.

Mangan, J. A., and James Walvin, eds. *Manliness and Morality: Middle-Class Masculinity in Britain and America, 1800–1940.* New York: St. Martin's Press, 1987.

The Man-Traps of New York: What They Are and How They Are Worked, by a Celebrated Detective. New York: Police Gazette, 1881.

Markus, Thomas. *Buildings and Power: Freedom and Control in the Origin of Modern Building Types.* London: Routledge, 1993.

———. *Order and Space in Society: Architectural Form and Its Context in the Scottish Enlightenment.* Edinburgh: Mainstream Press, 1982.

Marsh, Margaret. "Suburban Men and Masculine Domesticity." *American Quarterly* 40 (June 1988): 165–86.

Martin, Edward Winslow. *The Secrets of the Great City: A Work Descriptive of the Virtues and the Vices, the Mysteries, Miseries and Crimes of New York City.* Philadelphia: Jones, Brothers and Co., 1868.

Marty, Martin E. *Righteous Empire: The Protestant Experience in America.* New York: Dial Press, 1986.

May, Charles C. "A Post-War Construction Program: The Building Bureau of the International Committee of the YMCA." *Architectural Record* 45 (March and April 1919): 216–241, 325–342, respectively.

May, Henry. *The Protestant Churches and Industrial America.* New York: Harpers, 1949.

Mayer, Harold M., and Richard C. Wade. *Chicago: Growth of a Metropolis.* Chicago: University of Chicago Press, 1969.

McCabe, James D., Jr. *Lights and Shadows of New York Life: or the Sights and Sensations of the Great City.* Philadelphia: National Publishing Company, 1872.

McCarthy, Kathleen. *Noblesse Oblige: Charity and Cultural Philanthropy in Chicago, 1849–1929.* Chicago: University of Chicago Press, 1982.

McCarthy, Michael. "Politics and the Parks: Chicago Businessmen and the Recreation Movement." *Illinois State Historical Society Journal* 45 (Summer 1972): 161–62.

McDannell, Colleen. *The Christian Home in Victorian America, 1840–1900.* Bloomington: Indiana University Press, 1986.

McKenna, Rosalie Thorne. "James Renwick, Jr. and the Second Empire Style in the United States." *Magazine of Art* 44 (March 1951): 97–101.

McKinley, William, and Theodore Roosevelt. "The Association a National Defense." *Association Men* 26 (May 1901): 269–70.

McMillan, Neil, Jr. "Buildings That Express Ideals." *Association Men* 48 (May 1923): 222, 228, 232.

———. "Capitalizing on Our Building Experience." *Association Men* 45 (June 1919): 462–63.

McNamara, Brooks. *The New York Concert Saloon: The Devil's Own Nights.* Cambridge, Eng.: Cambridge University Press, 2002.

McTighe, Michael J. *A Measure of Success: Protestants and Public Culture in Antebellum Cleveland.* Albany: State University of New York Press, 1994.

Meikle, Jeffrey. "A Paper Atlantis: Postcards, Mass Art, and the American Scene." *Journal of Design History* 13 (2000): 267–86.

A Memorandum Respecting New York as a Field for Moral and Christian Effort among Young Men. New York: The Association, 1866.

Merritt, Russell. "Nickolodeon Theaters, 1905–1914: Building an Audience for the Movies." In *The American Film Industry,* edited by Tino Balio, 83–102. Rev. ed. Madison: University of Wisconsin Press, 1985.

Miller, Wayne G. "Churches Are Not What They Used to Be . . ." *American Architect* 140 (October 1931): 28–29.

Mjagkij, Nina. *Light in the Darkness: African Americans and the YMCA, 1852–1946.* Lexington: University of Kentucky Press, 1994.

Mjagkij, Nina, and Margaret Spratt, eds. *Men and Women Adrift: The YMCA and the YWCA in the City.* New York: New York University Press, 1997.

Moody, William R. *The Life of Dwight Moody by His Son.* New York: Fleming H. Revell, 1900.

Moore, R. Laurence. *Selling God: American Religion in the Marketplace of Culture.* New York: Oxford University Press, 1994.

Moore, William. *Masonic Temples: Freemasonry, Ritual Architecture, and Masculine Archetypes.* Knoxville: University of Tennessee Press, 2006.

Moran, Horace. "Interior Decoration: Its Present and Its Future." *Good Furniture* 10 (March 1918): 180–85.

Morgan, David. *Protestants and Pictures: Religion, Visual Culture, and the Age of American Mass Production.* New York: Oxford University Press, 1999.

Morriss, W. H. "The Association Building, or Headquarters." *Watchman* 8 (April 15, 1882): 116.

Morse, Richard C. *History of the North American Young Men's Christian Associations.* New York: Association Press, 1913.

———. *My Life with Young Men: Fifty Years in the Young Men's Christian Association.* New York: Association Press, 1918.

Morse, Verranus. *An Analytical Sketch of the Young Men's Christian Association in North America.* New York: International Committee of the YMCA, 1901.

Nadel, Jack. "The Y.M.H.A. and the Jewish Center." *Jewish Center* 1 (October 1922): 11.

Needham, Joseph. *Science and Civilisation in China.* Vol. 4, Part 2, *Mechanical Engineering.* Cambridge, Eng.: Cambridge University Press, 1965.

"Neil McMillan." *Michigan Society of Architects Monthly Bulletin* 27 (July 1953): 29.

Nelson, Dana. *National Manhood: Capitalist Citizenship and the Imagined Fraternity of White Men.* Durham, N.C.: Duke University Press, 1998.

Nelson, Donna Rae. "School Architecture in Chicago during the Progressive Era: The Career of Dwight H. Perkins." Ph.D. diss., Loyola University of Chicago, 1988.

"New Building of the Young Men's Christian Association of New York." *Association Monthly* 1 (January 1870): 1.

Newman, I. F. "How Can the Secretary Awaken a Sentiment for and Secure a Building in His Community?" *Watchman* 13 (June 15, 1887): 174.

Noll, Mark A. *A History of Christianity in the United States and Canada.* Grand Rapids, Mich.: Eerdmans, 1992.

Nolte, Claire E. *The Sokol in the Czech Lands to 1914: Training for the Nation.* Basingstoke, Eng.: Palgrave, 2002.

Oaklander, Christine I. "Studios at the YMCA, 1869–1903." *Archives of American Art Journal* 32 (1992): 14–22.

Oberdeck, Kathryn J. *The Evangelist and the Impresario: Religion, Entertainment, and Cultural Politics in America, 1884–1914.* Baltimore and London: Johns Hopkins University Press, 1999.

Otis, Harrison G. "The Financing of Memorial Buildings." *American City* 21 (August 1919): 103.

Ownby, Ted. *Subduing Satan: Religion, Recreation, and Manhood in the Rural South, 1865–1920.* Chapel Hill: University of North Carolina Press, 1990.

Page, Max. *The Creative Destruction of Manhattan, 1900–1940.* Chicago: University of Chicago Press, 1999.

Pai, Hyungmin. *The Portfolio and the Diagram: Architecture, Discourse, and Modernity in America.* Cambridge, Mass.: MIT Press, 2002.

Peel, Mark. "On the Margins: Lodgers and Boarders in Boston, 1860–1900." *Journal of American History* 72 (March 1986): 813–34.

Peiss, Kathy. *Cheap Amusements: Working Women and Leisure in Turn-of-the-Century New York.* Philadelphia: Temple University Press, 1986.

Pence, Owen E. *The Y.M.C.A. and Social Need: A Study of Institutional Adaptation*. New York: Association Press, 1939.
Perkins, Dwight. "The School Building as a Social Center, Part I & II." *The Brickbuilder* 24, 25 (December 1914, January 1915): 293–94, 1–7, respectively.
Perkins, Dwight, and Howell Taylor. "The Functions and Plan-Types of Community Buildings." *Architectural Record* 56 (October 1924): 289–304.
Perry, Clarence Arthur, and Marguerita Williams. *New York School Centers and Their Community Policy*. Russell Sage Foundation, Recreation and Education Department, no. 158. New York: Russell Sage Foundation, 1921.
Pollock, John. *Moody: The Biography*. Chicago: Moody Press, 1963.
Pond, Allen. "The Settlement House." *The Brickbuilder* 11 (July, August, September 1902): 140–45, 160–65, 180–85, respectively.
Pond, Irving K. "Buildings of the Young Men's Christian Association." *The Brickbuilder* 15 (January, March, April 1906): 28–29, 52–58, 68–77, respectively.
Power, Richard Lyle. "A Crusade to Extend Yankee Culture." *New England Quarterly* 13 (December 1940): 638–53.
Price, C. Matlack. "Architect and Decorator: The Relations between Two Specialized Professions." *Good Furniture* 4 (June 1915): 553–55.
Putney, Clifford. "Character Building in the YMCA, 1880–1930." *Mid-America* 73 (January 1991): 59.
———. *Muscular Christianity: Manhood and Sports in Protestant America*. Cambridge, Mass.: Harvard University Press, 2003.
"The Question Box." *American City* 2 (April 1910): 192, 194.
Ramsay, Charles G., and Harold Reeve Sleeper. *Architectural Graphic Standards for Architects, Engineers, Decorators, Builders and Draftsmen*. London: Chapman and Hall, 1932.
Rattner, Selma. "James Renwick." *Macmillan Dictionary of Architects*. 4 vols. New York: Free Press, 1982, 3:541–48.
Rayburn, R. L. "The Purpose of the New Type of 'Y.'" *Architectural Forum* 53 (August 1930): 151–52.
Reeseguise, Harry. "A. T. Stewart's Marble Palace: The Cradle of the Department Store." *New York Historical Society Quarterly* 48 (April 1964): 131–62.
"Remarkable Building Canvass Stories." *Association Men* 30 (March 1905): 269–70.
Richardson, Albert. *Garnered Sheaves: From the Writings of Albert D. Richardson*. Hartford, Conn.: Columbian Book Company, 1871.
Riess, Steven A. *City Games: The Evolution of American Urban Society and the Rise of Sports*. Urbana: University of Illinois Press, 1991.
Rifkind, Carole. *Main Street: The Face of Urban America*. New York: Harper & Row, 1977.
Risedorph, Kimberly A. "Reformers, Athletes, and Students: The YMCA in China, 1895–1935." Ph.D. diss., Washington University, 1994.
Robinson, Edgar M. "Provisions for Boys' Work in Association Buildings." *American Youth* 2 (August 1914): 195–257.
Rodgers, Daniel T. *The Work Ethic in Industrial America, 1850–1920*. Chicago: University of Chicago Press, 1974.
Rosenzweig, Roy. *Eight Hours for What We Will: Workers and Leisure in an Industrial City, 1870–1920*. New York: Cambridge University Press, 1983.

Rosenzweig, Roy, and Elizabeth Blackmar. *The Park and the People: A History of Central Park*. Ithaca, N.Y.: Cornell University Press, 1991.

Rotundo, E. Anthony. *American Manhood: Transformations in Masculinity from the Revolution to the Modern Era*. New York: Basic Books, 1993.

Ruskin, John. *The Seven Lamps of Architecture*. New York: Dover, 1989.

Ryan, Mary. *Cradle of the Middle Class: The Family in Oneida County, New York, 1790–1865*. Cambridge, Eng.: Cambridge University Press, 1981.

Saint, Andrew. *The Image of the Architect*. New Haven, Conn.: Yale University Press, 1983.

Sante, Luc. *Low Life: Lures and Snares of Old New York*. New York: Vintage Books, 1991.

Satterlee, Herbert. *J. Pierpont Morgan: An Intimate Portrait*. New York: Macmillan, 1939.

Schultz, Stanley. *Constructing Urban Culture: American Cities and City Planning, 1800–1920*. Philadelphia: Temple University Press, 1989.

Schwantes, Carlos A. *Vision and Enterprise: Exploring the History of the Phelps, Dodge Corporation*. Phoenix: University of Arizona Press, 2004.

Scobey, David. *Empire City: The Making and Meaning of the New York City Landscape*. Philadelphia: Temple University Press, 2003.

Shao, Qin. *Culturing Modernity: The Nantong Model, 1890–1930*. Palo Alto, Calif.: Stanford University Press, 2004.

Shaw, Diane. *City-Building on the Eastern Frontier: Sorting the New Nineteenth-Century City*. Baltimore, Md.: Johns Hopkins University Press, 2004.

Sinclair, Andrew. *Corsair: The Life of J. Pierpont Morgan*. Boston: Little, Brown, 1981.

Smith, Terry. *Making the Modern: Industry, Art, and Design in America*. Chicago: University of Chicago Press, 1993.

Smith, Timothy. *Revivalism and Social Reform: American Protestantism on the Eve of the Civil War*. New York: Harper & Row, 1957.

Smith-Rosenberg, Carroll. *Religion and the Rise of the American City: The New York City Mission Movement, 1812–1870*. Ithaca, N.Y.: Cornell University Press, 1971.

Snyder, Robert W. *The Voice of the City: Vaudeville and Popular Culture in New York*. New York: Oxford University Press, 1989.

Solomonson, Katherine. *The Chicago Tribune Tower Competition: Skyscraper Design and Cultural Change in the 1920s*. Cambridge, Eng.: Cambridge University Press, 2001.

Somers, Dale. "The Leisure Revolution: Recreation in the American City, 1820–1920." *Journal of Popular Culture* 5 (Summer 1971): 125–47.

Spain, Daphne. *How Women Saved the City*. Minneapolis: University of Minnesota Press, 2001.

Spann, Edward. *The New Metropolis: New York City, 1840–1857*. New York: Columbia University Press, 1981.

Spears, Timothy B. *100 Years on the Road: The Traveling Salesman in American Culture*. New Haven, Conn.: Yale University Press, 1997.

"Special Number on Club and Fraternal Buildings." *Architectural Forum* 45 (September 1928).

Srole, Carole. "'A Position That God Has Not Particularly Assigned to Men': The Feminization of Clerical Work, Boston, 1860–1915." Ph.D. diss., University of California, Los Angeles, 1984.

Stansell, Christine. *City of Women: Sex and Class in New York, 1789–1860.* New York: Knopf, 1986.

Stapleton, Kristin. *Civilizing Chengdu: Chinese Urban Reform, 1895–1937.* Cambridge, Mass.: Harvard University Press, 2000.

Stern, Robert A. M., Gregory Gilmartin, and John Montague Massengale. *New York 1900: Metropolitan Architecture and Urbanism, 1890–1915.* New York: Rizzoli, 1993.

Stern, Robert A. M., Gregory Gilmartin, and Thomas Mellins. *New York 1930: Architecture and Urbanism between the Two World Wars.* New York: Rizzoli, 1995.

Stern, Robert A. M., Thomas Mellins, and David Fishman. *New York 1880: Architecture and Urbanism in the Gilded Age.* New York: Monacelli Press, 1999.

Stitt, Edward W. "Evening Recreation Centers." *National Society for the Study of Education, Tenth Yearbook.* Vol. 50. Chicago: University of Chicago Press, 1912.

Strong, George Templeton. *The Diary of George Templeton Strong.* 4 vols. Edited by Allan Nevins and Milton Halsey Thomas. New York: Macmillan, 1952.

Strong, Josiah. "The Problem of the City." *Association Men* 33 (July 1908): 462–63.

Super, Paul. *Formative Ideas in the YMCA.* New York: Association Press, 1929.

"The Swimming Pool: Opinions about Its Use and Size." *Association Men* 31 (April 1906): 317–18.

Sypher, J. R. "The Need of Buildings Constructed for and Owned by the Associations, and the Plans for the Accumulation of Building Funds." In *Journal of the Proceedings,* Portland, Maine, July 14–18, 1869, 31–35.

Taylor, Graham Romeyn. "Recreation Developments in Chicago Parks." In *Public Recreation Facilities,* edited by Emory R. Johnson, 88–105. Philadelphia: American Academy of Political and Social Science, 1910.

Taylor, William R. *Inventing Times Square: Commerce and Culture at the Crossroads of the World.* New York: Russell Sage Foundation, 1991.

Thompson, Joseph. "The Association in Architecture." *Association Monthly* 1 (January 1870): 3–4.

Trachtenberg, Alan. *The Incorporation of America: Culture and Society in the Gilded Age.* New York: Hill and Wang, 1982.

———. *Reading American Photographs: Images as History, Matthew Brady to Walker Evans.* New York: Hill and Wang, 1989.

Tyler, M. C. "Natural vs. Artificial Gymnasiums." *Physical Education* 1 (June 1893): 214.

Valentine, Maggie. *The Show Starts on the Sidewalk: An Architectural History of the Movie Theatre Starring S. Charles Lee.* New Haven, Conn.: Yale University Press, 1994.

"Value of a Building." *Watchman* 6 (February 1, 1880): 39.

Van Slyck, Abigail A. *Free to All: Carnegie Libraries and American Culture, 1890–1920.* Chicago: University of Chicago Press, 1995.

———. "The Lady and the Library Loafer: Gender and Public Space in Victorian America." *Winterthur Portfolio* 31 (Winter 1996): 221–42.

———. "Managing Pleasure: Library Architecture and the Erotics of Reading." In *Library as Place: History, Community, and Culture,* edited by John Buschman and Gloria J. Leckie, 221–34. Westport, Conn.: Libraries Unlimited, 2007.

———. *A Manufactured Wilderness: Summer Camps and the Shaping of American Youth, 1890–1960.* Minneapolis: University of Minnesota Press, 2006.

Vidler, Anthony. "Architecture, Management, and Morals." *Lotus International* 14 (March 1977): 4–20.

———. "A Note on the Idea of Type in Architecture." In *The Building of a Club: Social Institution and Architectural Type, 1870–1905: A Study of the Precedents and Building of the University Cottage Club, Princeton*, by Anne W. D. Henry, ix–xxv. Princeton, N.J.: School of Architecture and Planning, Princeton University, 1976.

Waller, Gregory A. *Main Street Amusements: Movies and Commercial Entertainment in a Southern City, 1896–1930*. Washington, D.C.: Smithsonian Press, 1995.

Wanamaker, John. "Money for the Support of Our Associations—How Shall It Be Raised?" In *Journal of the Proceedings*, Washington, D.C., May 24–27, 1891, 81–90.

Ward, C. S. "The Association Building and Its Care." *Association Men* 34 (March 1909): 294.

———. "Where Shall the Gymnasium Be Located?" *Young Men's Era* 16 (May 15, 1890): 313.

Ward, Edward J. "The Schoolhouse as the Civic and Social Center of the Community." *Journal of the Proceedings and Addresses of the 50th Annual Meeting of the National Education Association* 47 (July 6–12, 1912): 436–49.

———. *The Social Center*. New York: D. Appleton, 1915.

Wegener, A. B. "Give Us Sunlight and Plenty of It." *Association Men* 36 (September 1911): 563.

Weiner, Deborah E. B. *Architecture and Social Reform in Late-Victorian London*. Manchester, Eng.: Manchester University Press, 1994.

Weisman, Winston. "Commercial Palaces of New York: 1845–1875." *Art Bulletin* 36 (December 1954): 285–302.

Weiss, Ellen. *City in the Woods: The Life and Design of an American Camp Meeting*. New York: Oxford University Press, 1987.

"We Rejoice over the Number of Association Buildings . . ." *Watchman* 10 (June 1, 1884): 121.

"West Side Y.M.C.A., New York, Dwight James Baum, Architect." *Architectural Forum* 53 (August 1930): 147–52, plates, 33–48.

Wharton, Annabel Jane. *Building the Cold War: Hilton International Hotels and Modern Architecture*. Chicago: University of Chicago Press, 2001.

"What Part of the Building Should Be Used by the Association?" *Watchman* 14 (July 1, 1888): 202–3.

"Where Should the Gymnasium Be Located?" *Watchman* 14 (June 15, 1888): 181.

Wiebe, Robert H. *The Search for Order, 1877–1920*. London: Macmillan, 1967.

Wilkie, T. J. "Association Boarding-Houses." In *Journal of the Proceedings*, Dayton, Ohio, June 24–28, 1874, 92–94.

Willard, Ashton R. "The Development of College Architecture in America." *New England Magazine* 16 (July 1897): 513.

Williams, M. C. "Our Greatest Building Era." *Association Men* 51 (January 1926): 233.

Willis, Carol. *Form Follows Finance: Skyscrapers and Skylines in New York and Chicago*. Princeton, N.J.: Princeton Architectural Press, 1995.

Willson, Meredith. *The Music Man*. New York: G. P. Putnam's Sons, 1958.

Wilson, Elizabeth. *The Sphinx in the City: Urban Life, the Control of Disorder, and Women*. Berkeley: University of California Press, 1992.

Winston, Diane. *Red-Hot and Righteous: The Urban Religion of the Salvation Army*. Cambridge, Mass.: Harvard University Press, 1999.

Winter, Thomas. *Making Men, Making Class: The YMCA and Workingmen, 1871–1920.* Chicago: University of Chicago Press, 2002.
Wodehouse, Lawrence. "Alfred B. Mullett." *Journal of the Society of Architectural Historians* 31 (March 1972): 22–37.
———. "Ammi Burnham Young." *Journal of the Society of Architectural Historians* 25 (December 1966): 268–80.
———. "W. A. Potter." *Journal of the Society of Architectural Historians* 32 (May 1973): 175–92.
Wohl, R. Richard, and Moses Rischen. "The Country Boy Myth and Its Place in American Urban Culture: The Nineteenth-Century Contribution." *Perspectives in American History* 3 (1969): 77–158.
Wood, Walter M. "Buildings of the Young Men's Christian Association." *The Brickbuilder* 14 (December 1905): 264–69.
———. *Young Men's Christian Association Buildings.* New York: International Committee of Young Men's Christian Associations, n.d.
Wosh, Peter J. *Spreading the Word: The Bible Business in Nineteenth-Century America.* Ithaca, N.Y.: Cornell University Press, 1994.
Wright, Gwendolyn. *Building the Dream: A Social History of Housing in America.* Cambridge, Mass.: MIT Press, 1983.
———. *Moralism and the Model Home: Domestic Architecture and Cultural Conflict in Chicago, 1873–1913.* Chicago: University of Chicago Press, 1980.
Yarnall, Elizabeth Biddle. *Addison Hutton: Quaker Architect, 1834–1916.* Philadelphia: Art Alliance Press, 1974.
"The Y.M.C.A. and the Y.M.H.A." *Men of New York* 41 (November 1926): 88, 96.
"The Y.M.C.A. Building, San Francisco." *Harper's Weekly* 13 (February 6, 1869): 81.
"Y.M.C.A. Building, Washington." *Harper's Weekly* 13 (May 8, 1869): 301.
Young Men's Christian Association. International Committee. *The Building Enterprise of a City Young Men's Christian Association.* New York: International Committee, 1919.
———. *How Does the Possession of a Building Benefit a Young Men's Christian Association?* New York: International Committee, 1888.
———. *Plan of a Canvass for a Young Men's Christian Association Building.* Pamphlet 86. New York: International Committee, n.d.
———. *Ten Reasons Why It Paid.* Pamphlet 202. New York: International Committee, n.d. [1880s].
"Young Men's Christian Association: New Building." *New York Times,* October 22, 1869, 4.
"Young Men's Christian Association: New Room Opening." *New York Times,* January 15, 1865, 3.
"The Young Men's Christian Association Building, Philadelphia, Penn." *American Architect and Building News* 2 (August 25, 1877): 273.
"Young Men's Christian Association Buildings." *Architecture & Building* 48 (April 1916): 55–64.
"The Young Men's Christian Association of Baltimore, Md." *Watchman* 5 (May 15, 1879): 109–110.
Young Men's Christian Association of Chicago. *New Central Building Souvenir: With New Year's Greetings.* Chicago: The Association, 1891.

"Young Men's Hebrew Association, 91st and Lexington Ave., New York, A. W. Brunner, Architect." *Architects' and Builders' Magazine* 2 (April 1901): 245.

"Young Women's Hebrew Association Building, New York, Louis Allen Abramson, Architect." *The Brickbuilder* 24 (February 1915): 50, plate 22.

Zald, Mayer N. *Organizational Change: The Political Economy of the YMCA.* Chicago: University of Chicago Press, 1970.

Zunz, Olivier. *Making America Corporate, 1870–1920.* Chicago: University of Chicago Press, 1990.

ILLUSTRATION CREDITS

Courtesy of Archives and Special Collections, Babson Library, Springfield College, Springfield, Massachusetts: Plate 11.

Copyright the Art Institute of Chicago, Chicago, Illinois: Figure 2.7.

Collection of the author: Figures I.1, 2.6, 3.19, 5.27.

Courtesy of Chicago History Museum, Chicago, Illinois: Figure I.5 (ICHi-50345); Figure 2.24 (ICHi-02916); Figure 3.3 (ICHi-31436); Figure 4.1 (ICHi-50344); Figure 5.19 (*Chicago Daily News* negatives collection DN-0008209).

Courtesy of Environmental Data Resources, Inc., Milford, Connecticut: Figure 3.16.

Courtesy of Greensboro Historical Museum Archives, Greensboro, North Carolina: Figure 3.15.

Courtesy of Kautz Family YMCA Archives, University of Minnesota Libraries, Minneapolis: Figures I.3, I.6, 1.1, 1.3, 1.6, 1.8, 2.5, 2.9, 2.14, 2.16–2.18, 2.20, 2.21, 2.25, 2.27, 2.29, 3.2, 3.4, 3.7, 3.8, 3.11, 3.12, 4.2–4.11, 4.14, 4.16, 4.20, 5.1, 5.2, 5.3, 5.6–5.13, 5.15–5.18, 5.20–5.25, 5.29–5.31.

Courtesy of Library of Congress Prints and Photographs Division: Figure 5.5.

Courtesy of The Metropolitan Museum of Art, New York: Plate 3.

Courtesy of the Museum of the City of New York, The J. Clarence Davies Collection: Figure 2.12.

Courtesy of New-York Historical Society, New York: Figures 1.11, 2.2, 2.26.

Courtesy of the Ninety-second Street YM-YWHA Archives: Figure E.1.

Courtesy of Pierpont Morgan Library, New York: Figure 1.7.

Courtesy of Prints & Drawings Collection, The Octagon, The Museum of the American Architectural Foundation, Washington, D.C.: Figure 2.11.

Courtesy of Cliff Smith YMCA Postcard Collection, Archives and Special Collections, Babson Library, Springfield College, Springfield, Massachusetts: Figures I.4, 3.9, 3.10, 3.13, 3.14, 3.18, 3.20, 4.12, 4.13, 4.19, 5.26; Plates 1, 6–10.

Courtesy of Ulrich Museum of Art, Wichita State University, Wichita, Kansas: Plate 4 (#1955.1.2).

Courtesy of Washington University Libraries, St. Louis, Missouri: Figures 4.15, 4.17, 4.18, E.2.

Courtesy of J. D. Weeks: Figure 3.17.

INDEX

Italic numbers refer to illustrations.

Abbott, Austin, 185
abolitionism, 19, 20
Abramson, Louis Allen, 188–89, *188*
Ackerman, Frederick, 164
Adams, Henry, 15–16
Adams, William, 34, 37–38
Adamson, Arthur Q., 153, 154
Adrian, Michigan, YMCA, 107, *107*
aesthetics: aesthetic features of the YMCA building: 44, 46, 112, 138–39, 167–71, 172, 173; architectural portraits, 74–75; whether aesthetics should be emphasized in YMCA buildings, 168–69
African-American men, xvii. *See also* "colored" YMCAs; segregated facilities
age of incorporation, xix, xx–xxi
agrarian system, xvi–xvii
AIA. *See* American Institute of Architects
Akron Plan, 67
all-male living environments, 124. *See also* masculine space
American Architect, 186–87

American City, The, 194–95
American Institute of Architects (AIA), tensions with YMCA, 177–79
Amsden, Jon, 42
annual reports, YMCA, 18, 19–20
apprenticeship system, 18, 32, 33, 143–44
architects: general practice, 146, 156, 160, 161, 165, 177; selection of, 171, 204n6; specialist architects, 101, 137, 153, 156, 160, 161, 164, 172, 173, 214–15n72. *See also* Building Bureau, YMCA; *and by individual firm or name*
Architectural Bureau, YMCA, 172
architectural evangelism. *See* environmental evangelism
architectural standardization: standardized building plans, 160, *161,* 163–64, *163,* 172; standardized national building system, 165–67, *165, 166,* 170. *See also* Building Bureau, YMCA; YMCA building models
architecture: and civic pride, 86, 97; feminist studies of, xvii; and meaning, 102; philanthropic, 41, 48, 144;

243

244 / INDEX

scientific or businesslike practice of, 139, 167–68, 179; spiritual dimensions of, 25; structuring behavior, 29, 171. *See also* building culture; YMCA building(s); *and architectural styles by name*
Arnold, Constable & Co. store, *46*
artists' studios, 52–53
Aspinwall, William H., 34, 41, *42*, 53, 82
Association Men, 111–12, *125,* 160, 170, 195; on the building campaign, 85, 97; manufacturers' ads in, 147, *148, 149*
Astor House Hotel, 29
Astor Place, 25–26, *26, 27*
athletics: athletic memberships in YMCA, 116; as a component of the YMCA, 23–24, 77, 115, *116*; and religion, 32, 70; and sporting subculture, 9–13. *See also* billiards rooms and tables; gymnasium(s); recreational facilities
Atlanta, Georgia, YMCA, 93, *94, 128*; gymnasium, 93
Atlanta Constitution, 93
A. T. Stewart's Cast Iron Palace, 28, *28,* 29
Augusta, Maine, YMCA, 100

Baltimore YMCA, 80, 81
banking industry, 18
Baum, Dwight James, 171, 172, 175
Beaux-Arts style, 138
Bederman, Gail, xvii, xix, 20, 21
Bentham, Jeremy, Panopticon of, 66–67. *See also* Panopticism
Bible House on Astor Place, 25–26, *26*
Bible study, 13, 14, 77, 99
Bierstadt, Albert, 65
billiards rooms and tables, 132, 135; in Brooklyn Central Branch YMCA ("Big Y"), 130, 132–35, *133, 134, pl. 7*; in commercial saloons, 9; Mrs. Morgan's donation to New York YMCA, 25, 132, 135; in YMCA buildings, 102, 111, 132–34, *133,* 135, 186, 193, 197, *pl. 7*
Birmingham, Alabama, YMCA, 97
boarding houses, 8–9, 19–20
Booth's Theatre, 50, 53–54, *53*

Boston YMCA, 81
Bowery culture, 26–27
Boyington, W. W., 78
Boys' Clubs, 194
boys' programs ("boys' work"): facilities separated from men's, 126–28, 149; playroom(s), 128–30, *129*
Brickbuilder, The, 162, 189
Bridgeport YMCA, gymnasium of, *119*
Bronx Union YMCA, 189; boys' log-cabin room, *129*
Brooklyn Central Branch YMCA ("Big Y"), 112, 133–35, *pl. 6, pl. 7*; billiards room, 130, 132–35, *133, 134, pl. 7*; boys' programs, 126–30, *129*; dormitories, 123–25, *124*; gymnasium, 128; hot cabinet baths, xix, *pl. 8*; "The Inn of Brooklyn Central," 133–34; lounging room, 131–32, *131*; as a model of residential YMCA, 122–23, *130*
Brown, William Harmon, 15
Building Bureau, YMCA, 177, 215n83; complete service (third phase), 165–67, *165*; free advisory service (first phase), 160–64; increasing control of the building process, 139, 156, 159–60, 165; paid advisory service (second phase), 164; planning division, 159–60; quality control efforts, 164; role in the larger Association, 167–71; split-fee structure, 171, 178–79, 214–15n72
Building Committee, New York YMCA, 5, 41–42, 43, 44–45, 48–49
Building Committees, local, 99, *134,* 146, 153
building culture, modernization of YMCA, 138–44, 153–56
building plans, YMCA, *17,* 52, 55, *56, 66, 67, 122, 130, 151, 175*; standardized plans, 160, *161,* 163–64, *163,* 172
building technology, YMCA buildings requiring specialized, 89–91, 137, 146–49, *154, 155,* 175
built environment, xvii, xx, xxi, 5, 103, 200, 208n50
Buttenheim, Harold S., 192

Calkins, Raymond, 195
campaign clocks, *158, 159*. See also fundraising and promotional campaigns
Candler, Martha, 193
capitalist culture, xxii, 1, 28, 34, 39, 71, 88, 196. *See also* corporate capitalism
Catholic organizations, 191, 194
Cedar Rapids, Iowa, YMCA, *122*
Central Committee, YMCA, 5, 84, 91; lodged in New York, 84–85, 91
Chappell, George S., 173
character building: gymnasiums as sites of, 116; as a YMCA goal, 3, *7,* 116, 124, 130, 209n10
Chauncey, George, xvii
Chicago Central YMCA, gymnasium, *120*
Chicago World's Fair, xxi, 74, 102, 114
Chicago YMCA (Farwell Hall), xxi, 78–80, *79, 113, 117,* 200n20, *pl. 9*; cultural and commercial space combined, 114; gymnasium and recreational facilities, 79, 116, 117–18, 120; location of, 114, 117–18, 120–21; locker room, 118–20; modeling a public role for YMCAs, 112; open to women on a limited basis, 79–80; revival hall converted to gymnasium, 115–16; skyscraper properties, 114–15; swimming pool, 117
China: YMCA construction in, 143–44, *145,* 152–53. *See also* Tientsin/Tianjin YMCA
Chinese Building Bureau, YMCA, *153,* 156
Christian clubhouse: New York YMCA the nation's first, 39, 73; vision of a, 34–35, 39, 75
Christian Commission, 13–14
Christian gentleman, 12, 16, 17, 19, 66
Christianity: "muscular Christianity," xix, 23, 115–16; practical Christianity, 91, 112; traditional Christian values, xviii, 39, 106; "unsectarian Christianity," 120. *See also* traditional evangelicals
churches, non-ritualistic, 186–87. *See also* institutional churches; *and individual churches by name*
Church of the Messiah, New York, 27–28
Cincinnati YMCA, 81, *118*
City Beautiful, YMCA buildings and the, 96–100, 135
civic model, 112, 122, 141, 160–63. *See also* YMCA building models
civic pride, 104, 159, 198; and architecture, 86, 97; civic ideals, 184; YMCA buildings promoted as civic assets, 96–102, 182, 195–96
civil religion, 182, 190
civil service, 18
Civil War: change in YMCA leaders during and after, 14–16; and effects of, 1–2, 13–16; YMCA reconstruction during, 21–26
clerks, xxi, xxiii, 1, 2–3, 12, 15, 32, 39, 57, 201n33; clerical work, 7–8, 18, 19–21, 201n33
Cleveland YMCA, 81, 124
Cliff Smith YMCA Postcard Collection, 105–6
clubhouse YMCAs, 121–22
Coe, George A., 170
Cohn, Louis H., 58
Cole, Thomas, 65; *The Cross and the World,* 66, *pl. 4*
Collins, Anson B., 14
"colored" YMCAs, xxi, 3, 23, 96, 141. *See also* African-American men; segregated facilities
Columbus, Ohio, YMCA, 24
Committee on Rooms and Attractions, YMCA, 31–32
community center movement, 182, 189–93; YMCA model influencing, xxiv, 189–93, *194*
Concert Hall Act, 27
Cone, Moses, 97–98
Confederate soldier, as a symbol of Southern manhood, 94–95
Conover, Elbert M., 187
consumerism, 6, 20, 21, 27, 29, 75, 198, 201n7
consumption of leisure, 25, 27, 29

control and surveillance features, 61–62, 66, *67*

conventions, YMCA, 162; International YMCA Convention, 93; Jubilee Convention, *87,* 162; Kansas YMCA State Convention, 141, *144*

Cooper Union building, 50, *50*

Cope and Stewardson architects, 92

corporate capitalism, xviii; changes in the structure of, xx–xxi, 16, 19, 168; consumerism, 6, 20, 21, 27, 29, 75, 198, 201n7; economic incorporation (period and acts of), xix–xxiii, 15–16, 21, 23, 32; employers' concerns regarding workers, xviii, 3, 5, 7, 8, 12–13, 18, 20, 21, 34, 182; goal of integrating religious ethics with, xviii, 6, 20, 108, 109; landscape and effects of, xvi, xix–xxi, 2, 6, 15, 17, 19–21, 97; spatial segregation and classification in, xx, xxi; YMCA attuned to corporate culture, xvi, xx, 2, 112, *120,* 168, 183

Cree, Thomas K., 91

criticisms of the YMCA: athletic facilities questioned, 27, 77–78, 115, 184; billiards tables questioned, 24–25, 132, 135; efficiency principle questioned, 170; as lacking neighborhood connection, 194–95; regarding policies on class and gender, 195

Daniels, John, 194–95

Danville, Illinois, YMCA, 100

Darling, T. G., 86, 89

Dean, Sherman W., 165, 170–71

Decatur, Illinois, YMCA, *110, 121*

depression of 1893, 99. *See also* Great Depression

Detroit Publishing Co. and Rotograph, 103

Dewey, John, 170–71

Dillard, Frank G., 186–87

Dissenters (British), 2–3

Dodge Jr., William E., 14, 16–17, *16,* 20, 22, 23, 25, 32, 34, 39, 40, 42–44, 50, 52, 62, 81–82, 84, 205n27, 209n4; as chair of the Building Committee, 44; role in designing the New York YMCA, 42–43

domestic sphere, 6, 9, 107, 208n38

donations, 13, 141, 152, 157, 192; for Chicago's Farwell Hall, 78; for construction of New York YMCA, 34–35; of Mrs. J. P. Morgan, 25, 132, 135. *See also* fund-raising and promotional campaigns

doorways and entrances, 121, 123, 130, 164, 173, *174;* separate for men and boys, 126–28, 149

dormitories: at the Brooklyn "Big Y," 123–25, *124;* producing income, 123–24; survey of, 162

Douglass, Paul, 185

Eau Claire, Wisconsin, YMCA, 100

economic conditions, xvi; depression of 1893, 99; Great Depression, 179, 197

educational philosophy, 170–71

efficiency, 170

elite men's clubs, 29, 31

employers: concerns regarding workers, xviii, 3, 5, 7, 8, 12–13, 18, 20, 21, 34, 182; decline of the apprenticeship system, 18, 32, 33, 143–44

Enlightenment philosophy, 7, 208n40

environmental evangelism, 5–6, 7, 71, *125,* 168, 170, 181, 186; as architectural evangelism, xxiv, 73, 84; spatial strategies of, xxiv, 5–6, 73, 204n6. *See also* evangelical Protestantism

European modernists, 179

evangelical Protestantism, 5–7, 10, 12, 14–15, 16, 18, 19, 23, 32; concerns of middle-class white evangelicals, 18–20; environmental evangelism, 5–6, 7, 71, 168, 170, 181, 186; evangelical culture, 3, 10; evangelical women, 19; philanthropist efforts, 18, 202n38. *See also* traditional evangelicals; YMCA

Evans, Herbert, 184

Farwell Hall. *See* Chicago YMCA (Farwell Hall)

Faulkner, William H., 103

Federal Bureau of Memorial Buildings, 192

feminine space, xix, 106; the parlor, 62–64, 130

Field, Marshall, 80
field of visibility, 66, *68*
Findlay, Ohio, YMCA, *127*
Finney, Charles Grandison, 5–6
First Methodist Episcopal Church, Wichita, 90
First World War. *See* World War I
Fishman, Robert, 6–8
Foochow, China, YMCA, 155, *156*, 159
Ford Motor Company, 139
Foster, George G., *New York by Gas-Light,* 9
Foucault, Michel, 66
fourfold plan of work, 23, 43, 77, 81, 99, 187
Frost, George, 82, 84
function and efficiency in architectural design, 43–44, 170, 179
fund-raising and promotional campaigns, 74, 85–87; appeal to mass psychology, 157–59; campaign clocks, *158, 159*; Greensboro campaign, 98–99, 158–59; investments in YMCA buildings, 138, *138*; invoking moral responsibility, 32–35; nationwide building campaign, 74, 85–87, 195–96; support from local elites, 138; support from women, *105,* 106–7, 109; systematic policies of, 157–59; for the West Side YMCA, 171; YMCA buildings depicted as civic assets, 96–102, 99, 100, 135, 182, 195–96. *See also* donations; international building efforts
furnishings, 2, 31, 44, 58, 68, 75, 102, 128, 132, 145, 152, 163, 189. *See also* interior design of YMCA buildings
Furnishings Service, *166,* 166–67, 174–75, 179. *See also* Building Bureau, YMCA

Galt, Ontario, YMCA building, 193
Gates, Herbert Wright, *Recreation and the Church,* 185–86
gay men, xvii
gender: formation of, xvii–xviii; gendered behavior, 9; ideology of, xix, xxii, 71
gendered space, xx, 39, 63, 75, 130, 182, 200n10; gendered geography, 6, 28, 39; masculine space (*see also* masculinity), 62, 63, 123, 124, 131; women's or feminine space (*see also* parlor), 6, 19, *62,* 200n10
general contractors, 155
general practice architects, 146, 156, 160, 161, 165, 177
Geneva, New York, YMCA, billiards table, *133*
Gerber, David, 24
Gladden, Washington, 85
Gotham style, 75, 82
Gothic–Second Empire style, 44
Gothic style, 12, 44–45, 46, 48, 49, 81, 82, 92, 173
Grace Church, New York, 27–28
Gramercy Square, New York, 40
Grand Junction, Colorado, YMCA, 100, *pl. 10*
Great Depression, 179, 197
Great War, the. *See* World War I
Greensboro, North Carolina, YMCA, 97–99, *98,* 100–102, *101*; billiards room, 145; as a civic institution, 100–101, *101,* 145–49; elite class as fundraisers for, 98–99, 158–59; gymnasium, 102, 145; site selection, 99–100
Griffen, Clyde, 201n33
Griffen, Sally, 201n33
Gropius, Walter, 139
Gustav-Wrathall, John, xvii, 106
gymnasium(s), YMCA, 81, 82, 93, *116, 118, 119, 120, 127,* 128, 191, 192, 197; attracting membership, 33, 70; at Chicago's Farwell Hall, 79, 116, 117–18, 120; construction and equipment, 147, 148–49, 152–53, 186; criticized by traditional evangelicals, 24–25, 27, 77–78, 115, 132, 184; at Greensboro, North Carolina, 102, 145; as masculine space, xvii, 135; at New York YMCA, 37, 43, 60, *60,* 80; as sites of character building, 116

Hammond, Halsey, 115
Harmon, Arthur Loomis, 174
Harper's Weekly, 74–77, *83,* 85
Hartford, Connecticut, YMCA, 100

Hatch, Stephen D., 31, 34, 41
Hatch Family, The (Johnson), 64, *pl. 3*
Hawthorne, George, 44, *45*
hierarchy: in corporate capitalist structures, *xviii,* xx–xxi, 16, 22, 168; in features of YMCA buildings, *xviii,* 22, 168, 182, 205n26
"His Home over There," (poster), 196, *pl. 11*
Home Insurance Building, Chicago, 114
homosocial world, xvii, 31, 79, 80
Hull House, 218n32
Hunt, Richard Morris, 51–52, 205n26
Hussey, Harry, 146–47
hybrid space. *See* religious-secular hybrid space

incorporation, xix–xxiii, 15–16, 21, 23, 32; age of, xix, xx–xxi. *See also* corporate capitalism
India, YMCA construction in, 143
Indiana, 81
Indianapolis, Indiana, YMCA, 81
institutional churches, impact of YMCA buildings on, 183–87
interior design of YMCA buildings, 3, 61, *166,* 168, 173, 208n38; furnishings, 2, 31, 44, 58, 68, 75, 102, 128, 132, 145, 152, 163, 189; Furnishings Service, 166–67, *166,* 174–75, 179
international building efforts, 137, 143; native cultures and, 144, 152, 154, 212n31
International Committee, YMCA, 73, 95, 100, 139, 141, 146, 152, 155–56, *157,* 213n48
International YMCA Convention, 93
Isenberg, Alison, 102
Italianesque style, 173

Jacksonville, Florida, YMCA, 94–95
Jallade, Louis, *67,* 161, 172, 188, 193, *194*
James, William, 170
Janesville, Wisconsin, YMCA, 104–5, *105*
Japan, YMCA construction in, 143
Jasper, William, memorial, 95, *95*
Jeanneret-Gris, Charles-Édouard (Le Corbusier), 139

Jenney and Mundie architects, 114–15
Jesup, Morris, 34, 82
Johnson, Eastman, *The Hatch Family,* 64, *pl. 3*

Kahn, Albert, 139
Kansas YMCA State Convention, 141, *144*
Kennedy, John S., 15, 203n73
Korea, YMCA construction in, 143
Kwolek-Folland, Angel, 46

labor-capital relationships, 19
Ladies' Mile, New York, xi, 27–29, 31, 37, 39, 41, 45, 62, 87
leadership, wartime change in YMCA, 14–16, 18, 25–26, 203n73
Le Corbusier, 139
leisure: consumption of, 25, 27, 29; legitimizing, 25, 33, 144; masculine, 9–12, 88, 131
"liberty" buildings, 192–93
London YMCA, 2–3, *4*
Louisville, Kentucky, YMCA, *116*

machine, metaphor of the building as a, 206n49
machinery, 30, 137, 147, 154. *See also* manufactured materials
Madison Square, New York, 40–41, *41*
"Main Street" YMCA building(s), 5, 73, 99, 108, 121, 141, 167, 190; investments in, 138, *138*
male identity, 2
"manhood factories," xvi, 68, 106, 168, 170, 182, 209n10
manufactured materials: machine components, 30, 137, 147, 154; specialized, 162
manufacturers, ads in YMCA print media, 147, *148, 149*
Martin, George Winslow, *The Secrets of the Great City,* 10, *10, 11*
Martin, Lewis, 155–56
masculine leisure, 9–12, 88, 131
masculine space, 62, 63, 123, 124, 131; and elite men's clubs, 29, 31; the parlor as, 62, 63–64; regimentation of, xxi; the YMCA as, xvii–xix

masculinity: models of manhood, xvii–xx, 9–13, 21; and "muscular Christianity," xix, 23, 115–16; and public life, 100; Southern white manhood, 94–95, 96; and urban bachelor subculture, 9–12
Masonic Temple(s), xviii, *30,* 122
mass culture, 111
McBurney, Robert, *22,* 50, 60, 62, 81, 84; *Memorandum,* 32–33; as New York YMCA general secretary, 22–23, 67–68, 123, 205n27; office at the New York YMCA, 67–68, *68, 69;* role in design of the New York YMCA, 42–43
McCabe, James, 26–27
McCormick Jr., Cyrus, 80, 116
McMillan, Neil, 159–60, *160,* 163, 164, 178–79, 213n46
memorial buildings, 192–93
Merchants of New York, The (Rossiter), *65*
Messer, Wilbur, 115, 196, 197
Metropolitan Museum of Art, 52
middle class, xxiv, 3, 28, 29, 62–63; urban, xxii, 42, 126
middle-class evangelicals, 5–7, 18–20
middle-class values, 6–7, 9, 12, 26, 35
middle-class women, 19
middle-class young men, YMCA mission focused on, 9, 12–13, 71, 88, 96, 100, 115, 122, 182, 187, 197
Middle East, YMCA buildings in, 143
Milwaukee YMCA, 125–26, *126*
Minneapolis YMCA, 97
modern city, 35, 184
modernity: cultural landscape of, xv, xxi, xxii–xxiii, 2, 96, 135; YMCA building as symbol of, xvi–xvii, 77, 91, 99, 109, 122, 144, 198. *See also* age of incorporation
Mogge, E. L., 171
Moody, Dwight, 77–80, *78*
Moody's Hall. *See* Chicago YMCA (Farwell Hall)
Moore, Laurence, 39
Moore, William, xvii
morality: associated with the domestic sphere, 6, 9, 107; capitalist culture threatening, xxii, 1, 28, 34, 39, 71, 88, 196; ideal of a moral capitalist order, 19, 32–35, 112; and "Mammon," xxiii, 28, 39; and masculine leisure, 27, 62, 111, 201n7
Morgan, J. Pierpont (J. P.), xxiv, 15, *17,* 17–18, 20, 22, 43; as railroad magnate, 98; role in building YMCAs, 32, 43, 53, 186; as treasurer of the YMCA, 27
Morgan, Julia, 200n10
Morgan, Mrs. J. P., donation of billiards table, 25, 132, 135
Morse, Richard C., 66
Morse, Verranus, 8, 24–25
multifunctional design, 43–44, 50, 54, 71, 78, 81, 112, 114, 120, 189, 208n40
Mundie, William, 114
Muscatine, Iowa, YMCA, 100
"muscular Christianity," xix, 23, 115–16

Nast, Thomas, 74
National Academy of Design, 40, *40,* 65
National Community Center Association (NCCA), 192
National Education Association, 191
national identity crisis, xix
National Park Bank building, 46, *47, 48*
nationwide building campaign, 73–74, 80–84; ended by the Depression, 197; promotional campaign, 74, 85–87, 195–96; vision originating in New York, 73–77, 84–85
Nebraska, YMCA building plans in, 141, *142*
neighborhood life, 191, 194–95
Nelson, Dana, xix–xx
New England Magazine, 184
New York: center of the national building campaign, 74–77, 84–85, 108–9; YMCA map of, *30*
New Yorker, 173
New York YMCA: members' evaluation of, 69–70; membership levels, 69–70; as the model of religious-secular hybrid, 69–70; Mrs. J. P. Morgan's donation of a billiards table, 25, 132, 135; the public and press on, 68–71; site (re)location, 26–27, 31, 39–49
New York YMCA building features, *36, 37,* 55, *56, pl. 2;* artists' studios, 55;

Association Hall, 55, *55*; design of, 42–45, *45*, 46–49, *59*; grand piano, 32; gymnasium, 37, 43, 60, *60*, 80; lecture hall, *61*, 75; library, 58, *59*, 62, 64–65; McBurney's domain, 67–68, *68*; as the national headquarters, 37–38; the parlor, 58, *58*, 62–64, *64*; Parthenon frieze, 58; reading room, 33, 43, *57*, 57–58, *63*; reception room, *56*, 57–58, 66–67; staircases, 61; street-level stores, 55; vertical structure of, *54*, 54–55

non-ritualistic churches, 186–87

North Italian Gothic style, 173

Ohio, YMCA planning in, 81

older men, 119, 127

older YMCA buildings, 128, 141

Omaha, Nebraska, YMCA, 80, 83, *84*, 87–88; religious-secular boundaries blurred, 88–89

Orne, Henry, 188

panic of 1873, 199n3

Panopticism, *67*, 71, 130, 168, 186, 187; Bentham's Panopticon, 66–67

Parkersburg, West Virginia, YMCA, 105–6

parlor: associated with femininity, 62; depictions of, 63–64, *pl. 3*; disappearance of, 130–31; in the New York YMCA, 58, *58*, 62–64

patriarchal family, 63–64

Peabody, George Foster, 96

"people's palaces," 29

Petrie, George H., 3

Philadelphia chapter of the AIA, 177

Philadelphia YMCA, 81, *81*, *140*; as cultural satellite of New York YMCA, 80; gymnasium, 81

philanthropy, 12, 18, 19, 53, 184, 202n38, 204n6; philanthropists, 34, 96, 203n73, 204n6

Philippines, YMCA construction in, 143

physical needs, 23, 77

Physical Training, manufacturers' ads in, 147

Pittsburgh chapter of the AIA, 177

Pittsburgh, Pennsylvania, YMCA, 124

Plessy v. Ferguson, 96

policies, YMCA, xxiii, 79, 125, 169; of building, 139, 144, 157, 165, 167–68; on class and gender, 119, 195; of fundraising, 157–59; toward the poor, 183

Pond, Allen, 218n32

Pond, Irving K., 147, 218n32

pool. *See* billiards rooms and tables; swimming pools

Portland, Oregon, YMCA, *xiv*, xx

Portugal, YMCA construction in, 143

Postcard Exchange Map, *pl. 5*

postcards: architectural representation in, 102–3, *104*, *pl. 5*; featuring YMCA buildings, *105*, *107*, *pl. 5*; image of YMCA enhanced by, 103–8

Poughkeepsie, New York, YMCA, 81

practical Christianity, 91, 112

progressive, national conceptions of, 96

promotional campaigns. *See* fundraising and promotional campaigns

Protestant American church: challenges to, 21; influences by YMCA recreational approach, 183–87; and progressive clergy, 33–34

Protestant evangelism. *See* evangelical Protestantism

Protestant values, xviii

Pyne, Percy R., 15

railroad transportation, 98, 102–3, 141, *143*, 152, 182

Rayburn, R. L., 163

Reconstruction period, xx, 1, 20, 73, 91, 93

recreation: competing with commercial venues, 33, 186, 191–92; providing a moral and middle-class venue for, 38, 122, 125, 146; "respectable," 198; role of, in religious life, 183–87; vice areas facing young urban migrants, 8–9, 10–12, *10*, *11*, 26–27, 111–12

recreational facilities: quality of YMCA, 185, 186; non-YMCA centers, 181, 183–87, 190, 191–92, 193, 194, 198. *See also* gymnasium(s)

religious-secular hybrid space, 31, 37, 49, 69–70, 112, 135, 183, 187; cultural and commercial space combined, 114;

hybrid building efforts, 25, 38–39, 88–90; New York YMCA as model of, 69–70; religion and civic functions combined, 90, 97, 100–101; religion and commercial orientation combined, 6, 19, 71, 74, 78, 87–88; religious and leisure or athletic functions combined, xix, 9, 20, 32, 70, 75, 77, 81; respectability of hybrid approach an early issue, 23, 24, 75; socioreligious buildings, 70, 182

Renwick Jr., James, 41–42, *42*, 44–45, 48–49, 61, 67

Republican political fervor, 51, 73, 77, 80, 95, 143

residential YMCA model, 122–24, 131, *131*. *See also* YMCA building models

residential YMCAs, 122–23, *124, 125, 126*; dormitories, 123–25; housekeeping services, 125

respectability: respectable leisure, 144, 198; respectable living spaces, 123

revival hall, shrinking role of, 115–16

revival meetings, 5, *6*, 13, 77, 79, 115

Richardson, Henry Hobson, 92

Richmond, Virginia, YMCA, 91–92, *92*

Rochester, New York, YMCA, 186

Rockefeller Jr., John D., 96

Rodenz, Mrs. William, 104, *105*

Romanesque style, 92, 114–15, 173

Roosevelt, Theodore, xvi, 116, 209n9

Rosenwald, Julius, 96, 141

Rossiter, Thomas Prichard, *The Merchants of New York*, 65

Ruskin, John, 44

Russia, YMCA buildings in, 143

Salvation Army, 194

San Francisco YMCA, 80, 81–82, *83*; gymnasium, 82

Savannah, Georgia, YMCA, 94–95

Scobey, David, 73

Scottish Enlightenment philosophy, 7, 208n40

Second Empire style, 45–47

Second Great Awakening, 3, 5

secular faith, 182, 190

segregated facilities: "colored" YMCAs, xxi, 3, 23, 96, 141; in Southern YMCAs, 94–96. *See also* African-American men

separate spheres, 6–7, 71

sermon pictures, *65*, 65–66

settlement houses, 194

Shanghai Building Bureau, YMCA, *153*, 156

Shattuck and Hussey architects, *xii, 98*, 101, 145, 146–47, 148, 149, *151*, 152, *153*, 193, 212n32, *pl. 1*

Shelton Hotel, 174

site location, xxii, 78, 81, 88, 95, 114, 165, 208n38; Greensboro YMCA, 99–100, 101; New York YMCA, 26–27, 31, 32, 39–49, 53

small town YMCAs, 87–91

Smith, Cliff, YMCA Postcard Collection, 105–6

social centers, 181, 182, 190, 196; YMCA model influencing, xxiv

social/community center movement, 181–82, 189–93

social control, 62; in design of the New York YMCA, 61–62, 66, *67*; visual control, 66–67, *68*

social fellowship, 186

Social Gospel doctrine, 183–85

socialization, 35, 61

socioreligious buildings, 70, 182

Southern Railway, 98

Southern YMCAs, 93, 96–102; segregation and, 94–96. *See also individual YMCAs by city*

space: feminine space, xix, 106; spatial segregation and classification in the landscape of capitalism, xx, xxi; women's space, 6, 19, 200n10. *See also* gendered space; masculine space; religious-secular hybrid space

specialist architects, 101, 137, 153, 156, 160, 161, 164, 172, 173, 214–15n72

spirituality, 25, 38–39. *See also* religious-secular hybrid space

sporting subculture, 9–13. *See also* athletics

standardized building plans, 160, *161, 163*, 163–64, 172

standardized national building system,

165–67, *165, 166,* 170. *See also* YMCA building models
Stewart, A. T., Cast Iron Palace, 28, *28,* 29
Stone, Joseph, 98–99, 158–59
Strong, George Templeton, 16
Studer, A. G., 162
Sunday school(s), 5, 12, 18, 34, 67, 183, 204nn3, 6
swimming pools, 192; standards for, *163*; in YMCA buildings, 80, 111, 112, 117, 155, 174, 186, 188

Taylor, Frederick Winslow, 139
technologies, YMCA buildings requiring specialized, 89–91, 137, 146–49, *154,* 155, 175
Thompson, Joseph P., 38–39
Tientsin/Tianjin YMCA, *136,* 149–53, *150, 151*; gymnasium, 149, *150,* 152–53, 155
Tonawanda, New York, YMCA, *91*
Trachtenberg, Alan, xx
traditional Christian values, xviii, 39, 106
traditional evangelicals: criticizing gymnasiums, 24–25, 27, 77–78, 115, 132, 184; opposing leisure and aesthetic components, 43–44; in the YMCA split with progressive forces, 24–25
transportation technology, 74
Trollope, Anthony, 74
Trowbridge and Ackerman architects, *131,* 131–32, *pl. 6*
Tsinanfu, China, YMCA, 154
turnverein organization, 23–24, 202n52
Twenty-third Street and Fourth Avenue, New York, xxi, *40*
Tyng, Stephen, 24

Union League Club, 14, 29, *30,* 31, 34–35, 50, *51,* 51–53
Union Pacific Railroad, 141
urbanization, xvii
urban landscape, xvii, xxix, 33, 39, 74; YMCA buildings' impact on, xvi, xxii–xxiv, 71, 84, 87, 91, 109, 111, 135, 143, 182

urban life, xx, 7, 9, 78, 181, 183, 184; the modern city, 35, 184
urban middle class, xxii, 42, 126
urban migrants, *7,* 8, 9, 10, 25, 91, 106–7, 108

Van Slyck, Abigail A., 208n38
vice areas: faced by young urban migrants, 8–9, 10–12, *10, 11,* 26–27, 111–12;
Victorian Gothic style, 44, 46
Villee, A. J., 162
visual control, 66–67, *68*

Ward, Edward, 190–93
wartime change in YMCA leadership, 14–16, 18, 25–26, 203n73
Watchman, The, 85
Weidensall, Robert, 85, 91, 141
West Indies, YMCA construction in, 143
West Side YMCA, New York: design plans, 171–72, *173,* 174–75, *175, 176*; fund-raising for, 171; lobby of, *175, 176*; Mediterranean-style furnishings, 174; a model of aesthetic design, 171, 172; response of the architects and press to, 175–77; the social room, 174–75
white-collar work, 19–21. *See also* clerks
Wichita Falls, Texas, YMCA, 90, *90*
Wight, Peter Bonnett, 44, 46, *47*
Williams, George, 2–3
Wilson, Meredith, *The Music Man,* 132
Winter, Thomas, xvii
women, xvii, 10, 18, 80; associated with the domestic sphere (*see also* parlor), 6, 200n7; emergence in public sphere, xvii, 21; as evangelicals, 19; fund-raising and support for the YMCA, *105,* 106–7, 109; genteel women, 26, 28, 63, 75, 82; inferior status of, xx, xxvi, 19, 95; and the YMCA, 13, 79–80, 202n53
Women's Christian Temperance Union, 114
women's space, 6, 19, 200n10
Women's Temple, 114
Wood, Walter M., 162
working-class men, xvii

World's Fair, Chicago, xxi, 74, 102, 114
World War I, 169–70, 194, 196, *pl. 11*;
and memorial community centers, 192
Wyckoff, Jacob, 15
Wyckoff, Walter, 173

"Ya Got Trouble" (Wilson), 132
YMCA (Young Men's Christian Association): attuned to corporate culture, xvi, xx, 2, 112, *120,* 168, 183; developing a new approach during and following the Civil War, 21–26; as an evangelical Protestant organization, 1, 3–5, 12–13, 20, 23, 195–96; goals and plan of work, 23, 43, 71, 81, 99, 187, 191; increasing secularization of, 70–71, 135; membership policies, 190, 195–96; mission focused on middle-class young men, 2–3, 9, 12–13, 25, 26, 71, 88, 89, 96, 100, 108, 115, 122, 182, 187, 197; modernist ideas of respectable leisure (*see also* Christian clubhouse), 84, 111, 115–16, 144, 182–83; origins of, 2–9; pragmatic ideas a challenge to traditional evangelicals, 24, 27, 77–78, 115, 132, 184; split between orthodox and progressive forces, 24–25; transformed from a voluntary group to a national built network, 73–74, 181; wartime changes in leadership, 14–16, 18, 25–26, 203n73. *See also* criticisms of the YMCA; policies, YMCA
YMCA annual reports, 18, 19–20
YMCA building(s), *xii, xx,* 100, 101, 144–45, 146, 197–98, *pl. 1, pl. 10*; as civic institutions, 95, 100–101, *101,* 111; given local meanings, 109; impact on the urban landscape, xvi, xxii–xxiv, 71, 84, 87, 91, 109, 111, 135, 143, 181, 182–83; as "Main Street" buildings, xv–xvi, xxiv, 5, 73, 99, 108, 121, 141, 167, 190; as a new kind of urban institution, 21, 39, 208n38; periods of boom and decline in construction of, xv, *xvi;* renovation of older buildings, 128; suburban construction, 197. *See also* international building efforts; nationwide building campaign
YMCA building design(s), xii–xxiv, 81, 130–31, 135, 147; building plans, *17,* 52, 55, *56,* 66, *67, 122, 130, 151, 175*; exterior styles, 29, 44, 50, 81, 168–69, 173; imitated by subsequent builders, xxiv, 182–83, 186, 189–93; specialized designs and skills required, 89–91, 137, 146–49, 155, 175. *See also* architectural standardization; Building Bureau, YMCA
YMCA building models: aesthetic model, 171–75; civic model, 112, 122, 141, 160–63; clubhouse YMCAs, 121–22; residential YMCA, 122–24, 131, *131*
young men: as evangelical focus of the YMCA, 3, 12–13, 25, 26, 89, 108; faced with a variety of recreational pursuits, 8–9, 10, 111–12; middle-class, 9, 12–13, 71, 88, 96, 100, 115, 122, 182, 187, 197; the needs of, xvi, 1–2, 119; as urban migrants, 2, *7,* 7–8, 9, 10, 25, 91, 106–7, 108
Young Men's Christian Association. *See* YMCA
Young Men's Hebrew Association (YMHA), YMCA model influencing, xxiv, 187–89, 217n25
Young Women's Christian Association (YWCA), *xx,* 123, *180,* 182, 192, 200n10
Young Women's Hebrew Association (YMHA), 188, *188,* 189

PAULA LUPKIN is assistant professor in the Sam Fox School of Design and Visual Arts at Washington University in St. Louis, where she teaches architectural and urban history.